Labor Politics in North Africa

The Arab uprisings of 2010 and 2011 had a profound effect on labor politics in the region, with trade unions mobilizing to an extent never before seen. How did these formerly quiescent trade unions become militant? What linkages did they make to other social forces during and after the revolutions? And why did Tunisian unions emerge cohesive and influential while Egyptian unions were fractured and lacked influence? Following extensive interviews, Ian M. Hartshorn answers these questions and assesses how unions forged alliances, claimed independence, and cooperated with international groups. Looking at institutions both domestically and internationally, he traces the corporatist collapse and the role of global labor in offering training and new possibilities for disgruntled workers. With special attention to the relationship with rising Islamist powers, he also examines the ways in which political parties tried to use labor, and vice versa, and provides a detailed study of the role of labor in ousting the first Islamist governments.

Ian M. Hartshorn is an assistant professor in the Department of Political Science at the University of Nevada, Reno. His research focuses on trade union politics both internationally and domestically, with a focus on the recent transitions in the Arab Middle East broadly, and Egypt and Tunisia specifically. He has several ongoing research projects looking at the strategic decisions made by trade unionists, the role of global labor in affecting transitions to and from authoritarianism, and the role of organized interests in constitutional assemblies.

Labor Politics in North Africa

After the Uprisings in Egypt and Tunisia

IAN M. HARTSHORN
University of Nevada, Reno

CAMBRIDGE
UNIVERSITY PRESS

University Printing House, Cambridge CB2 8BS, United Kingdom

One Liberty Plaza, 20th Floor, New York, NY 10006, USA

477 Williamstown Road, Port Melbourne, VIC 3207, Australia

314–321, 3rd Floor, Plot 3, Splendor Forum, Jasola District Centre, New Delhi – 110025, India

79 Anson Road, #06–04/06, Singapore 079906

Cambridge University Press is part of the University of Cambridge.

It furthers the University's mission by disseminating knowledge in the pursuit of education, learning, and research at the highest international levels of excellence.

www.cambridge.org
Information on this title: www.cambridge.org/9781108426022
DOI: 10.1017/9781108351157

First published 2019

Printed and bound in Great Britain by Clays Ltd, Elcograf S.p.A.

A catalogue record for this publication is available from the British Library.

Library of Congress Cataloging-in-Publication Data
Names: Hartshorn, Ian M., 1985- author.
Title: Labor politics in North Africa : after the uprisings in Egypt and Tunisia / Ian M. Hartshorn.
Description: New York : Cambridge University Press, 2018. | Includes bibliographical references and index.
Identifiers: LCCN 2018029212 | ISBN 9781108426022 (hardback : alk. paper) | ISBN 9781108444385 (pbk. : alk. paper)
Subjects: LCSH: Labor unions–Political activity–Egypt. | Labor unions–Political activity–Tunisia. | Corporate state–Egypt. | Corporate state–Tunisia. | Egypt–Politics and government–1981-2011. | Egypt–Politics and government–2011- | Tunisia–Politics and government–1987-2011. | Tunisia–Politics and government–2011-
Classification: LCC HD8786 .H37 2018 | DDC 322.20962–dc23
LC record available at https://lccn.loc.gov/2018029212

ISBN 978-1-108-42602-2 Hardback

For the martyrs of the revolution
and
Giulio Regeni

Contents

vii

Acknowledgments

First and foremost I'd like to thank those who took the time to speak with me: workers, activists, unionists, politicians, and everyday citizens of Egypt and Tunisia, as well as specialists from across the world. I sincerely hope my analysis accurately captures your experience and contributes in a material way to your continued wellbeing. Your efforts have impressed the world.

Thank you to my research assistant, interpreter, first sounding board, and friend Ashraf Ayadi. Seeing Tunisia through your eyes and those of your colleagues in civil society informs this book. Leaders like you make me hopeful for Tunisia. Thank you also to Ahmed Khader, my interpreter in Egypt, who helped me navigate the hectic days in the first eighteen months after the revolution. Also, much appreciation goes to Hajer Ayadi for assisting with the final interviews for the book.

Thank you to my fieldwork comrades with whom I shared the pleasures and pains of being far from home and thinking big thoughts: Meir Walters and Susan Ellis (who literally put a roof over my head), Adi Grief, Rachel Sternfeld, Steven Brooke, Christine Cuk, Hoda El-Mahdy, Teresa Meoni, and Amanda Rogers.

I was fortunate to begin graduate school with some of the smartest people I've ever met and am proud to count Thea Riofrancos, Begüm Adalet, Emma Hayward, and Chelsea Schafer among my friends. I benefited from the support and wisdom of my friends further along in their research and career at Penn and elsewhere: Jon Argaman, Chris Russel, Eric Trager, David Bateman, Ryan Grauer, Kaija Schilde, Rosella Capella Zielinski, and Barbara Elias. Special thanks to David Faris and Stacey Philbrick Yadav who made connections and offered support that made this book possible.

Thanks to my friends that walked the grad student/adjunct/early career road with me: Dan Moak, Sarah Cate, Emmerich Davies, Josh Darr, Danielle Hanley, Isabel Perera, Jim Ryan, Nick Seltzer, Todd

Smith, Susanne Martin, Amy Pason, and Jessie Clark. Thanks to my colleagues at UNR who taught me how to make teaching and research work and created opportunities for me to do both, especially Bob Ostergard, Bill Eubank, Kristen Kabrin, and Eric Herzik.

Special appreciation to the scholars who have trod similar ground in international labor and North African politics, especially Teri Caraway, Susan L. Kang, Dina Bishara, Eva Bellin, and the late Marsha Pripstein Posusney. I hope I have acknowledged throughout the book my deep debt to your research.

Thanks to my early mentors, Steve Stamos, Chris Harth, and Rivka Ulmer at Bucknell University. Early stages of this project were shaped by the support of Julia Lynch and Robert Vitalis and it continues to bear the hallmarks of their thinking. I am forever indebted to Rudra Sil for his guidance, support, and solidarity first as his student, then as his advisee, and now as his colleague and friend.

Thanks to the individuals and institutions that supported and funded this work, notably the University of Pennsylvania; the University of Nevada College of Liberal Arts Scholarly and Creative Activities Grant Program; Ed Mansfield and the Christopher H. Browne Center; Rogers Smith and the Penn Program on Democracy, Citizenship, and Constitutionalism; the Project on Middle East Political Science; and the University of Pennsylvania Center for Teaching and Learning. Much appreciation to the institutions that allowed me to conduct research in their facilities, especially the American University of Cairo and the archives of the International Labor Organization. Thanks to the Grand Sierra Resort in Reno, Nevada, for (mistakenly) giving me a dozen free nights at their hotel, which I used as a writing retreat over my first two years in the west. Thanks to La Colombe coffee for keeping me awake to write the dissertation this book is based on. Thanks to Western New Mexico University and the Miller Library for giving me a home base while I finished my revisions.

Thanks to my students at Drexel University, the University of Pennsylvania, St. Joseph's University, Bryn Mawr College, Germantown Friends, and the University of Nevada, Reno. Your thoughtful questions and scholarship made this work better. Thanks especially to my doctoral students Nataliia Kasianenko, Jeffrey Griffin, and Janicke Stramer-Smith.

It sometimes felt like the final steps were the hardest, and I benefited from the help of my editor, Maria Marsh, and the team at Cambridge

University Press, who saw something in this project even when I did not. Thanks also to the anonymous reviewers who made this manuscript stronger. I appreciate the editorial support of Kelli McGhiey, and index help from Wes Palmer and Nigel Quinney. The mistakes that remain, despite their heroic efforts, are all mine.

Thanks to my sister, Erin, my first friend and truest supporter. Thanks to my dad, Bruce, who values knowledge in all forms and about all topics. Thanks to my mom, Sandee, who took me to my first strike and taught me that when we fight we win. My only regret about this book is that you are not here to see it.

Words can't express the thanks I have for my heart, Allison, who changed everything for the better. I never knew life could be as good as it is with you. Thank you for being there and orchestrating this project's successful conclusion. Thank you for sharing me with it for so long. I'm all yours now, forever.

1 | Trade Union Politics before and after the Arab Uprisings

In September 2015, Egyptian workers gathered in a specially designated "protest zone" in Cairo to protest a new civil service law that would create layoffs and reduce wages. They were corralled by security services, and many were arrested. Buses were stopped en route. The protests lacked the support of the country's "official" trade union, which had spent much of the previous year promising an end to industrial action to curry favor with the new regime. The "unofficial" independent unions, which held so much promise during the 2011 revolution, had largely fallen into infighting. They had achieved few of the demands they put forward in either the strike wave that emerged in the 2000s or the uprising that followed.

At the same time, trade unionists in Tunisia were being awarded the Nobel Peace Prize along with fellow civil society activists. The General Secretary of the "official" union was visiting the United States as a guest of the AFL-CIO and being hailed as one of the people who saved Tunisia. Over the previous few years, workers enjoyed multiple raises, including an increase to the minimum wage and an unprecedented influence over the government. Unionists held sway in the streets and in the halls of power.

Just ten years before the 2010–11 revolutions, these results were unthinkable. Both Egypt and Tunisia had regime-backed trade union confederations. Deals struck in the 1950s and 1960s created compliant unions that were "corporatized" to aggregate and channel the demands of their members in specific ways. The years before the revolutions saw a rending of the corporatist pact that maintained labor peace followed by a wave of labor militancy in each country. Despite these similar histories, each country diverged on labor after the revolutions. How did formerly quiescent trade unions become militant? What linkages did they make to other social forces during and after the revolutions? Why were Tunisian unions cohesive, unified, and influential in the transition while Egyptian unions were fractured, co-opted, and lacking influence?

Why Egypt and Tunisia?

The project is motivated by two puzzles. First, how did unions in Egypt and Tunisia become involved in revolutionary politics? Second, how did Tunisian unions manage to become influential actors while Egyptian unions barely survived? The answers are based on scores of interviews in each country. On the first question, I find that the methods used to "constrain" and "channel" workers' issues while also opening up the economy to free market forces shaped their participation in protest politics. For the second, I turn to how the trade unions split apart, and whether those splits were irrevocable.

Egypt and Tunisia might appear an unlikely pairing at first. Egypt has almost twice the land mass of France with a population in excess of 95 million. Tunisia's entire population could fit in greater Cairo. Despite this, as two of the earliest and most decisive transitions in the wave of revolutions known as the "Arab Spring," Egypt and Tunisia yield the most complete cases to understand the role of trade unions in regime transition in the recent era. The countries also share specific strategies of labor management, which make them more comparable. Each country faced an economic and political crisis in the 1980s and used structural adjustment, a package of policies promoted by international lenders including the World Bank and International Monetary Fund, within a few years of each other. Both countries also saw periods of sustained worker unrest in the run-up to their revolutions.

In their choice of ways to "handle" the problem of working-class demands, Tunisia and Egypt are also not alone.[1] Regime-backed corporatism was a popular technique in postcolonial states throughout

---

[1] Christopher Candland and Rudra Sil, eds., *The Politics of Labor in a Global Age: Continuity and Change in Late-Industrializing and Post-Socialist Economies*, 1st edition (New York, NY: Oxford University Press, 2001) explores the results of globalization in a variety of non-Western countries. This work builds on the efforts outlined here to understand the withdrawal of the state and the reaction of labor to new economic policies of diverse states. This argument militates against the "convergence" theory where states are seen as moving inexorably toward similar policies.

the world.[2] The conflict between these policy packages (corporatism and structural adjustment) ripped apart the coalitions that kept each country's regimes in power. With elements of these policy packages combining to cause conflict around the world, understanding what factors affect outcomes in the two selected cases, which saw such broad waves of contentious politics that the regimes actually fell, helps us better understand other countries.

Definitional Issues

Both Tunisia and Egypt saw trade union organizations survive revolutionary change. While the revolutions themselves had multiple causes, a failing political economy is frequently recognized as a contributor.[3] Trade union organizations, in various capacities, sought to "push back" changes that happened from the 1980s on.[4] I use the term "trade union organization" to mean any institution whose main purpose is to deal with workers' issues. In each instance, the country has a trade union organization that predates the recent revolutions, which, in accordance with Teri Caraway's research, I call the "legacy" union. Caraway has carried out the most important work on "legacy" trade unions in a series of articles theorizing why some legacy unions manage to retain power while others falter following major transitions.[5] Caraway cites legacy union strength, method of incorporation, and mobilization of competitors as keys to understanding whether a legacy union

[2] See also Rudra Sil, "Globalization, the State, and Industrial Relations: Common Challenges, Divergent Transitions," in T. V. Paul, G. John Ikenberry, and John A. Hall, eds., *The Nation-State in Question* (Princeton, NJ: Princeton University Press, 2003).

[3] For more on how even Islamist parties have relied on appeals framed economically see Tarek Masoud, *Counting Islam: Religion, Class, and Elections in Egypt* (New York, NY: Cambridge University Press, 2014).

[4] I also draw on the Polanyian tradition of looking at efforts to "embed" economic change in protective social structures, as well as social movements that seek to reclaim labor rights from economic forces. See ibid.

[5] Doug Brown, "The Polanyi-Stanfield Contribution: Reembedded Globalization," *Forum for Social Economics* 40, no. 1 (April 1, 2011): 63–77; Ronaldo Munck, "Globalization, Labor and the 'Polanyi Problem,'" *Labor History* 45, no. 3 (August 2004): 251–69.

will dominate the post-transition labor scene.[6] This book builds on Caraway's framework to look at a related issue: how union movements, broadly conceived, succeed in advancing their agenda and influencing transitions, or fail to do so. I use the term "legacy union" for the Egyptian Trade Union Federation (ETUF) and the Union générale tunisienne du travail (UGTT), and the term "competitor union" or "independent union" to describe alternative trade union organizations in each country.

This book puts forth the idea of "corporatist collapse." Corporatist collapse is failure of the corporatist structure to manage its basic duties. Two of these were "top-down" duties: coordination and quiescence. Coordination meant harmonizing goals and strategies among the "social partners" of labor, capital, and government. Quiescence meant limiting industrial action, practicing wage restraint, and not resisting the regime. Two other duties were "bottom-up" duties: aggregating and advocating. Aggregating means bringing together workers through a predetermined channel. This could be to endorse government policy or weigh-in on decisions. Advocating meant actually obtaining some concessions for the members of the corporate body (wage increases or job security for workers, tax cuts or protection for business). Corporatist collapse came about because of structural adjustment, flexibilization, and the loss of political power suffered by trade union organizations.

Structural adjustment policies generally focused on macroeconomic performance. Loans from international financial institutions (IFIs) looked to stabilize financial markets, correct trade imbalances, create or reform banking sectors, and move workers into private enterprise while reducing debt. These policies were applied to many of the least developed and middle-income countries facing economic crises during the 1980s and 1990s.

Flexibilization, a long-term goal of the IFIs to correct perceived problems in the labor market, is a global phenomenon. While the restrictions on the "ideal" flexible labor market vary from country to country, the goal is consistent. Employers seek maximum liberty to hire and fire workers, reassign their tasks, increase or

---

[6] Teri L. Caraway, "Pathways of Dominance and Displacement: Explaining the Dominance of Legacy Unions in New Democracies Comparative Insights from Indonesia," *Comparative Political Studies* 41, no. 10 (August 2007): 1371–97.

diminish their production quotas, and set their wages. Despite the difficulties in implementing flexibilization in countries with strong unions, the process had been applied in Europe, Asia, and Latin America.

Political power loss for unions operated both grossly and subtly. Both the ETUF and the UGTT lost their central role in helping to decide how the political economy of the state should function. New leaders sought support from business and emerging middle classes and felt comfortable pushing unions aside. Labor issues were often solved in the courts, a process called judicialization, which removed the important role once played by the unions.

Incorporation, as used in this book, deals with the rhetorical claims unions make about their earlier history. Regime changes and liquid-ation of leadership structures in both Egypt and Tunisia eliminated any consistent material resources for the trade union organizations. Both were dependent on the state. Despite that, the rhetoric of their founding remained important, and in the UGTT's case was reinforced during periods of militancy, and reshaped by rank-and-file activists as a call-to-arms.

In authoritarian regimes like Egypt and Tunisia it is in some ways easier to spot trade union politics than in advanced democracies. Prior to the revolutions, Egypt and Tunisia lacked political parties working with unions, or strong campaigns for national office. We can track the relationship between union, state, and business over the years with some clarity. On the other hand, authoritarian regimes are opaque. Statistics like strike rate, union density, and wages are harder to get. More sophisticated attempts to assess trade union "power" remain challenging.[7] For the purposes of this chapter, political power of trade unions means the organizations' capacity to influence policy decisions that affected workers. Older studies have described Egypt and Tunisia as having powerful trade unions.[8] This book will show how that power broke down.

---

[7] Christian Lévesque and Gregor Murray, "Understanding Union Power: Resources and Capabilities for Renewing Union Capacity," *Transfer: European Review of Labour and Research* 16, no. 3 (August 1, 2010): 333–50.

[8] Hishaam D. Aidi, *Redeploying the State: Corporatism, Neoliberalism, and Coalition Politics*, Reprint edition (New York, NY: Palgrave Macmillan, 2012).

Puzzle 1: Corporatist Collapse

How did a system designed to channel workers' complaints, limit their actions, and give them some say in governance break down and allow workers to get swept up into revolutionary action? While corporatism has several goals, it is at its core a system of interest aggregation. Interests and demands are organized into hierarchical, exclusive corporate bodies. Generally, these include the state itself, a business association, and a trade union organization. In both Egypt and Tunisia, these corporate bodies reinforced a system of repression. Police, intelligence, and the military kept the population from activity that threatened the regime. In both countries the corporate bodies were linked directly to dominant political parties, which provided resources through patronage networks and mobilized voters for sham elections. These trade union organizations prevented potential rival movements (political parties, communist organizations, Islamist movements, factions of the dominant regime) from using workers as a base from which to challenge the status quo. Despite these apparent advantages for the continued dominance of the corporatist system, it entered a slow collapse in the 1990s and 2000s.

The three factors highlighted here – structural adjustment, flexibilization, and political power loss for trade union organizations – alienated workers. Many workers did not even know they were in a union. Union elections were corrupted, and union leaders either could not or would not push for benefits for their workers. Increasingly, workers did not have union representation. As both countries drew strength and domestic control from their relationship to unions, a cornerstone of regime stability was undermined. In both countries, union activists began a wave of strikes, sit-ins, and protests. The wave of labor militancy introduced new tactics and strategies of contestation. The collapse of the trade union–based benefits system both alienated labor and angered rank-and-file trade unionists. This left the state with little capacity to either address demands or channel discontent. Both countries saw new independent unions emerge, competing for influence with workers and further eroding confidence in the legacy unions.

Puzzle 2: Divergent Outcomes

How did trade unions in Egypt and Tunisia produce such radically different outcomes in the reconsolidation of new regimes following the uprisings of 2011? With both countries having used similar management techniques prior to the revolutions, the relative success of the Tunisian trade union movement, and the relative failure of the Egyptian trade union movement, is surprising. The second half of this book explores the reasons for these differences.

I propose three key variables in understanding the differences in relative union strength in Egypt and Tunisia. These variables – external links, internal links, and legacy of incorporation – combine to produce what I term the trade union movement's "position" in the transition process. This position predicts how much of an impact the trade union will have on the transition itself. The most extensive of these variables is internal linkages, which covers how the trade union movement relates to various forces within the country.

Argument

Pre-Uprising

Media accounts date the "Arab Spring" to the self-immolation of Mohammed Bouazizi on December 17, 2010 following a humiliating exchange with a government official. Bouazizi became emblematic for many of the aspects later claimed by the revolutionary movements both in his home country and abroad, enshrined in the names used for the revolutions themselves: The Dignity Revolution or The Youth Revolution. Twenty-six years old and facing a police state, Bouazizi fit these descriptions. He was, however, also a resident of the economically neglected interior of the country, and a member of the economically frustrated generation that grew up under aging autocrat Ben Ali that was promised economic development and higher education. The initial conflict with a government representative was over his precarious livelihood, selling fruit in the street.

Another interior region, south of Bouazizi's home, faced a major revolt in 2008. The Gafsa mining basin rose up in a major strike, followed by sit-ins, hunger strikes, and marches. The groundswell of labor militancy forced labor's peak institution in the country, the UGTT, to react to the newly militant labor sector. The Gafsa strikes introduced new repertoires of contention, and were the most sustained challenge to the Ben Ali regime in more than twenty years. The system of corporatist control that held Tunisia's laborers in check was breaking down, and it was not the only Arab country experiencing the problem.[9]

While Egypt was neither the starting point nor the most destructive of the "Arab Spring" uprisings, given the country's historical role in the region, it may have been the most important. The media narrative, especially in the United States and Europe, focused on information technology and the sudden emergence of social media and internet-based activism as a source of real revolutionary potency. Signs in Arabic and English reading "Facebook" and "Twitter" were splashed across American newspapers and TV screens. It seemed for some to be vindication for their hope for a cyber utopia that would upend existing political structures. Despite this, some individuals with a longer history of both research and activism in the country saw other causal agents. Some pointed to the unexpected fracturing of the coercive state apparatus.[10] Others identified the political economic component of the revolution, including scarcity, unemployment, and privatization. While aspects of the Egyptian revolution were novel, the breakdown of certain key regime support structures had taken place in several countries with varying outcomes. Prior to and during the revolution, Egypt witnessed the collapse of the corporatist labor structure and the emergence of labor organizations as a revolutionary sector in society. The bargain struck between labor and the regime was rent, and new relationships were (and continue to be) negotiated.

The processes undergirding corporatist collapse in Egypt mirror those in Tunisia. Like Tunisia, balance of payments issues, coupled

---

[9] Scholarly inattention to ground-up social movements is common. Despite this, some research on social and labor unrest was ongoing before and after the revolution brought renewed interest. Notable among them is Joel Beinin, "Workers' Protest in Egypt: Neo-Liberalism and Class Struggle in 21st Century," *Social Movement Studies* 8, no. 4 (2009): 449–54; Joel Beinin, *Workers and Thieves: Labor Movements and Popular Uprisings in Tunisia and Egypt* (Stanford: Stanford University Press, 2016).

[10] Eva Bellin, "Reconsidering the Robustness of Authoritarianism in the Middle East: Lessons from the Arab Spring," *Comparative Politics* 44, no. 2 (January 1, 2012): 127–49.

with diminishing political rents, forced Egypt to agree to a structural adjustment package in the 1990s. Many segments of this neoliberal turn were delayed until the mid-2000s, when the emergence of a new political faction, including President Hosni Mubarak's son, came to power. The public sector in Egypt, like in many developmentalist states, was massive. The bureaucracy of the country swelled under President Gamal Abdel Nasser's rule, as free education produced a cohort of young people with middle-class aspirations. Government jobs were used to soak up excess labor, and Nasser-era nationalization created a need for more bureaucrats. The public sector was the main source of unionized labor inside the ETUF, the country's single legal trade union confederation. Nasser used the trade union movement to bolster his rule, despite rocky beginnings. The bureaucratic middle class, dependent on government jobs, formed a core support structure for the regime. By embracing structural adjustment agreements under pressure from the international financial institutions, Mubarak began a slow process of eroding this power base.

Structural Adjustment

The fracturing of the old labor pact was born of three main factors in Tunisia and Egypt: structural adjustment reforms, flexibilization, and the political power loss of the trade unions. While each country followed its own internal logic and political necessities, the broad patterns closely match.

While originally recommended as part of the structural adjustment plans that accompanied IFI loans in the 1980s, the neoliberal reforms in Tunisia were rolled out in stages based on political feasibility and crony capitalism.[11] The reforms served to change the role of the state in governance. While the state continued to intervene, it no longer sought primarily to ensure employment or bolster labor-heavy enterprises. The ramifications of neoliberal reforms were partly perceptual and partly practical. With the turn toward capital-intensive industries, trade unionists felt the government had abandoned its pro-labor position, rhetorically enshrined in the abandonment of the term "socialist"

---

[11] The World Bank, "Tunisia – Structural Adjustment Loan Project" (The World Bank, May 20, 1988), http://documents.worldbank.org/curated/en/469511468311960320/Tunisia-Structural-Adjustment-Loan-Project.

from official discourse.[12] On the practical side, the "upgrading" of the economy as it was called in national plans did little to increase the wages or broaden the employment of the working class.

The core of the "Economic Reform and Structural Readjustment Program" Egypt entered into in 1991 was a contraction of the public sector. State assets were sold off, wages stagnated, and layoffs became more common, all while the government dramatically shrunk the number and kind of state subsidies.[13] State investments in health care and education were also walked back. State employees were constrained on all sides, by rising prices for services previously provided by the state and the potential of being fired at any moment. The first years of the privatization program were marginally successful; however, the mid-2000s saw a renewed effort. The 2000s saw a significant increase in the rate of privatization, peaking in 2005–6 with sixty-five companies worth over 1.4 billion LE privatized. Not coincidentally, the following year saw the emergence of a wave of labor protests as workers felt the effects of mass privatization.

Flexibilization

Flexibilization, which has come to be described as "the overall ease with which employers are able to employ or dismiss workers" could perhaps be more harshly and accurately defined by what it is opposed to.[14] A 2003 ILO report defines it as opposition to "labour 'rigidities'

---

[12] The definitive English-language study of Tunisia's political economy is Eva Bellin, *Stalled Democracy: Capital, Labor, and the Paradox of State-Sponsored Development*, 1st edition (Ithaca, NY: Cornell University Press, 2002). In it Bellin explicates the "developmental paradox" of the authoritarian state, by which the forces nurtured by the state have the power to push back against it. A second "democratic paradox" emerges that limits the states' willingness to democratize. This book builds on Bellin's thesis, looking at one of the forces she identified as "ambivalent" to democracy, labor, and addressing its actions when the chance for democracy became real.

[13] The definitive work on the ETUF's historical relationship to the state can be found in Marsha Pripstein Posusney, *Labor and the State in Egypt: Workers, Unions, and Economic Restructuring* (New York, NY: Columbia University Press, 1997). Posusney is prescient on the crises that emerged in the years following the book's publication. She identifies two levels, one of elite co-optation and one of broader working-class "moral economy."

[14] Rudra Sil, "The Battle over Flexibilization in Post-Communist Transitions: Labor Politics in Poland and the Czech Republic, 1989–2010," *Journal of Industrial Relations* 59, no. 4 (September 1, 2017): 420–43.

such as protective labour legislation, collective bargaining agreements and codified regular employment."[15] Eliminating labor legislation, collective bargaining, and regular employment was a prima facie assault on labor.

In Tunisia, flexibilization primarily took the form of easing employment protection legislation. While negotiations on this topic began in the early 1990s, revisions to the labor code did not take effect until the end of the decade, in which reforms were introduced to make it easier to lay off workers and to increase short-term and temporary contracts. The public sector was a stronghold of trade unionism in Tunisia, and the process of privatization that began in the late 1980s diminished the strength of the UGTT and also its capacity to serve as an interest aggregator.[16] The UGTT put up little sustained resistance to the structural adjustment plans instituted in the late 1980s, or to the intensification of privatization in the 1990s, signing new pacts with the government in 1993.[17] In 1996, the Tunisian labor code was amended to make layoffs for economic and technological reasons more flexible. While rather unsuccessful (an African Development Bank report states only 5.4 percent of workers as of 2007 were laid off for such reasons), the change demonstrates the continued erosion of unionized workers' privileged position.[18]

Flexibilization reforms in Egypt were focused primarily on selling off state owned enterprises (SOEs). The process itself was politically untenable through much of the 1990s, and debt forgiveness for the regime's support of the 1991 Iraq War allowed Mubarak to delay its

[15] Job Creation and Enterprise Department Kim Van Eyck; InFocus Programme on Boosting Employment through Small Enterprise Development, "Flexibilizing Employment : An Overview," Working paper, April 1, 2003, www.ilo.org/empent/Publications/WCMS_117689/lang–en/index.htm.

[16] At the onset of privatization and structural readjustment, the public sector accounted for a third of employment in the country. Public sector and public-run enterprise employment in Egypt was also a third of the economy. International Labour Office and International Institute for Labour Studies, *Tunisia: A New Social Contract for Fair and Equitable Growth* (Geneva: ILO, 2011); Ragui Assaad, "The Effects of Public Sector Hiring and Compensation Policies on the Egyptian Labor Market," *The World Bank Economic Review* 11, no. 1 (1997): 85–118.

[17] Eva Bellin, "Contingent Democrats: Industrialists, Labor, and Democratization in Late-Developing Countries," *World Politics* 52, no. 2 (January 1, 2000): 175–205.

[18] Natsuko Obayashi, *Tunisia: Economic and Social Challenges beyond the Revolution* (Tunisia: African Development Bank, 2012).

implementation. SOEs were a legacy of the socialist period of the country's development that saw guaranteed public employment as an answer to persistent poverty, as well as a way to build support in the lower-middle class. While the guarantee of governmental employment for college graduates had been dubious for decades, the official turn to privatization and shrinking of government payrolls alienated trade unionists.

For workers not laid off in the sale of SOEs, flexibilized labor laws served to threaten their employment. Flexibilization was passed in labor reform laws in 2002, after years of negotiation. Like their Tunisian counterparts, these laws served to make it easier to fire (and hypothetically hire) workers who had previously been protected by union-backed contracts. Additional flexibilization clauses were provided to foreign businesses willing to locate within the country, effectively guaranteeing a union-free workplace for multinational firms.

Political Power Loss
Given the pivot to capitalism, and loss of public sector and SOE jobs, it is unsurprising that trade union organizations lost their influence with the government in both Egypt and Tunisia. Once given pride of place among corporatized actors on issues of trade, subsidies, and wages, labor was increasingly pushed out of the leadership position it enjoyed in the 1960s.

In the 1970s and 1980s the Tunisian government resorted to bald-faced repression of the UGTT. The sharp repression of the UGTT following the food riots of 1984 served to repress the leadership of the organization without addressing the discontent of rank-and-file members. Ben Ali's bloodless coup in 1987 led to renewed hopes for liberalization, but the new leader decimated the UGTT leadership, replacing it with his own preferred candidates. The UGTT was no longer a true political player at the national level for the remainder of Ben Ali's regime. With an increasingly quiescent leadership, the UGTT rank and file were alienated from their own union. Some advocates began agitating for an independent trade union as early as 2006, with a sustained effort since 2008 that was not recognized and actively repressed by the government.[19] During the Gafsa crisis in 2008, the first sign of cleavage in the trade union movement (rank and file vs. leadership cadres) emerged, with local and regional leaders taking a

---

[19] Habib Guiza, CGTT Leader, interview with author, July 2013.

militant line when their leadership did not. The same process would come to define the union response to the revolution two years later.

By the mid-2000s, the need to exclude unions from new multinational projects was almost unnecessary. In Egypt the ETUF had fallen from its privileged status in previous years. Despite legal guarantees that the organization would have a say in the political economy of the country, the organization failed to make an impact on the post-2005 "government of businessmen" assembled by the regime. Furthermore, the interpenetration of the security services guaranteed that no authentic worker-representative was elected to positions of authority in the union. Where the Ben Ali regime satisfied itself by decapitating restive leadership in Tunisia, Mubarak opted to rig elections down to the rank-and-file level, ensuring that the ETUF was wholly ineffective. Many workers touched by the strike wave that began in 2007 had never communicated with their union representative and many did not realize they were members of a union. This left workers not only disaffected and disconnected, but also open to mobilization and even radicalization by more militant and vocal organizations.

In both countries, leadership pivoted to business elites. Whole sections of the political apparatus were restructured to promote business and attract international investment.[20] Egypt bolstered their ties to business by disempowering the bureaucracy and placing more power with a businessman-filled cabinet. The Tunisian government had a functioning business interlocutor to deal with, unlike its counterpart in Egypt. The L'Union tunisienne de l'industrie, du commerce et de l'artisanat (UTICA) served to aggregate the interests of employers. As the regime took on a more business-minded frame, it grew closer to UTICA leadership, damaging its relationship to the UGTT.[21]

The Egyptian and Tunisian revolutions revealed the deep divisions in the countries' political and economic functioning. Years of reforms produced surprising results. Instead of undercutting trade unionism, the structural adjustment and labor flexibilization projects opened the door to a new militant cadre of labor union activists. In Egypt, many of

---

[20] Tamir Moustafa, *The Struggle for Constitutional Power: Law, Politics, and Economic Development in Egypt* (Cambridge: Cambridge University Press, 2009).

[21] Eva Bellin, Stalled Democracy: Capital, Labor, and the Paradox of State-Sponsored Development, 1st edition (Ithaca, NY: Cornell University Press, 2002).

these activists left the ETUF or organized outside of it, creating new trade union organizations. In Tunisia, most stayed inside the UGTT but increasingly pressed its leadership for change. Both countries would see the opportunity for substantial reformation of the political economy following the 2010–11 crises.

Post-Uprising Egypt and Tunisia

Following the revolutionary moment, the trade union movements in Egypt and Tunisia were faced with differing cleavages. Tunisia's rank-and-file unionists had risen up and forced their leadership to make a decisive break with the old regime. Egypt's unionists instead faced the choice of staying in the ETUF or joining one of the new independent unions. Within a few months, Egyptian workers faced not only this choice, but additionally the choice of several competing independent union federations. Both countries saw some concessions by the newly consolidating regimes in the form of pay increases in Tunisia and government appointments to trade union leaders in Egypt.

New political actors arose in Egypt and Tunisia as well. Tunisian unions had to deal with new political parties, including leftist, centrist, and Islamist parties. Egyptian unions also sought ties to political parties, while also having the added danger of a dominant military apparatus running the country. Fractured movements were left vulnerable to co-optation or sidelining. Egypt's constitutional process reserved seats for "unionists," though determining who deserves that label is contested. Tunisia's constitutional process was based on elected parties. Both countries faced Islamist parties, with Egyptian independent unions having made some common cause with members of the Muslim Brotherhood (running in elections as the Freedom and Justice Party or FJP) in the past, while Tunisian unions were largely alienated from the Ennahda Movement (running as the Party of the Ennahda Movement).[22] These differing situations produced surprising results. Throughout the transition, three main

---

[22] According to Wolf, Rachid Ghannouchi was the main catalyst of a brief, largely unsuccessful effort by Islamists to join the UGTT in the 1980s. While it is true that Islamist members have always been part of Ennahda, it has been *organizationally* alienated from Islamist groups in the country. Anne Wolf, *Political Islam in Tunisia: The History of Ennahda*, (Oxford: Oxford University Press, 2017).

factors influenced whether unions would win the day or be alienated again as regimes reinstitutionalized: internal linkages, external linkages, and a legacy of incorporation.

Internal Linkages

The toppling of the regimes did not bring to power the revolutionary forces that had called for their ouster. In Egypt, a military coup led to a military government with an appointed civilian cabinet. The military leadership lasted just over one year, and saw the issuance of several constitutional decrees, as well as a Presidential election, passage of new laws, formation of a constitutional committee, and the seating (and later dismissal) of the first postrevolutionary parliament. At each step of these processes, independent trade unions attempted to press their advantage and shift the political balance in the country. These interests set them apart from the approach of the Mubarak regime, and they worked to secure labor quiescence through cooptation. The army fiefdom was not to be touched, by the old regime, activists, or rising political powers in the Islamist movement.

Labor faced the rising Muslim Brotherhood and its Islamist allies. The Muslim Brotherhood economic plan was broadly market-driven. The Muslim Brotherhood was a tentative ally of independent trade unions in the pre-revolution era. Muslim Brotherhood offices hosted independent trade union conferences, and pressed for independence from the state as part of a broader struggle, and leading trade unionists ran for parliamentary seats on the Brotherhood list in the first post-revolution election. Despite this history of solidarity under Mubarak, the Muslim Brotherhood pursued a policy of coopting existing governmental structures, as opposed to their wholesale reorganization. To this end, several Brotherhood leaders entered the ETUF. In addition to facing the government, independent unions was forced to tangle with an effort to re-craft the old corporatist regime with new, Islamist, management. Following the June 30 popular uprising and military coup that unseated President Mohammed Morsi, independent trade union leaders were once again placed in positions of power in the new military-backed government, but once again faced challenges in their ability to achieve real change in the system.

Trade unionists in Tunisia faced a different situation than their counterparts in Egypt. The UGTT constituted the largest civil society group in Tunisia, with offices throughout the country. While political parties were scrambling to make headway in the postrevolutionary chaos, the UGTT established itself as the nationalist counterweight to the emerging Islamist movement. Unlike in Egypt, the Ennahda had no historical ties to the trade union movement and relations between the two were nearly nonexistent. When Ennahda came to power in a power-sharing arrangement with two other parties, the UGTT set itself up as the nongovernmental opposition, holding occasional strikes and protests over Ennahda policy. Despite this, the union was able to close a major social pact with support from the international community, and fend off the emergence of independent trade unions. With the fate of the government uncertain, and pervasive insecurity claiming the lives of two union-affiliated leftist leaders in 2013, the UGTT pushed forward its national dialogue with renewed support.[23] The national dialogue helped organize a governmental transition, establish new election timelines, and pass Tunisia's first postrevolutionary constitution. These new internal ties, weak and coopted in Egypt, and independent and flexible in Tunisia, were bolstered by differing international ties to what I term global labor.

External Linkages

Global labor consists of several organizations with some overlapping and contrasting policies.[24] The International Labor Organization is a United Nations specialized agency "devoted to promoting social justice and internationally recognized human and labour rights, pursuing its founding mission that labour peace is essential to prosperity."[25] The International Trade Union Confederation is the world's largest trade

---

[23] The best ground-up analysis of UGTT action during the revolution itself is provided in Hèla Yousfi, *Trade Unions and Arab Revolutions: The Tunisian Case of UGTT*, (New York: Routledge, 2018). Yousfi extensively quotes UGTT activists and leaders. While generally describing the UGTT as more independent than I have here, Yousfi's outstanding work highlights the discontent within the union before and during the revolution.

[24] Here I draw on the work of Keck and Sikkink on transnational advocacy networks (TANs). While global labor is in some ways distinct from the traditional TANs they discuss, in that there is more agency and purpose in global labor's decisions, they do function in like TANs in many dimensions, forging linkages, disseminating practices, and building new norms Margaret E. Keck and Kathryn Sikkink, *Activists beyond Borders: Advocacy Networks in International Politics* (Ithaca, NY: Cornell University Press, 1998).

[25] "Mission and Objectives," accessed April 18, 2013, www.ilo.org/global/about-the-ilo/mission-and-objectives/lang–en/index.htm.

union confederation, with a mission of representing workers world-wide.[26] The Global Union Federations are sector-based international groupings of trade unions, strengthened by the breakdown of old Cold War divisions throughout the 1990s. In addition to these explicitly international organizations, domestic trade union organizations often have the capacity and interest to operate across borders. Included in this group are the AFL-CIO's Solidarity Center, the Danish Confederation of Trade Unions (LO), the British TUC, and the governmental affiliated institutions like the German stiftungs.

In Egypt, we see an external linkage to global labor based on "pluralism." Various organizations pushed trade union pluralism as a foremost goal. This meant that disgruntled unionists were encouraged to form their own unions, and incentivized to do so with money and rhetorical support. Trade unions regularly explicitly invoked their right to form unions under ILO conventions that Egypt had signed. Independent union organizations promoted the idea of pluralism to disgruntled unionists, having picked up the term and rights-based framing from global labor.[27] The ETUF was seen as irredeemably corrupt and controlled by the regime. This process created a feedback loop. Global labor changed the incentives, promoting the formation of new federations. New federations competed for global attention.[28]

In Tunisia, global labor prioritized "cohesion" among trade union activists. The UGTT was cast as an important social actor, worthy of support. In addition, explicitly discouraging the creation of independent labor organizations, global labor failed to provide capacity building and money that was given to their Egyptian counterparts. This left disgruntled trade unionists to make the logical choice to work "within" the system.

---

[26] For more on the differing pressures put on labor markets by IFIs and the ILO, see Mark Anner and Teri Caraway, "International Institutions and Workers' Rights: Between Labor Standards and Market Flexibility," *Studies in Comparative International Development* 45, no. 2 (June 1, 2010): 151–69.

[27] Trade unionists embrace of rights-based language, and invocation of international agreements to defend their rights matches the arguments made in Susan L. Kang, *Human Rights and Labor Solidarity: Trade Unions in the Global Economy* (Philadelphia: University of Pennsylvania Press, 2012).

[28] Efforts to obtain the attention of potential funders in global labor reflect the "bidding" process outlined in Clifford Bob *The Marketing of Rebellion : Insurgents, Media, and International Activism* (Cambridge; New York: Cambridge University Press, 2005).

Incorporation

Finally, the UGTT was able to draw on a deep well of rhetoric from its historical incorporation and stories it told about that process. This well of revolutionary and nationalist legitimacy was refreshed in the 2011 uprising when militant rank-and-file members joined the revolutionary process, at first to the chagrin, and later to the benefit, of union leadership. By claiming its role in both the independent and revolutionary struggles, the UGTT was able to place itself above the fray of politics. This history of the UGTT's role during independence is real, and it was put forth as a key to legitimacy during the dark days of Ben Ali's repression by some rank-and-file activists.[29] The UGTT had broad-based support during its early years. Despite this, an elite deal was cut to wed the UGTT to the regime, a pattern maintained throughout the state's history.[30]

The ETUF, on the other hand, did not have this "imagined" history of militancy. It mostly justified its existence on what it was able to extract from the regime, and from the benefits it enjoyed under previous governments. Its decision to offer quiescence and even repression in the face of revolutionary change made it hard to justify to its own dissident members its future as a national organization.

These three factors, external links, internal links, and incorporation, combined to form what I term a "federation vs. federation split" in the trade union movement in Egypt. Incentivized by global labor, under constant threat of cooptation, and with no strong script based on incorporation, trade unions in Egypt fractured into competing federations, unable to present a united front on any issue. In-fighting was both personal and political and multiple attempts to bring trade unionists together failed. These failures resulted in trade unions in Egypt having a limited impact on transitional politics, and explain their weak role to this day.

The same factors were important to the "rank and file vs. central split" that emerged in Tunisia's reconsolidation process. External linkages in Tunisia were geared toward the legacy union. Internal links to

---

[29] Here I draw on the critical junctures literature first put forth by Ruth Collier and David Collier, *Shaping the Political Arena : Critical Junctures, the Labor Movement, and Regime Dynamics in Latin America* (Princeton, NJ: Princeton University Press, 1991).

[30] Douglas E. Ashford, "Neo-Destour Leadership and the 'Confiscated Revolution,'" *World Politics* 17, no. 2 (January 1, 1965): 215–31.

political movements and parties in Tunisia were based on flexible linkages. The trade union movement eschewed calls for it to form a political party, or declare a formal alliance with any new political faction. It did not endorse an electoral list and its leadership generally avoided positions within the government. The urge for competition was focused instead internally, to competitive elections within the trade union structure. As the fortunes of various political actors rose and fell, the trade union movement was able to serve as a steady interlocutor between political parties, a pattern that became critical as the transition was threatened with instability.

Each of these variables – external linkages, internal linkages, and incorporation – became salient in the months after the revolutions. Both countries faced another change of regime, as Islamists who won early elections were forced to step down. Trade unionists in each country sought to benefit as much as possible from the reversal of fortunes, especially in the legal and constitutional drafting processes.

Pacts and Parliaments

In addition to those factors discussed in the previous sections, Tunisian trade union organizations in general, and the legacy union the UGTT, benefited from two unlikely institutional arrangements. Tunisian political elites made a fateful decision early in the transition. The National Constituent Assembly (NCA) was elected with participation of political parties. Since the UGTT chose not to form a political party, it had no official representation in the NCA. Egypt's constitutional assembly was mixed with some seats selected by the parliament with other seats reserved for "experts" and "representatives." These "representatives" were supposed to express the interests of several groups in society: youth, religious figures, and unions. At first, one might assume that formal representation in the parliament would benefit unions. It in fact did the opposite. The UGTT spent time building street power, holding strikes, and forging flexible ties to political parties. The ETUF, which was the federation that received the seats, became more of a site of contestation itself, with different forces fighting over it, and the seats it held. Furthermore, many of the seats for "unions" went not to working-class organizations, but to elite syndicates for groups like lawyers and doctors. Tunisian workers benefited from their exclusion, while Egyptian workers had no authentic mechanism for aggregating their demands to the (several) constitutional assemblies formed.

A second institutional factor that helped the UGTT is similarly paradoxical. The UGTT had little formal history with the Islamist movement in Tunisia. While it certainly had members with Islamist leanings, they often kept these political commitments to themselves. The leadership of the organization was thoroughly secular. Trade unions in Egypt, on the other hand, had a long history with Islamists in Egypt. Elite syndicates, including engineering and medicine, long had Islamist members in leadership positions, and the institutions were a forum for Muslim Brotherhood activism. Independent unions had made common cause with Islamists against the repression of the Mubarak regime in its final years, and many trade unionists in the countries had ties to either the Brotherhood or Salafi strains of Islamist thought. Despite these differences, with Tunisian unions alienated from Islamism, and Egyptian unions at least familiar with it, Tunisian unions fared far better in the long run in their relationship to the Islamist Ennahda Party than Egyptian unions did in their relationship with the Islamist Freedom and Justice Party (FJP). The reasons for this surprising outcome, explicated more in Chapter 6, include both structural and attitudinal differences between the trade union movements. The ETUF became a battleground for competing forces, and the Muslim Brotherhood worked to preserve it as a base of institutional power. The UGTT became a bulwark of secularism following the transition, and Ennahda was forced to grapple with it both in the streets and in negotiations. Egyptian trade unionists often expressed dismay at the actions of Islamists, when Tunisian trade unionists expected little of them and were not disappointed.

Methodology and Sources

This book draws its data from a set of original interviews conducted from 2011 to 2017, primarily in Egypt and Tunisia, with supplemental and follow-up interviews among global labor activists in Lebanon, Belgium, Switzerland, and the United States. Interviews were not sampled but instead aimed for a comprehensive picture of elite decision-making among relevant organizations. Leadership of the major competing trade union factions in Egypt and Tunisia were included. Disgruntled trade union activists were also interviewed in an attempt to better understand the basis of their decision to break away or not. I observed plenaries and side-meetings held during the 23rd General Congress of the UGTT.

Interviews began semi-structured and evolved into an open-ended structure with those interview partners who were available for multiple conversations. Early interview partners also shaped and drove the research project itself, producing different questions from the outset when compared to later interviews. Interview topics also evolved as a function of the political realities on the ground. At different points in the transition, topics became more or less sensitive, necessitating cutting certain lines of questioning for the safety of all involved.

International interviews focused on those organizations active in each country. Political instability led to some organizations only being actively involved for certain periods. Several representatives from the International Labor Organization, the International Trade Union Confederation, were interviewed, along with leadership of Global Union Federations and other elements of global labor.

Archival research was conducted at the ILO Archives in Geneva and in the publicly accessible records, which include inquiries, communications, and reports of Committees of Experts. Archival records provided historical context to situate the changing position of the ILO to the national trade union confederations in each country. Secondary source research included government-run and independent periodicals in the newspaper archives of the American University in Cairo.

Interviews in each country following the uprisings also evolved to include direct observations of planning and strategizing sessions for trade unions, as well as strikes, and protests. These included the first national strike following the seating of the postrevolutionary government in Tunisia. These observations allowed for less structured opportunities for engagement and discussion with workers, both individually and collectively. For some, circumstance did not allow the collection of identifying information beyond a union or party affiliation. For elite interviews, name and affiliation are provided in the appendix. Interviews were conducted in English, Arabic, and French, with simultaneous interpretation support from research assistants when necessary.

Organization of the Book

The remaining chapters address the two cases of Egypt and Tunisia in two time periods: the period of corporatist collapse and neoliberal reforms (roughly the 1990s and 2000s in each country) and the reconsolidation of new regimes in the aftermath of the 2011 uprisings

(2011–16). Points of similarity and divergence are highlighted. Broader theoretical implications are explored in the conclusion.

Chapter 2 looks at the difficulties that Egypt faced in the early 1990s and 2000s while undergoing corporatist collapse. It addresses the adoption of structural adjustment, labor flexibilization, and the loss of union power. It explores the early decisions of global labor in Egypt, and the beginning of the federation vs. federation trade union cleavage in the country.

Chapter 3 addresses the outcome of corporatist collapse and revolution in Egypt. I argue that federation vs. federation split in Egypt conditioned how much influence union organizations could have. I explain the internal linkages to new political forces, as well as how external linkages continued to impact the union movement. Finally, I address how incorporation influenced rhetoric to allow fracture in Egypt.

Chapter 4 reviews corporatist collapse in Tunisia, and how the UGTT became a restive sector active in the revolution. It analyzes the results of structural adjustment, and how Tunisian workers responded to new pressures in the 1990s and 2000s.

Chapter 5 addresses how Tunisian workers differed from their Egyptian counterparts, managing to heal the rifts of a rank-and-file vs. central leadership split that differed from the federation vs. federation split in Egypt. It also addresses the emergence of the National Dialogue that would see the trade union movement in a guiding position during the revolution.

Chapter 6 explores how new labor relations were codified in the constitutional processes in each country. It also extends the story into the first postrevolutionary regime transitions. Both instances involve the removal of Islamist incumbents, with trade union organizations making uncomfortable alliances with potentially long-running ramifications.

Chapter 7 extends this study in several directions: our understanding of the Arab Uprisings, corporatism and its relationship to contentious politics, and the future of labor incorporation in an era of neoliberalism. It also looks at historical cases from around the world that may be fruitful in considering new ideas for corporatist collapse and labor-mediated transitions.

2 | *Corporatist Collapse in Egypt*

Historical Corporatism

Dominant narratives of the Arab Uprisings have focused on a number of factors: authoritarian rule, corruption, and economic inequality among them. All played a role in the prelude to the revolutionary moment, but the most surprising element was the failure of the very institutions designed to protect the regime from falling. Police, military, intelligence, and party discipline all needed to fail in some way or another to bring this about.[1] An underexplored institution is the corporatist labor system, which sought to ensure labor quiescence in each regime. By managing and coopting labor writ large – workers, shop floor activists, elected union leadership – in pyramidal, interest-aggregating structures, Egypt and Tunisia, and to varying degrees other countries in the region, sought to prevent politicized strikes and issue-linkage seen in the revolutions. These corporatized unions were supposed to channel dissent into manageable directions and keep it from spilling into the street. They failed. The top-to-bottom failure of this structure, along with its unintended consequence of pushing dissent in new directions, I term corporatist collapse. This collapse was caused by a fundamental incongruence. Corporatist structures were born in a domestic and international period in which socialist and centrally planned economies could be married to "pro-labor" (in the sense of higher wages and protected rights) and centrally coordinated corporatist bodies. The slow breakdown of these socialistic and centrally planned systems shattered the bargains that undergirded the corporatist system. Structural adjustment, flexibilization, and the erosion of the political power of the union federations removed their ability to "aggregate and advocate for workers."

---

[1] Mona El-Ghobashy, "The Praxis of the Egyptian Revolution," *Middle East Reports*, no. 258 (Spring 2011).

Instead, workers found other outlets for their grievances, or turned on the unions themselves.

This chapter seeks to move beyond the economic costs and benefits of neoliberal reforms to explain how these policies disrupted the equilibrium of the Mubarak regime and eventually helped bring about its downfall. First, I will address the nature of historical corporatism, including how this arrangement of policies produced state–labor relations in Egypt. Next, I will explore structural adjustment, the wave of internationally endorsed economic and political changes enacted from the 1980s until, with halting progress, the 2000s. From here, I review the main causal variables in "corporatist collapse" structural adjustment, flexibilization, and the erosion of political power of the unions.

While modern trade unionism emerged in Egypt as early as the 1890s, legally recognized union confederations only emerged in the mid-twentieth century.[2] The Egyptian Trade Union Federation (ETUF) was founded in 1957 during the early years of Gamal Abdul Nasser's regime. Nasser sought to consolidate his control, and the establishment of a peak institution to channel worker's issues was a part of this effort. The establishment of the ETUF followed Nasser's land reforms, the crackdown on the Muslim Brotherhood, and the nationalization of the Suez Canal as the new regime centralized administration and removed alternative power bases in the country. Workers had called for their own national union federation for several years, but these efforts had been thwarted by the former regime. A communist-supported proto-confederation planned a founding congress, only to have it interrupted by the Free Officer's Coup of 1952. The Free Officers' relationship to organized labor was strained from the beginning. The regime's reaction to labor unrest at Kafar Al-Dawwar was the execution of two of the strike leaders.[3]

Nasser's coup took place at the same time as ongoing labor agitation in the country. Nasser's regime sought to direct all nationalist and independent-minded political forces into his revolution. A close relationship formed between the ETUF and the national movement headed by Nasser. Leaders of the transit workers' union were convinced (and

---

[2] Joel Beinin and Zachary Lockman, *Workers on the Nile: Nationalism, Communism, Islam, and the Egyptian Working Class, 1882–1954* (Princeton, NJ: Princeton University Press, 1987).

[3] Joel Beinin, *Workers and Peasants in the Modern Middle East* (Cambridge: Cambridge University Press, 2001).

possibly bribed) to support a general strike supporting Nasser during his internal power struggle with Mohammed Naguib.[4] Later, the ranks of the trade union swelled with the Nasserist nationalizations of the early 1960s, which created far more government employees, the vast majority of whom were eventually unionized.

In Egypt, workers were given a voice in industrial organization, with seats reserved for them on management boards of nationalized companies. Strikes were banned, and dispute resolution was channeled through the ETUF. Under the new Nasserist laws, any union with three-fifths of workers in a union was effectively a "closed shop" with all workers considered members of the union, and open to dues collection. Unions were given a mission of protecting worker interests, providing for health and wellbeing, and staying out of politics and religious activities.[5]

Despite restrictions on "political work," the ETUF was promised a share of political power in the national constitution promulgated in 1964. It guaranteed them a reserved number of seats in the national assembly, along with farmers, totaling 50 percent. To be certified a "worker," and therefore eligible for workers' seats in the assembly, one had to receive recognition from the ETUF, placing them in yet another position of power. The slate of laws passed with the new constitution in 1964 also enhanced the ETUF's corporatist nature. Twenty-five national industries were defined, and organizing within them was confined to one hierarchical union.[6]

These early centralizations had several useful outcomes for workers. First, the labor market was rendered more rigid, with restrictions on how and when a worker could be dismissed by an employer. The mediation and arbitration system established in the early 1950s in Egypt biased cases toward workers. Compulsory arbitration was a double-edged sword, allowing more workers to obtain their demands while undercutting the ability to hold strikes.[7]

---

[4] Hazem Kandil, *Soldiers, Spies, and Statesmen: Egypt's Road to Revolt* (London and Brooklyn, NY: Verso, 2012), 39.
[5] Ibrahim Ahmed Kamel, "The Impact of Nasser's Regime on Labor Relations in Egypt" Ph.D. diss. (University of Michigan, 1970).
[6] Ibid.; It is interesting to note that currently the ETUF covers twenty-three unions, a surprising level of consistency. "Egyptian Trade Union Federation Official Website," *Unions*, accessed May 1, 2014, http://etuf-egypt.org/en/elnekabat.
[7] Kamel "The Impact of Nasser's Regime on Labor Relations in Egypt," 43.

In the first years of his revolution, Nasser's government used state policy in support of his political base, including land reform, subsidies, and unionization. These commitments, however, were based largely on political exigencies rather than carefully considered policy. Many of the subsidies used were not in fact directed at the urban poor or subsistence farmers, but were focused at the lower-middle class and up, a political calculation designed to ensure quiescence.[8] The subsidies and nationalized industries faced increased pressure through the 1960s, compounded by military expenditures during and after the 1967 Arab–Israeli war.

Egypt faced a set of related and interlocking economic issues in the 1970s that threatened the corporatist bargain of restrictive labor contracts, political influence, and pro-worker policies from the previous decades. Egypt experienced a moment of labor militancy at this time as well. Following the death of Nasser and his replacement by another member of the RCC, Anwar Sadat, the regime changed as well. Sadat's shift in economic policy, called *infitah*, or opening, was driven by both domestic economic concerns and military competition with Israel. Understanding these moments of militancy is important to understanding what came after. In a process that has been repeated many times in Egypt, the new President sought to tackle the domestic budget, a major portion of which was subsidies, the so-called social price that supported the old Nasserist system.

Sadat's policy of economic openness, free market reform, and economic orientation toward the West and away from the Soviet Union alienated some of the socialist members of Nasser's regime, many of whom enjoyed strong ties to the trade union movement. Despite this, the close ties to the ETUF survived Sadat's purges and the "Corrective Revolution" of 1971. The reorientation of political structures included a call for new trade union elections. Despite the fact that this governmental decree interfered with internal affairs, the union elections have been described as free and fair. Sadat's chosen leader assumed both the Presidency of the ETUF and the role of Minister of Manpower in 1972. Communist activists were excluded from the ETUF, and multiple factions eventually emerged in the upper echelons of the organization.

[8] Iliya Harik, "Subsidization Policies in Egypt: Neither Economic Growth nor Distribution," *International Journal of Middle East Studies* 24, no. 3 (1992): 481–99.

These tendencies took different positions on Sadat's opening but were eventually sidelined in favor of Sadat loyalists. In this environment, the Trade Union Law 35 of 1976 was promulgated. Egyptian unions have been dealing with its ramifications ever since.[9]

The late 1970s saw the further subjugation of the ETUF to the new National Democratic Party, the successor institution to Nasser's Arab Socialist Union. The ETUF followed government policy while working class activism shifted to independent groups, many of who were rounded up, especially after 1977's disastrous bread riots. Foreshadowing later liberalizations, Sadat removed bread subsidies that many working and lower-middle class Egyptians relied on. The subsequent riots shook the regime and led to a crackdown on left-wing activists. The combination of the new law that strengthened the hierarchical nature of the ETUF, the crackdown on left-wing labor activists from the organization, and unions' inability to protect the subsidy scheme despite their legislated role in economic governance set the stage for the coming battles over economic reform and trade unionism in the country.

Subsidy reform is directly tied to labor politics both practically and in the mind of many workers. In discussions with trade unionists after the 2011 revolution, workers often complained of the prices of basic goods not in terms of the actual cost, but in terms of the inability of their wages to keep up with cost increases. It is challenging to disentangle labor and food price protests.[10] Successive generations of Egyptian leadership, including the Sadat regime and that of Hosni Mubarak which followed it, recognized that economic opening increased the chance of currency swings. Loans from the international financial institutions (IFIs) meant increased pressures to rein in governmental spending. Wage restraint was offset by a robust subsidy scheme, which what little remained of the "left" fought to preserve. During the late 1970s, communists and socialists were arrested or coopted to make

---

[9] Marsha Pripstein Posusney, *Labor and the State in Egypt: Workers, Unions, and Economic Restructuring, 1952–1996* (New York, NY: Columbia University Press, 1997).

[10] Todd Graham Smith, "Feeding Unrest: Disentangling the Causal Relationship between Food Price Shocks and Sociopolitical Conflict in Urban Africa," *Journal of Peace Research* 51, no. 6 (November 2014): 679–95.

sure the country did not have an active left-wing to resist market-based reforms in other sectors.

Structural Adjustment and Renewed Crisis

Sadat's turn to economic openness, coupled with increased aid from the United States following the successful implementation of the Camp David Accords, delayed the need for more thoroughgoing reforms in the early 1980s. Sadat's successor, Hosni Mubarak, faced many of the same pressures. The country faced an economic decline, including "massive fiscal and current account deficits, high inflation rates, negative interest rates, accumulated external debts, and high open unemployment."[11] Fears of growing urbanization, soaring public sector employment, and the threat (partially enacted in 1991) of Egypt's many expatriate workers returning home led to near constant concern over employment.[12] While many of these pressures existed in the 1970s, they were only exacerbated by the economics and politics of the late 1980s and early 1990s. With loans from IFIs, the state undertook a structural adjustment with the goal of fixing its economic troubles. The goals of this program, according to a postmortem conducted by the African Development Bank, included:

Stabilisation (sic) of the economy in order to restore macroeconomic balance and reduce inflation; structural adjustment to stimulate medium and long term growth; modification of social policies to minimize the adverse effects of economic reform on the poor and vulnerable groups. The structural adjustment policies were aimed at reforming public enterprises and liberalizing all prices, including interest rates.[13]

---

[11] African Development Bank Group, "Egypt: Economic Reform and Structural Adjustment Program Project Performance Evaluation Report (PPER)," May 15, 2000, www.afdb.org/fileadmin/uploads/afdb/Documents/Evaluation-Reports/05092259-EN-EGYPT-ECONOMIC-REFORM-AND-SAP.PDF.

[12] Bent Hansen and Samīr Muḥammad Raḍwān, *Employment Opportunities and Equity in a Changing Economy: Egypt in the 1980s: A Labour Market Approach: Report of an Inter-Agency Team Financed by the United Nations Development Programme and Organised by the International Labour Office* (Geneva: International Labour Office, 1982).

[13] African Development Bank Group, "Egypt: Economic Reform and Structural Adjustment Program Project Performance Evaluation Report (PPER)."

The 1991 Economic Reform and Structural Adjustment Plan (ERSAP) was negotiated by the government of Egypt and the IFIs.[14] The ERSAP itself secured a rather paltry loan, amounting to a standby agreement worth approximately $372 million. This agreement, along with participation in the United States-led Gulf War against Saddam Hussein's Iraq, however, led to a Paris Club debt forgiveness plan worth over $19 billion. The World Bank signed an agreement worth $520 million, and private debtors wrote off over $10 billion. A side agreement that eliminated more than $7 billion in military debt was no doubt particularly attractive to military leadership.[15] While the ERSAP would eventually have serious ramifications for workers, its initial terms were focused on other sectors of the economy. Egypt had been in arrears to other Arab states for loans received in the 1970s since 1979, and from the United States since the mid-1980s. The United States estimated arrears had reached over $4.3 billion in 1986.

The ERSAP was designed to remove imbalances in the economy. Action focused on exchange rates, monetary policy, and fiscal policy. The fiscal reforms were balanced between increased taxation and decreased spending, with most spending cuts coming from reform of the subsidy system. The prices of a basket of common goods were liberalized, including agriculture, transportation, and energy, but leaving the popular and politically necessary subsidy for flour. Petroleum and energy costs both increased substantially.[16] The market logic that undergirds the structural adjustment program called for privatization of state-owned enterprises (SOEs) and a reduction of public sector employment. The 1990s saw little progress on this front. During this time, the percentage of all employees in the public sector remained consistent, and from a macroeconomic view, the increase in private sector jobs should have reduced any simmering labor tension, but this view obscured reality on the ground.

The Egyptian government's "unruly corporatism" struggled in the 1980s and 1990s to include small-scale farmers and fishers.

---

[14] Timothy Mitchell, "No Factories, No Problems: The Logic of Neo-Liberalism in Egypt," *Review of African Political Economy* 26, no. 82 (December 1, 1999): 455–68.

[15] John Williamson and Moshin Khan, *Debt Relief for Egypt?* (Washington, DC: Peterson Institute for International Economics, November 2011).

[16] Philibert Afrika, "Critical Factors in Three Successful Structural Adjustment Programmes" (African Development Bank, November 19, 2001).

Privatization of some SOEs in these sectors alienated workers in them who were outside the ETUF structure. As in alienated sectors of the more formal labor market, alternative institutions emerged to deal with the problems, including the Land Center for Human Rights. Karam Saber, a leader of the group, stated "We started in 1996, bringing together lawyers and farmers against landlords and discussing rights. We established relationships with village associations. We expanded to include workers who were fired in 1998." When asked to describe the main problems, Mr. Saber described several aspects of the structural adjustment plan that harmed these workers: "The government sells the land through a public auction [and] ownership is an issue. Water access and irrigation are a problem. Government doesn't give loans or subsidies for crops, the laws protecting prices are gone, so prices are cheap. Loans can double and banks are merciless."[17] What Mr. Saber describes as a crisis for workers was the very success of the ERSAP in Egypt. Positive interest rates, a reduction in government subsidies, and a reformed macroeconomic environment were exactly the goals of the program.

Despite brewing labor unrest, the ERSAP results were impressive: GDP growth per year swelled to over 5 percent, inflation went from 22 percent to 9 percent, interest rates became positive, and the elimination of so-called social prices for a variety of goods eased the deficit problem.[18] The macroeconomic indicators were often touted in the media and to international bodies as signs of the success of the structural adjustment program. Little attention was paid, at the time, to the political or social ramifications of these reforms.

The ERSAP, and the regime, envisioned macroeconomic stabilization leading to a flourishing private sector. Despite the regime of liberalization and reduced inflation, Egypt's private sector struggled. The proposed mechanism to "soften the blow" of structural adjustment was the Social Fund for Development (SFD). This institution was designed to provide small loans, fund small-scale development projects, and directly support the poor and extremely poor. The SFD in Egypt cost more than $650 million in the first six years of its existence. The target, however, was largely the least-developed regions of the

---

[17] Karam Saber, Director of Land Center for Human Rights, interview with author, October 2012.

[18] African Development Bank Group, "Egypt: Economic Reform and Structural Adjustment Program Project Performance Evaluation Report (PPER) May 16, 2000."

country, often with admirable results. The benefit rarely went to those who the Egyptian government's original subsidy scheme focused on: working poor, public sector, and urbanized workers. In addition to the loss of their "social prices" these workers would also soon face new threats to their job security.

Flexibilization

While the concept of "labor market rigidity" dates to the 1940s, its inverse did not become a major policy prescription until the 1980s. Flexibilization has been defined as "changing work practices by which firms ... seek flexible employment relations that permit them to increase or diminish their workforce, and reassign and redeploy employees with ease."[19] While structural adjustment often focuses on macroeconomic issues, an IMF report from 1990 includes a section on "Structural Adjustment Defined" and states " ... a number of industrial countries have taken important steps toward improving efficiency, including major tax and financial reforms, privatization, and measures to enhance the flexibility of labor markets."[20]

For Egypt, a less "rigid" and more "flexible" labor market meant the regime taking significant steps against their own, previously bolstered trade unions. The trade unions' raison d'etre was to "tighten" the labor market, making it harder to fire workers or reassign them to other tasks. To the extent flexibilization was pursed for other benefits, such as de-skilling the workforce and reducing their salaries, especially in the public sector, trade unions were even more under attack. The very regimes that had propped up strong jobs with reliable work contracts now sought to create weaker job protections across the board. The ETUF worked to slow or stop the implementation, but in many ways was dealt damaging blows to its ability to aggregate and advocate for its members. Without the ability to help workers in these vital issues, the unions lost the loyalty of these members, allowing for problems to become outright contention in the decades that followed.

---

[19] Katherine V. W. Stone, "Flexibilization, Globalization, and Privatization: Three Challenges to Labor Rights in Our Time," SSRN Scholarly Paper (Rochester, NY: Social Science Research Network, August 11, 2005), http://papers.ssrn.com/abstract=781249.

[20] "1990 International Monetary Fund Annual Report," April 30, 1990, www.imf.org/external/pubs/ft/ar/archive/pdf/ar1990.pdf.

Flexibilization in Egypt went hand in hand with privatization. SOEs were the bulwark of unionization in many postcolonial states that used corporatism. These workers enjoyed the most privileges and were the hardest to fire or reassign. Moving these employees to the private sector removed this problem. Privatization was appealing to the IFIs for several reasons: It promised a quick influx to government coffers running at consistent deficits, permanently removed workers from the government payroll, and held the promise of greater efficiency for the economy. Flexibilization was both a way to encourage privatization (companies would want to buy government assets only if it was easy to hire and fire workers) and an outcome of privatization (private sectors workers enjoyed fewer protections than public sector workers.) The results, however, were mixed.

For Egypt, Law 203 of 1991 sought to privatize 314 companies under government control. In 11 years, only 190 of those companies actually completed privatization.[21] Privatization averaged around 15 companies per year, a rate that the IFI's viewed as anemic.[22] The Egyptian bureaucracy, the main beneficiary of the nationalization of corporate assets under Nasser, worked to slow down the privatization scheme. Furthermore, even Mubarak recognized the potential damaging effects of privatization if it led to mass layoffs, an almost certainty for low-performing businesses. The president was quoted as saying that these privatizations could be carried out without any loss of jobs, a highly unlikely scenario. In addition to presidential hesitancy, the entire architecture of the state had a vested interest in the status quo, with leaders enjoying fiefdoms that provided remuneration both legal and illicit. As a result, the privatization scheme moved slowly.

Workers, unsurprisingly, were concerned with their fate in the new, privatized economy. The ETUF, guaranteed a position in negotiating economic policies in the country, sought to constrain the government's actions through negotiations. Despite this, the organization had abandoned most of the traditional tools of trade unionism to accomplish its goals. Strikes conducted at this time were largely wildcat and without

---

[21] USAID Privatization Coordination Support Unit, "The Results and Impacts of Egypt's Privatization Program: Special Study August 2002."

[22] Karim Badr El-Din, "Privatization: A Key to Solving Egypt's Economic Woes," Text, Voices and Views: Middle East and North Africa, March 11, 2014, http://blogs.worldbank.org/arabvoices/privatization-key-solving-egypt-s-economic-woes.

union support. Elections were increasingly penetrated by security services, with more militant members prevented from running. The trade union law was amended in 1995 to ensure that the old guard of the ETUF, loyal to the Mubarak regime, could extend their terms.

The mechanism charged with mitigating the fallout of economic reforms, the SFD, increasingly focused on "new entrants" to the work force, including recent college graduates and women.[23] This was an evolution of the purpose of the institution, which initially called, at least in part, for "labor intensive public works Sub-projects, including ... improvement of rural roads and of water supply ... irrigation canals ... refurbishing of buildings." This original component of the SFD was envisioned as a "sponge" for excess labor from two sources: returning Egyptian workers from Iraq following the fall out of the Gulf War, and newly "flexibilized" government employees. The transition from young and middle-aged low-to-moderate skilled men to women and high-skilled college graduates of both sexes changed the target.

Some researchers have described Egypt as a successful case of trade union pushback on neoliberal reforms.[24] However, the purges of the 1970s had effectively removed the most militant members from the ETUF, leaving only those more compliant to regime

---

[23] Human Development Department, "Social Fund for Development: Micro and Small Enterprises Support Project" (African Development Bank, August 2006), www.afdb.org/fileadmin/uploads/afdb/Documents/Project-and-Operations/EG-2006-096-EN-ADB-BD-WP-EGYPT-AR-SFD-MSES-PROJECT.PDF.

[24] The author states that the ETUF had "substantial influence" on this process. The most generous interpretation of this assertion is that the success of the ETUF eroded over time; a less generous interpretation might be that Paczynska is incorrect in this key area. Paczynska states that the ETUF enjoyed financial independence from the regime as a result of reforms in the 1970s. While this is formally true, it fails to correctly characterize the fact that both the state and the trade union confederation had become subservient to Mubarak's National Democratic Party. Paczynska argues that the ETUF successfully managed the transition to a more open economic system by constraining the actions of the Egyptian government: Agnieszka Paczynska, *State, Labor, and the Transition to a Market Economy Egypt, Poland, Mexico, and the Czech Republic* (University Park, PA: Pennsylvania State University Press, 2009). A more thoroughgoing account is provided by Posusney, who argues that rank-and-file members were never mobilized in a way to truly resist privatization, with ETUF elites simple seeking to preserve the status quo. Marsha Pripstein Posusney, *Labor and the State in Egypt: Workers, Unions, and Economic Restructuring, 1952–1996* (New York, NY: Columbia University Press, 1997).

demands. It is true, however, that the late 1980s and early 1990s saw a slowdown in the administration of the privatization and liberalization programs. However, this can be attributed to bureaucratic inertia, as middle management faced the prospect of losing their positions, more than a real institutionalized resistance from the ETUF. This is perhaps most notable in the steel and railroad strikes that took place at this time, which all happened outside the union's auspices.

Egypt turned to new neoliberal strategies to flexibilize the workforce, while also attracting international investment money. The government tinkered with a number of different "industrial zones." This model focused expansion away from the crowded capital and into new areas. Some new cities had specific economic incentives attached to them, including limited tariffs, tax abatements, and, most notably, flexible labor standards. These special economic zones that fell under various sets of legal designations have been created in Egypt since the 1970s. Qualified Industrial Zones (QIZs) enjoy a preferential trade arrangement with the United States on the condition that a certain percentage of their products are made in Israel. While some of these QIZs are remote, much of their workforce commutes from the more densely populated areas.[25] These areas explicitly advertise in English-language websites the more "flexible" labor codes used in them, including short-term contracts and limits on unionization.[26] Some reports suggest that ETUF-affiliated unions were effectively nonexistent in the special economic zones.[27]

While organizations and activists pushed for revisions to Law 35 of 1976 that defined the role of the ETUF, they also hoped for amendments to a 1980s-era labor law that laid out basic terms of employment. Agitation began in the 1990s for a new labor law from several directions. Employers and international firms wanted labor flexibilization and a unified labor law that would be attractive to

---

[25] Shamel Azmeh, "Labour in Global Production Networks: Workers in the Qualifying Industrial Zones (QIZs) of Egypt and Jordan," *Global Networks*, January 1, 2014.

[26] *Business Laws*, www.gafinet.org/LawsLibrary/Forms/En_AllItems.aspx? lawtype=Business%20Laws#first.

[27] "Report on the Seminar of World Trade Agreements and Their Impact on the Egyptian Textile Industry and Workers 9–10 April 2005" (CTUWS, April 10, 2005).

business as opposed to the labyrinthine regulations in place at the time. Trade unionists and activists wanted a "balanced" law that protected workers' rights, including the right to strike. By almost all indications, employers fared better than workers under the new law.

Law 12 of 2003 had several "flexibility" clauses. Prior to the unified labor code it created, termination of workers was a complicated and difficult affair. Effectively, workers had to be guilty of malfeasance to be dismissed, and business needs were not acceptable grounds for termination. Law 12 changed this. Employers were now allowed to set a probationary period of three months, during which a worker could be terminated at any time. After the probationary period, the new law permitted fixed-term contracts after which workers could be terminated, with or without cause, at any time. These fixed-term contracts were renewable indefinitely, and workers report having been kept on them for decades. Employers were obligated to give notice of two months, with extended notice for longer-serving employees, and pay a severance package. Furthermore, labor disputes, previously settled by a tripartite commission, would be reviewed by a labor court made up of at least one representative of the union, one representative of the business, one representative of the ministry, and one judge, swinging the tripartite nature in favor of the business-friendly state.[28] These changes amounted to a revolution in the way labor relations were conducted in the country.

Despite the increased flexibility for employers, workers also obtained a renewed commitment on the right to strike, albeit under the auspices of the ETUF only. In reality, the ETUF almost never authorized a strike or other collective action. The reconfirmation of the right to strike was an easy concession for the government to make, as it would require the agreement of the quiescent ETUF leadership, already deeply enmeshed in the Mubarak regime. Once again, labor disputes were pushed out of the formal system and into wildcat strikes, which became a regular occurrence by the mid-2000s.

[28] "Law 12/2003 Book Four 'Collective Labour Relationships,'" available at: www.egypt.gov.eg/english/laws/labour/.

Political Power Loss

Along with the neoliberal reforms in the form of structural adjustment and the privatization and flexibilization schemes, the Egyptian regime worked to reduce the political power of the ETUF. The bread riots of the 1970s may have delayed, but did not deter, the regime from pursuing cost-saving reforms to domestic expenditures. The decision to introduce structural adjustment, and with it labor flexibilization and privatization, did not introduce labor militancy, but was fuel on a smoldering fire. The relative difficulty faced by the ETUF leadership in stemming any of the economic changes carried out by the regime was prefigured by their own militant members' inability to get the ETUF to endorse their basic wage demands in the late 1980s. Major strikes affected vital sectors, including steel and railroads. Workers demanded increased wages primarily, and security services were used to put down the unrest. The strikes of the late 1980s in steel and rail transit launched the careers of several activists who would grow in power as the neoliberal turn continued in the 1990s and 2000s.

From this point forward, work on trade union issues largely shifted to the NGO/legal sector. While the torch of worker's rights continued to be carried by some of the small opposition parties, such as Tagammu, these parties were largely coopted by the regime and kept on a short leash. Activism was forced out of the official political and trade union sector and into outside advocacy groups. This process had actually started in the late 1970s when activists like Saber Barakat formed independent committees to address worker issues following the *infitah*.[29] When these independent committees were excluded from the ETUF, a cadre of activists outside the formal system emerged. While law explicitly banned forming unions, formation of other "entities," like NGOs and law centers, was easier. Giving these entities legal character allowed activists to maintain bank accounts, and begin to receive money, including from the international community.[30]

The rise of nonunion organizations, such as the Hisham Mubarak Law Center, clearly demonstrated the diminishing benefit to workers in using the existing dispute resolution mechanism of the ETUF. Each of these groups opted to push labor disputes into the judicial system.

---

[29] Saber Barakat, Activist, interview with author, April 1, 2012.
[30] Adel Badr, Activist interview with author, April 2012.

Ironically, the growing judicialization in Egypt across the legal spectrum was itself a function of neoliberal reforms. Impressively, these labor advocates managed to gain some traction in the courts even as the administrative mechanisms were collapsing.[31]

Those interested in supporting labor rights set up new organizations outside the auspices of the ETUF.[32] Despite the fact that the ETUF was the exclusive trade union in the country, nongovernmental organizations remained legal (despite intermittent harassment). Kamal Abbas, an activist and leader of the seminal strikes of the 1980s in the steel and rail industries, established the Center for Trade Union and Worker Services (CTUWS) in 1991. Abbas managed to attract limited support and national attention for the strikes, despite their suppression by security forces, by enlisting help from the small opposition parties that remained in operation at the time. While repressed by state media, the liberal Wafd Party's newspaper, foreshadowing the sometimes awkward alliance of leftists and liberal opposition groups that would plague Mubarak's later years, reported on the strike.[33] Abbas also pioneered gaining international attention for workers' issues in the country, receiving the French Republic's Human Rights Prize in 2000.[34] Other activists, like Elhamy Elmergany, who first became active during Sadat's crackdown, helped organize a younger generation of workers. In an interview, Elmergany cites the railroad strike of 1986 and steel strike of 1989 as turning points in which the ETUF demonstrated that it had "turned against workers."

---

[31] For more on the growing judicialization within the country, especially in the upper echelons of the legal system, see Tamir Moustafa, *The Struggle for Constitutional Power: Law, Politics, and Economic Development in Egypt* (Cambridge: Cambridge University Press, 2009). Moustafa argues that the judicialization of the country was born of the need to provide more secure property rights for multinational corporations.

[32] Nicola Pratt, "Maintaining the Moral Economy: Egyptian State – Labor Relations in an Era of Economic Liberalization," *The Arab Studies Journal 8/9*, no. 2/1 (October 1, 2000): 111–29.

[33] "الرئيس يطلب تقرير عن اضطر ابات مصانع الحديد و الصلب بحلوان العمل المتقون ينفون الاتهامات التي جهتها لهم اجهزة الامن" (The President Requests a Report on the Strike at the Iron and Steel Factories in Helwan While Workers Deny the Charges Leveled against Them By the Security Services)," *Wafd*, August 4, 1989; "اضطرابات في مصانع الحديد و الصلب بحلوان" (Disturbances in Iron and Steel Factories in Helwan)," *Wafd*, August 3, 1989.

[34] Kamal Abbas, CTUWS Founder, interview with author, April 2012.

The CTUWS focused its efforts on the two sectors of the Egyptian economy most damaged by liberalization policies: the public sector and the new industrial sectors. In the public sector, CTUWS opened an office in Mahalla el-Kubra, the home of the largest spinning and weaving plant in the country, long a hotbed of trade union activity. The main office opened in Helwan, the industrial heart of southern Cairo, home to a slew of public and private light and heavy industrial plants. Over the following years, the organization expanded to Tenth of Ramadan City, a new industrial city originally conceived in 1977. The organization situated itself as the representative of the industrial worker, challenged by privatization in the public sector and flexibilization in the private sector.

The move to NGOs didn't go unnoticed by the government, which, in addition to its regular campaign of harassment, amended the NGO law in 2002 to read:

The concerned administrative quarter shall refuse with substantiated decision, the request for registration of the society's summary of statutes if it transpires to it that the society's purposes include the exercise of one of the following activities: ... 3) ... any unionist activity the exercise of which is restricted to unions according to the Unions Law.

Since the union law gave unions a broad mandate to generally assist workers, almost no NGO that did so could be legal.[35]

After the arrest of striking workers, activist lawyers argued that strikes, even in so-called critical sectors, were legal regardless of ETUF support. They invoked Egypt's status as a signatory of ILO Convention 87 – Freedom of Association and Protection of the Right to Organise. This convention covers union independence from government and employer intervention. Egypt signed it, and a spate of other ILO conventions, in the late 1950s during the consolidation of the Nasser regime. The novel argument seemed unlikely to gain traction at the time, but later Egypt's signatory status would play a major role in labor disputes.[36]

---

[35] Law on Non-Governmental Societies and Organizations, No. 84 of the Year 2002, www.icnl.org/research/library/files/Egypt/law178-2002-En.pdf.

[36] "Convention C087 – Freedom of Association and Protection of the Right to Organise Convention, 1948 (No. 87)," accessed May 1, 2014, www.ilo.org/dyn/normlex/en/f?p=NORMLEXPUB:12100:0::NO:12100:P12100_ILO_CODE:C087.

From the perspective of early structural adjustment in the 1990s, Ellis Goldberg predicted that strife would soon return to state–labor relations in Egypt. He wrote,

As public goods become private again, the state will have to choose between two courses of action. One would be to allow workers in groups to again struggle for a share in the division of income... The other would be to restrain the workers' movement to the extent possible in the hopes that an unequal division of the national income will shift the burdens of development to the working class.

For a long time Egypt took the latter of Goldberg's two options, leaving the trade union movement to suffer a malignant neglect. Workers neither faced a legitimate collective bargaining structure nor the benefits of government-mandated perks. Just as in a previous era one could question the independence of the trade union movement given its influence with the government, in the 2000s one could question whether there was really a "business community" or "employer's association" with which to bargain, when the most powerful capitalists in the country were closely tied to the regime. It instead restrained trade union influence by limiting its ability to reach workers in the new industrial sectors.

Some of this loss of power was organic. The loss of public sector jobs, the restrictions on unionization at private sector work sites, and the weakening of the labor codes meant that unionized workers were fewer and those that remained were less likely to see their union as a legitimate aggregator of their grievances. The regime also took decisive decisions to remove labor and the labor-oriented from positions of power with a goal of more deeply entrenching neoliberal reforms in the governing apparatus. The erosion of the ETUF's influence hobbled the union's ability to "aggregate and advocate" on behalf of its workers. The historic bias toward workers, enacted by Nasser to win the support of labor in the country in the 1960s, began to shift to capitalists instead. The desire to attract foreign direct investment gave capitalists increasing political influence in the country.

Unlike Sadat's purges of the 1970s, the increased use of security services in the 1990s had a chilling effect not only on those who were politically active with communist and socialist ambitions but on any worker advocate interested in pushing for change. The institution of the ETUF itself became ineffective, and it started from the bottom up. While some token resistance may have remained at the elite level, shop-floor representation broke down entirely. The administrative dispute resolution system, while still technically "stacked" toward labor, with two representatives from the labor side, one independent adjudicator, and one corporate representative, began to tilt heavily toward businesses.

The Mubarak regime was rocked by more protests early in the new millennium, including major protests against Israel's conflicts with Palestinians. The return to street politics was met by increasing security focus, with US support, in the post-9/11 era. Emboldened by a new tranche of debt forgiveness spurred by Egypt's membership of the "Coalition of the Willing" that invaded Iraq in 2003, Mubarak rolled out a cabinet reshuffle with a business focus. Egypt's 2004 cabinet shuffle was heralded as a new era of economic policy making. Ahmed Nazif was named prime minister and formed a cabinet of business-minded neoliberals. Nazif, despite being over 50 years old, was the youngest-ever prime minister of the country, and his cabinet was seen as a "changing of the guard." Several of the new ministers, had careers working in the IFIs. Others were deemed "technocratic" and were Western educated. Several others came out of Egypt's private business sector, including Rasheed Mohammed Rasheed of Unilever, who was named minister of foreign trade and Industry, and hotel magnate Ahmed Alaa El-Din Amin Al-Maghrabi, who was named minister of tourism.

Despite the turn to business elites, the ETUF retained one position in the cabinet for itself. In the 1980s and 1990s, the government maintained the tradition of promoting to the ministry of manpower a leading executive of the ETUF. Ministry officials often returned to the ETUF after their term in the ministry. This feedback and revolving door of union and government leadership reinforced regime loyalty and control by the government's National Democratic Party (NDP). The majority of ETUF leadership was also leaders of Mubarak's party, as was the minister of manpower in the 2000s.

Evidence from the leaders themselves demonstrates that, instead of being a source of power for the working classes, having trade union leaders so close to the regime was a detriment. Despite assertions that the interest of workers was being considered, eventually even regime officials had to concede that business interests in the privatization program were outweighing the concerns of the working class.[37] While leaders stated that the closeness with the regime was a necessary affair, later events would prove this to be empty talk.[38] In 2004, an official of the ETUF, Aisha Abdel Hadi, became minister of manpower.[39] Abdel Hadi distinguished herself by being one of the most prominent women in the Egyptian regime, not only serving as the only woman trade unionist to lead a national union but also one of the only women in the NDP's Political Bureau. Her ties to the union were only exceeded by her ties to the regime.

From the regime's perspective, its installation of ETUF officials in the ministry of manpower and its consolidation of control over both institutions with NDP officials should have allowed control over work protests that would threaten government interests. It did not. From the perspective of the workers, the ETUF's close ties to the regime were supposed to be able to constrain and limit the excesses of neoliberal reforms when those reforms would be damaging to workers. They could not. In both cases, grievances did not move through the preordained channels of aggregation. Instead of moving up through union infrastructure, the problems were pushed into legal channels, where judicialization throughout the 2000s had greatly empowered Egyptian courts, or into the activist sector, where labor militancy was on the rise. These efforts were independent of the formal union structure and supported by NGOs that the government had managed to intimidate, but not coopt.

The new cabinet completely eschewed effective trade union leaders or working-class activists. Ironically, while it oversaw the liberalization of the Egyptian economy, it also rubber-stamped the faux-liberalization of the political system. A constitutional amendment in 2004 called for competitive presidential elections for the first time in the Mubarak regime's history. Mubarak had already won referendum votes four times after being appointed by the NDP-controlled parliament. Despite this supposed liberalization, many candidates were banned from running, in addition to the ban on a Muslim Brotherhood

---

[37] "Woman Minister Allays Worker's Fears," available at www.algomhuria .net.eg/egyptian_mail/m4/.

[38] "Aisha Abdel Hadi: A Labor of Love," available at http://webcache .googleusercontent.com/search?q=cache:http://weekly.ahram.org.eg/2001/532/ profile.htm.

[39] Azza Khattab, "Cabinet: A Reader's Guide," *Egypt Today*, August 11, 2004.

candidate. Even this was insufficient, and reports of irregularities were widespread during the election itself. The election also saw the emergence of broad opposition to Mubarak's continued rule. The decision to rig the election, producing the relatively "limited" win for Mubarak of only 88 percent of the vote, left disgruntled activists more confident than ever that Mubarak was incapable in bringing about democratic reform. Security services crackdowns on the nascent protest movement, and the preelection arrest and trial of Ayman Nour, leader of the liberal opposition party Al-Ghad, only enhanced this notion.

With the establishment of labor flexibility, as well as liberalized labor practices with regard to foreign companies through the special economic zones, Egypt was ready to prepare a new round of privatizations. While privatization had been planned since 1991's ERSAP, several major industries remained off the chopping block. In the mid-2000s, Egypt faced a reduction in rents it received from the United States. The late 1990s saw the finalization of the "glide-path" agreement, in which the United States changed its funding package to both Israel and Egypt. Egypt wound up receiving over $400 million less in aid from the United States every year. These and other pressures pushed the state back toward privatization.

The failures of Egypt's labor management system are multifaceted. During interviews conducted from 2011 to 2013, workers repeatedly expressed their frustration with the ETUF and official unions. More surprising than the fact that these workers found their unions ineffective is that they found their unions nonexistent. Repeatedly, workers reported having been members "on paper" of the official union but having never received advice from a union official, participated in an election, or been informed of any rights. This does not mean, however, that if workers were informed of the activities of the union they would have been satisfied with the responses of the organization. The proto-unions and activist groups that emerged in the 1990s and early 2000s were able to use the absence of the unions as a recruiting tool. This was bolstered by the fact that formal sector workers, regardless of how active their unions were, had union dues automatically deducted from their pay. These workers saw no benefit from a union they were paying for. Furthermore, the rise of the NDP and the continued flexibilization of labor in the country eroded any sense of union identity.

The ETUF's inability to provide for its members was on display, as unauthorized strikes became the norm in the country. In the first major strike of the 2000s in Mahalla El-Kubra, labor activist Sayyid Habib describes the reaction to the plant's general strike. "On the second day, the NDP came to negotiate. We realized that the textile union was against the workers. Only on the third day did leadership of the ETUF arrive."[40] Worker activists were disconcerted to find the lack of support among their labor leadership. In an attempt to pressure the ETUF representatives, activists on the ground circulated a democratic petition to withdraw confidence in their union. From the beginning, the efforts of striking workers were supported by the CTUWS.

In addition to workers being unaware of, or lacking confidence in, their trade union representatives, many also reported a desire to be "put under a ministry," looking for some mechanism of government accountability.[41] Workers from various industries report being told that labor problems could only be solved by intervention from representatives of the controlling ministry. Some of this may have been buck-passing by the ETUF, but the structure of Nazif's reform government is also to blame. One of the neoliberal reforms made under Nazif was the empowerment of the cabinet. This reform was encouraged by the IFIs for the sake of efficiency and by Western democracy promoters as a way of shifting power from Mubarak's inner circle to a new "technocratic" leadership. This efficiency may have worked for businesses, but it undercut the traditional aggregation of labor complaints that had undergirded the corporatist system. Nazif managed to "hollow out" the bureaucracy. He passed reforms that left ministerial officials' positions redundant, but left the officials themselves in place saying, "Although we cannot fire them, at least they are not in the way. In the recent reform of customs, we made about 6000 people redundant but without firing them. Now you (a businessman) just don't go to these people any more, you don't need to. They are just sitting

---

[40] Sayyid Habib, Mahalla Activist, interview with author, November 2012.

[41] Workers in petroleum, transportation, and tax collection all discussed their issues in terms of wanting closer ties to the ministry. When asked if they had a preference in ownership, some stated that they would like to see nationalization, while the majority claimed that access and action on problems were their main concerns. The desire for full nationalization cannot be rejected wholly, however, as can be seen in the popularity of Hamdeen Sabbhi, a Nasserist politician who ranked a surprising third in the 2012 presidential elections. Sheikh Tariq, Activist, interview with author, March 2012. Mohammed Al-Amm, Activist, interview with author, April 2012.

there." While Nazif was correct that a "businessman" might not need bureaucratic interlocutors, workers still did.[42]

The close ties of union leadership, technocratic government, and business elite created what one International Labor Organization official called "social monologue" instead of "social dialogue" or "tripartite bargaining." The ETUF focused attention on broader issues, including the generation of the new labor law and reforms to the state pension scheme, while bread and butter issues of shop floor workers devolved to lower level committees. The chronic interference in union elections meant that local unionists were selected for their loyalty to the NDP as opposed to legitimately representing their colleagues.

In the face of neoliberal reforms and an eroded labor management structure, workers undertook several efforts in an attempt to pressure the regime into meeting their demands. Workers at Mahalla attempted a vote of no confidence, which at first seemed to rouse the attention of the NDP and ETUF but did not lead to a resolution of their problems. Unauthorized, or "wildcat," strikes were a standard practice and faced varying degrees of repression. Following the Mahalla strike, international organizations took an interest in trade union activity outside the ETUF, while, at the same time, workers in Egypt pursued international agreements as an avenue to push back on the regime.

Egypt is a signatory to dozens of ILO regulations, which hypothetically have the force of law within Egypt. As a state seeking international recognition and support, Egypt has long been an active participant in international organizations, be it the nonaligned movement under Nasser or various UN bodies under Mubarak. ETUF leaders held positions inside the ILO. Despite this affiliation, relations soured in the aftermath of the Mahalla strike. Working through the CTUWS, workers increasingly pressed their claims on the regime in the language of international agreements. Surprisingly, the two ILO conventions most often referenced by workers are 87 and 98, two conventions that center on freedom of association and bargaining, signed in 1954 and 1957, respectively. One might wonder why a set of 50-year-old ILO conventions suddenly became the legal justification provided by trade unionists against the regime. One ILO activist said forthrightly that

---

[42] The Banker Editor, "Optimistic Engineer of Egypt's Fate – The Banker," April 4, 2005, www.thebanker.com/World/Africa/Egypt/Optimistic-engineer-of-Egypt-s-fate?ct=true.

"[W]ithout local move(ment), we can't do anything. After Mahalla we had something to support and show solidarity (with)."[43]

The adoption of the language of ILO conventions was pervasive. Not only was it invoked by independent unionists, but eventually also by the ETUF, who wielded it against their own opponents during the transition process. Professional activists and shop-floor level unionists began to mobilize the rhetoric of international guarantees, ILO conventions, and core freedoms afforded under international law. New elements combined in the mid-2000s to increase the relevance of ILO conventions. Workers in a variety of fields point to Kamal Abbas and the CTUWS as the source of their knowledge on ILO conventions. CTUWS undertook training sessions throughout the country, focusing both on the new industrial cities exempted from labor policies and the older industrial cities, including those with nationalized industries, constrained by neoliberal reforms. The organization was good at directing the frustration of workers into a specific narrative, one of international rights and obligations. This reframing attracted the attention of global labor, which provided some cover for the CTUWS when it faced frequent harassment from the security apparatus.

Besides security harassment, the regime showed little capacity for actually addressing worker frustration. The ETUF initially tried to pay off workers who went on strike, promising back pay and bonuses. The efforts were untenable. One of the goals of the privatization scheme was to pay for government payroll. By regularly paying special bonuses to deal with striking workers, the government would never achieve this goal. The regime pressured the ETUF to control its errant members, but the union had lost its capacity to do so.

While focusing on attempts to curry favor with the NDP leadership, the ETUF had failed to develop the skills of its own worker cadres. International attempts to boost capacity, from institutions like the Friedrich-Ebert Stiftung in Germany, failed. Instead of regularly sending freely elected worker representatives to special training sessions in negotiation and strategy, the union sent the same organizational apparatchiks, leaving union leadership ill-suited to negotiation.[44] Truly militant members frustrated with the ETUF's complicity with regime decisions moved into nascent pro-worker organizations outside

---

[43] Mohammed Trabelsi, ILO Representative, interview with author, October 2012.
[44] Ibid.

the union structure. These nascent independent organizations scored their first major victory in 2007.

Kamal Abu Eita, the leader of the first successful public sector workers' strike in recent Egyptian history and future minister of manpower, is from the post-Nasser generation. Graduating from college in 1976, Abu Eita was among the first generation to receive free college education, a hallmark of the Nasserist system. He joined the swelling ranks of the public sector, serving for over twenty years in the tax collection division of the ministry of finance. A persuasive speaker, Abu Eita had a background as a student activist. He served with the official trade union, representing his ministry until the fraudulent elections of 2006.

While hardly the first rigged elections in Egyptian trade union history, the 2006 elections were notable for three reasons. First, angry workers could turn to an increasingly independent media to explain their grievances. Second, workers' organizations like the CTUWS were on the ground monitoring the situation and reporting on abuses. Third, union leaders denied positions of power for their activism drew on new activist networks to push back on both the regime and the ETUF.

Both Abu Eita and Abbas were skilled in promoting their efforts using new media. Satellite television grew in popularity in Egypt throughout the late 1990s and the early 2000s. Like other Arab countries, news channels like Al Jazeera drew viewers in part because of their round-the-clock coverage of the US-led wars in Afghanistan and Iraq. Print media also saw increased opening in the mid-2000s. Al Masry Al Youm started publishing in 2004 and became known for its independence. Trade union activists, including the CTUWS, took advantage of increased press freedom by complaining about the fraudulent 2006 elections at the headquarters of the Egyptian Journalists' Syndicate, a common spot for the airing of public grievances that might otherwise attract a security crackdown.

In 2006, CTUWS was also on the ground in multiple cities tracking and reporting on the various violations associated with the elections. In addition to unethical rejection of candidates and ballots, the CTUWS documented acts of intimidation and violence in polling places throughout the country.[45] Certificates stating trade union membership

---

[45] CTUWS, "Facts About the Trade Union Elections for the Term 2006–2011," 2006.

were denied members, disenfranchising voters and stopping potential candidates for trade union office. The complaints were sufficient to gain the attention of the International Labor Organization, whose Committee of Experts cited them in an annual report.[46]

Finally, the trade union leaders exiled from the formal union structure had new forms of contention to call on to push their cause. The year 2004 saw the emergence of the Kefaya movement (also called the Egyptian Movement for Change). Kefaya had formed in part from the antiwar movement of 2003 and sought to challenge what was then seen as the inevitability of hereditary succession of the Egyptian presidency. Kamal Abu Eita was a leader of the movement and imported some of its street politics to the trade union movement.

Corporatist Collapse and the New Repertoire of Contention

In the year following the fraudulent elections, Abu Eita sought to organize workers around the issue of pay inequality. Workers in the real estate tax collection division were paid different salaries depending on which section of the Egyptian government they reported to. The ministry, however, was uninterested in labor issues. Abu Eita marched thousands of striking workers to the ministry of finance. When this protest failed, he relocated to the minister's house. When this also failed, he moved it to the ETUF headquarters itself. The sit-in next moved to the People's Assembly and grew to thousands of workers and their families. Abu Eita and his leadership team made good tactical decisions and had a flair for the dramatic. Their protests, which had been planned since the late summer of 2007, culminated in an open-ended sit-in in December. Abu Eita threatened to add to the already massive traffic jam brought on by the holiday of Eid Al-Adha by booking "most of the taxis in the city."[47]

Seizing and holding public space with large numbers without government sanction emerged as a tactic in the 2000s. After several days, the government capitulated. Workers received more than a 300 percent

---

[46] International Labour Office, *Record of Proceedings* (Geneva: International Labour Organization, 2008).

[47] While the threat to book "most the taxis" may be an exaggeration, as there are over 80,000 in Cairo, Abu Eita did threaten to invite entire families to join workers at the sit in, taking the issue-strike into a more general protest. Kamal Abu Eita, EFITU Founder, interview with author, April 2012.

raise in addition to bonus pay. The reporting structure was reorganized with the promise that they could report directly to a ministry, further demonstrating the centralization and hollowing out of the bureaucracy and the inability of the ETUF to successfully aggregate demands. Perhaps the most damning demonstration of diminished confidence in the ETUF was the decision by the strike committee to move forward with a plan to formulate an independent union. Shockingly, Minister of Manpower Aisha Abdel Hadi recognized this union, in part due to ILO pressure. Within the following months, plans were drawn up and organizing committees formed for independent unions representing tax, health, and education of workers.

The expansion of labor unrest from the industrial heartland of Mahalla El-Kubra to the streets of downtown Cairo was a dramatic escalation. A network of activists was forming that linked politically savvy youth and long-time worker activists. Both the strike at Mahalla El-Kubra and Abu Eita's strike for tax workers revealed the complete collapse of Egypt's corporatist system. Workers from both the industrial and bureaucratic sectors were dissatisfied with the reforms carried out by the Nazif government. The labor discontent breached the banks of the ETUF and resisted intervention by the NDP. The taboo on independent unions had been broken with full international support.

Before and after Mahalla El-Kubra's strike of 2007 and Abu Eita's declaration of an independent trade union, strikes broke out throughout the country. Perhaps tellingly, ILO records on strike data end abruptly in 2003 after having been reported since 1988.[48] The labor unrest has been recorded by the Land Center for Human Rights (itself a pro-labor organization funded in part by global labor organizations) and numbered in excess of 3,000 strikes with as many as a million participants.[49] Even if exaggerated, this demonstrates a startling uptick of organizing outside of the ETUF structure. The ETUF had abandoned the strike weapon so completely that even strikes its leadership

---

[48] "LABORSTA Internet: 9A (Yearly Data) (E)," accessed February 11, 2015, http://laborsta.ilo.org/STP/guest.

[49] Joel Beinin and Frédéric Vairel, *Social Movements, Mobilization, and Contestation in the Middle East and North Africa* (Redwood City, CA: Stanford University Press, 2011); Beinin, Joel and The Solidarity Center, *Justice for All: The Struggle for Workers Rights in Egypt* (New York, NY: The Solidarity Center, 2010).

deemed positive, like the long-standing strike in the Tanta Flax facility, were not officially endorsed.[50]

The wave of contentious labor politics that started with industrial workers in Mahalla and civil servants in Cairo spread outward through the country. Locations that had already worked with the CTUWS were hotbeds of activism and included the special economic zones set up throughout the country where labor had been particularly "flexibilized" in the previous years. Abu Eita's independent union worked to support white collar and bureaucratic workers rendered idle by the Nazif government's effort to sideline them.

The crackdown on independent unionists in the 2006 elections led to their total alienation from the ETUF and the emergence of independent unions. The protest vote against the NDP reached its highest level ever in the parliamentary elections of 2005, with more seats going to independent candidates affiliated with the Muslim Brotherhood than ever before.[51] Nazif's government of businessmen had eliminated the small number of concessions that had been granted to the ETUF in the past in an effort to maintain worker quiescence.

The regime turned to criminalizing dissent. On the labor front, Kamal Abbas was sentenced in 2007 for speaking out about corruption, a move largely seen as an attempt to silence the CTUWS, was sued for running an illegal organization, and the office of the Real Estate Tax Collectors independent union was shuttered briefly. Outside the main cities, where independent media and international observers had a protective effect on organizers, the regime was freer to use heavy-handed tactics. A general strike, planned and organized for April 6, 2008 and based in Mahalla, was effectively aborted through intimidation. Plain-clothed police (often called "bultagaya" or "thugs" in local parlance) intimidated workers. The idea for a general strike was promulgated in part by online activists using blogs and social media. This marked the emergence, similar to one seen in Tunisia, of young, politically savvy activists linking their cause to more remote

---

[50] Hussein Megawar, later indicted for violent attacks during the revolution, cited it as a positive example to his US embassy interlocutors in 2009. "Cable 09CAIRO2380 (Comparison)," cabledrum, accessed February 11, 2015, www.cabledrum.net/diff/09CAIRO2380.

[51] Sharon Otterman, "Muslim Brotherhood and Egypt's Parliamentary Elections," Council on Foreign Relations, December 1, 2005, www.cfr.org/egypt/muslim-brotherhood-egypts-parliamentary-elections/p9319.

trade union organizers. The 2010 parliamentary elections were blatantly stolen, and references to political reform were eliminated from the NDP platform.[52] Mubarak's promise to abolish the much-hated emergency law was broken.[53] The changes on the political front directly affected workers, as many labor leaders joined with political dissidents to organize against the Mubarak regime.

At the same time that the regime sought tighter political controls, the labor movement sought to press the advantages it found in industrial action into the political sphere. Kamal Abu Eita became a leading member of the Karama Party, a leftist, Nasserist party founded in the late 1990s. Hamdeen Sabbahi, a populist former parliamentarian who often agitated for workers' rights and a state-planned economy from a Nasserist perspective, headed the Karama party. Both were also members of the Egyptian Movement for Change (Kefaya). Kefaya emerged in late 2004 and served as a national anti-Mubarak front. The name literally means "enough" in Arabic, a call for the end of the excesses of the Mubarak regime, especially the decision to change the constitution in 2005 and the constant speculation that Egypt would experience hereditary succession for the first time since the 1952 Revolution. Kefaya managed to unite nationalist, liberal, leftist, and Islamist groups around the idea of not extending Mubarak's rule. The organization served as a key transmission mechanism for new types of contention developed by its disparate members. Labor activists were early and active leaders in the organization.[54]

Perhaps the most notable "labor" organization that emerged from the early phase of labor unrest in the late 2000s is the April 6th Movement. This youth movement involved many of the younger members of Kefaya and draws its name from the failed general strike

---

[52] Amr Hamzawy and Michele Dunne, "The Egyptian Parliamentary Elections: Facts and Figures," http://egyptelections.carnegieendowment.org/2010/11/28/the-egyptian-parliamentary-elections-facts-and-figures.

[53] Michael Slackman, "Egyptian Emergency Law Is Extended for 2 Years," *The New York Times*, May 11, 2010, sec. World / Middle East, www.nytimes.com/2010/05/12/world/middleeast/12egypt.html.

[54] For more on Kefaya, see Nadia Oweidat et al., *The Kefaya Movement: A Case Study of a Grassroots Reform Initiative* (Santa Monica, CA: Rand, National Defense Research Institute, 2008), https://www.rand.org/content/dam/rand/pubs/monographs/2008/RAND_MG778.pdf. The paper does an excellent job revealing the origins of the organization, but mistakenly suggests that Kefaya inspired labor strikes. Labor leaders from early strikes never mention Kefaya as an inspiration but welcome its support later on.

planned for Mahalla El-Kubra in 2008.[55] Despite their name, these activists had rather limited ties to actual activists in Mahalla. One activist described them as "taking the name without supporting the workers."[56] The group brought increased attention to labor issues and served to connect young political activists who used the Internet with workers' leaders, despite a sometimes-tense relationship. The emergence of organized opposition dovetailed nicely, especially in the labor sector, with a general withdrawal of international support for the ETUF.

In addition to its reduced capacity internally, the ETUF faced new challenges internationally. Just as alternative workers' organizations like CTUWS adopted the rhetoric of international institutions, these same institutions sought to move away from the ETUF. Directed originally through the Africa-American Labor Center and its successor organization the Solidarity Center, funds had flowed to ETUF projects from the AFL-CIO since 1979. The National Endowment for Democracy and USAID funded many of these projects. The relationship with the Solidarity Center focused on skills training and strategic planning, especially around issues of economic restructuring. Even early assessments recognized the diminished legitimacy of the ETUF, with one report in 1992 stating, "[M]any trade unionists ... see the need for a truly independent trade union movement. But old practices and arrangements die hard. Perquisites and privileges at the disposal of the government flow easily to those who are government supporters first, and trade unionists second." Despite this, the same report noted, "[I]n spite of the Egyptian trade union history, its unions are surprisingly democratic in the election of officials. Large numbers of individuals were candidates in the last election, and there was a high turnover rate." By the 2000s, this was no longer the case as the strike wave threatened worker quiescence; trade union elections were corrupted completely to remove more militant representatives. The last Solidarity Center grant was allowed to expire in 2003, and the Solidarity Center office was shut down soon after. A perception emerged among leadership at the Solidarity Center that the close relationship between American labor and the ETUF was damaging and corrosive, not allowing

---

[55] Ironically, April 6, 2008 was a nonevent. While workers called for a strike, state security rounded up many of the leaders of the proposed strike. The government marshaled the full forces of its repressive apparatus to prevent a general strike.

[56] Sayyid Habib, Mahalla Activist, interview with the author, November 2012.

Solidarity to view the ETUF with the critical eye it deserved, describing its local office as "enmeshed with the ETUF."[57] One official stated that the activities of the Solidarity Center and other international supporters would never end, as no one was willing to "work themselves out of a job." The pivot away by the American trade union movement did not go unnoticed by the ETUF, and it complained about it to the US Embassy as late as 2009.[58] The ITUC, formed in 2006 from the merger of earlier trade union confederations, rejected the application of the ETUF. The Global Union Federations (GUFs) also moved away from their Egyptian affiliates at this time, recognizing the ETUF's diminished capacity and increasingly corrupt nature. External legitimacy helped the ETUF to both maintain internal discipline (both through prestige and directing foreign funds and travel to loyal members) and increase its influence with the government of Egypt, which was particularly sensitive to international opinion. The loss of this support only strengthened the hand of independent trade union activists, who organized even more earnestly at the end of the decade.

Labor activists attempted to gather their potential allies into a coordinating committee that would oversee the movement for labor rights. While this coordinating committee had little effect on the state's labor laws or ETUF domination, it served a secondary purpose of bringing diverse activists together and disseminating the successful techniques of trade unionists to other groups. The members included minor parties like Tagammu, Ghad, and Karama, as well as NGOs like the Hisham Mubarak Law Center. Finally, the group brought together the nascent independent trade unions, including Abu Eita's tax collectors and the weavers of Mahalla. While not formal members, the Muslim Brotherhood attended these meetings and provided the coordinating committee with office spaces in which to conduct meetings.[59]

Labor protests provided opportunities for individuals disconnected from the regime's systems of control and threatened by the regime's policies to come together. The inability to aggregate and advocate on the part of workers, born of limited influence in the regime, corrupted

[57] Heba El-Shazli, Former Solidarity Center Representative, interview with author, February 2013.

[58] "Cable 09CAIRO2380 (Comparison)."

[59] Other groups included the Socialists Center, the Land Center, and Kefaya itself. Khaled Ali, *Together for Unleashing Trade Union Liberties: A Campaign Launched by HMLC*, 2009.

elections that brought in compliant leadership, and a long-term alienation of labor led to workers bolting the ETUF for new structures. This process was not totally unpredictable. Bellin wrote as early as 2000 that organized labor's declining position vis-à-vis other workers and strained relationship with the state could lead it to being a democratizing force for the country. The instinct was correct, though at the time the mechanism was opaque. Labor did help push for an opening in the system, but not through a reform of the ETUF's position. The ETUF itself was challenged by labor unrest and its inability to restrain it.

Perhaps the most important goal Nasser and later Sadat and Mubarak hoped to achieve in the corporatist system established with the ETUF was not so much to bring in labor support, but to prevent that support from flowing elsewhere. The NDP, in its Mubarak incarnation, did not so rely on workers' active participation or support in regime maintenance. The party managed to organize electorally to ensure broad margins for Mubarak's sham elections only. The ETUF simply needed to ensure that its membership did not actively support something other than the status quo. By the time the strike wave reached its zenith in the late 2000s, the ETUF could no longer guarantee this. While the fears of workers joining a communist party en masse had faded, and the Muslim Brotherhood's effective cooptation into regime maintenance precluded their ascendancy with organized labor, workers were beginning to push for more fundamental changes to the system. These changes did not require the emergence of a major political party to challenge the NDP.

While labor cannot be seen as a vanguard, the practices of mobilization, cross-ideological coalitions, and independent media focus would be taken up by other protesters. The demands of labor, including fair wages and social justice, would be taken up more broadly. These techniques were disseminated not just by an increasingly pluralistic media (including social media, independent newspapers, and satellite television) but also through coordinating committees and umbrella organizations like Kefaya. Mass mobilizations in central Cairo squares became prevalent during the anti-Iraq War protests of 2003, which the regime tacitly supported. Abu Eita's tax collectors perfected this technique during their multi-day sit-in outside the government's offices in downtown Cairo. The same group pioneered mass petitioning in support of their independent status, a technique later copied after the revolution by the Tamarod movement.

The use of social movements, and networking with internet-savvy youth activists like April 6th, was also a hallmark of labor demonstrations. Kamal Abbas tells a story of begging independent editors and youth activists to come and cover Mahalla's early strikes, coordinating groups with diverse interests around the issue of heavy-handed police repression.[60] By 2010, he no longer needed to beg. Independent trade unions had successfully vied for the attention of international institutions and were adept at attracting the attention of both domestic and international media. Their coordinating committees already had the makings of a revolutionary coalition that would take and hold Tahrir Square, including technologically savvy youth, hardened protesters, Islamists, socialists, and liberals.

It would be a grave misstep to ignore the role of the Tunisian Revolution in sparking the events that began on January 25 and culminated in Mubarak's departure. January 25, National Police Day, took place deep into Tunisia's crisis, with Ben Ali already having been ousted, and the "liberation caravans" riding from the entire country to the capital. Workers had been instrumental in the fight, and even in the first revolutionary government, had been given major concessions, as the rump of the RCD attempted to reconstitute the regime without Ben Ali. The process was heartening to Egypt's potential revolutionaries. Many of the protest groups who geared up for January 25, or mobilized later in response to police brutality, were involved in workers' activism. Kefaya, the Revolutionary Socialists, and youth wings of the Wafd and the Muslim Brotherhood all marched on the revolution's first day. Despite laying the groundwork for much of the uprising, workers' organizations did not join in immediately. Kamal Abu Eita marched on January 25, in his role as a Kefaya member and leader of the small Nasserist Karama Party.

Unlike its independent counterparts, the ETUF mobilized almost immediately in reaction to the protests. On January 27 it issued a statement calling on all unions to resist any effort at holding a strike in support of protests that had coalesced in Tahrir Square. The statement was a direct reaction to the call for more protests on January 28, which would come to be known as "Angry Friday." ETUF President Hussein Megawar, one of Mubarak's top lieutenants, was involved in the efforts to push back the protest wave and organize individuals to

---

[60] Kamal Abbas, CTUWS Founder, interview with the author, November 2012.

attack protesters. Despite this, reports abound from around the country that workers, many thousands of whom were already on strike when the revolution started, picked up the revolutionary mantle and brought it to the shop floor.

An assemblage of independent workers' organizations gathered in Tahrir Square on January 30, 2011. Only five days after the outbreak of what would come to be known as the January 25th Revolution, and two days after "Angry Friday," a group of workers from several of the independent trade unions that had emerged in the late 2000s arrived in Tahrir Square to declare a new labor confederation, the Egyptian Federation of Independent Trade Unions (EFITU). Eleven days later, strikes broke out around the country. Some explicitly declared solidarity with the protests in Tahrir, while others simply pressed their advantage on more prosaic issues, including wages, contracts, and working conditions.[61] Some reports suggest that tension spread to military production facilities, consistent with ongoing labor strife documented there by the CTUWS prior to the revolution.[62] Regardless of the extent, the possibility of labor unrest added to the atmosphere of chaos in the country.

The ETUF was unable to calm the strike wave, ongoing since 2006, which now threatened to link protesters in Cairo with workers around the country. Reflecting on the independent unionists' call for a general strike, one ETUF leader said the federation's main goal was "protecting worksites" not "major changes."[63] Hussein Megawar was later indicted for organizing the notorious "Camel Day" attacks, which saw sword-wielding, camel-riding thugs attacking protesters in Tahrir. As the regime often used the ETUF to gin up or tamp down protests, this accusation is not as absurd as it first seems, despite Megawar's later acquittal. Reports also suggest that Megawar, seeing the writing on the

---

[61] Emad al-Arabi, Media Coordinator for EFITU, interview with author, November 7, 2012.

[62] It is worth noting that there is some disagreement on independent unionists' activism in the military production factories. It is possible this is a result of the sensitive nature of this type of organizing. Even with the EFITU, reports have differed on the extent of coordination with workers operating inside military-run organizations.

[63] Mostapha Rostum, ETUF Representative, interview with author, March 24, 2012.

wall, told union presidents to solve disputes and keep workers quiet.[64] The report is revelatory in that it suggests even Megawar, the organization's long-serving president and Mubarak crony, was unaware of how limited the ETUF's capacity to control strikes was. This legacy of quiescence and conspiracy against the revolution would be the ETUF's legacy during the reconsolidation phase.

Conclusion

From the early 1990s through an unprecedented strike wave starting in the mid-2000s, Egypt's corporatist system collapsed. Its national trade union confederation, the ETUF, lost its ability to aggregate the demands of workers and advocate for those demands. Under the influence of structural adjustment, the Egyptian government reset the terms of the state's political economy. Flexibilization led to worker alienation and less dependence on the union. Leadership of the union tried desperately to hold on to some semblance of political power, losing ground year over year. Fearing worker unrest, the regime sought to corrupt union elections, leaving the institution even less able to respond to its members. By the mid-2000s workers were organizing outside the structure of the ETUF, pushing for new NGOs, unions, and movements to redress their grievances. The new tactics developed in part by these unionists would be put to remarkable effect in the 2011 revolution.

---

[64] Hossam el-Hamalawy, "#Jan25 Megawer: The Regime's Man," *@3arabawy* (blog), accessed February 16, 2015, http://arabawy.org/23675/egyworkers-jan25-megawer-the-regimes-man.

3 | Egypt's Failures to Reconsolidate Corporatism

Egyptian unions faced a massive headwind in attempts to achieve their objectives. These objectives, roughly cohesive since the early 2000s, included noninterference in trade union affairs, a role in shaping the political economic bargain in the country, a reformed labor law, and a minimum wage increase. The goals were shared by disgruntled workers of all stripes: those outside unions, those in the ETUF, and those in the nascent independent union movement following in Abu Eita's footsteps in the late 2000s. The most powerful change among workers in the revolution was the idea that old structures could be changed. For the first time since the 1950s, the ETUF had to compete for workers, as did the new independent unions. Each carried the baggage of their past performance, and enjoyed different claims to legitimacy. Each had to find new ways to relate to rising social and political forces within the country. And finally, each had different relationships to the transnational advocacy network I have termed "global labor." The incentives provided by these external linkages, combined with the constraints of legitimacy and constant efforts at cooptation, left trade unions in Egypt fractured and weak during the transition, with few of their goals achieved.

Incorporation and Legitimacy

The ETUF brought over 60 years of history and public perception to the Egyptian revolution. Having discussed the ETUF's origin, and the breakdown in its ability to aggregate and advocate, I have argued that the union could once provide some outlet for workers' grievances, and that this had eroded sharply in the 1990s and 2000s. Some scholars have argued that the ETUF showed some capacity, while others have suggested that even analyzing it as a union is an exercise in futility. Alexander and Bassiouny suggest that the union was little more than a wing of the party.[1] Perhaps less important than what the ETUF "was," is how it thought of itself and the narratives open to members in justifying certain actions. These historical legacies, and the stories around them, limited options open to the union, and deprived its leadership of a disciplining rhetoric used effectively by their counterparts in Tunisia.

Collier and Collier's *Shaping the Political Arena* looms large in any study of the mobilization and politicization of labor.[2] While their main focus was on Latin America, many of the ideas contained in the 1992 classic are relevant for the Middle East as well, from colonial legacy to authoritarianism to labor incorporation. The book also shaped the field of comparative politics more broadly, providing a grammar of institutionalism that persists to this day.

Per Collier and Collier, the historical legacy of a critical juncture is, in fact, what makes that juncture critical. They write "[T]he importance or lack of importance of a critical juncture cannot be established in general, but only with reference to a specific historical legacy." The authors go on to distinguish between "constant causes" and "historical causes," aligning the latter with critical junctures. Constant causes are those that are repeated, pushing institutional arrangements on an ongoing basis. Historical causes are those that crystalize political institutions and set a new pattern. Incorporation of labor into a dominant political system clearly sets a "historical cause" for a country's political economy.

In the instances of Egypt and Tunisia, the periods of historical labor incorporation are quite clear. They began in the 1940s in each country, when domestic, rather than colonial, workers began to organize to push against owners, the state, and colonial powers. From these similar origins, Tunisia and Egypt diverge sharply. Tunisia's national trade union, the UGTT, coalesced prior to independence, and gave shape and political weight to the nationalist independence movement. The

---

[1] Agnieszka Paczynska, *State, Labor, and the Transition to a Market Economy Egypt, Poland, Mexico, and the Czech Republic* (University Park, PA: Pennsylvania State University Press, 2009); Anne Alexander and Mostafa Bassiouny, *Bread, Freedom, Social Justice: Workers and the Egyptian Revolution* (Chicago, IL: Zed Books, 2014), respectively.

[2] Ruth Collier and David Collier, *Shaping the Political Arena: Critical Junctures, the Labor Movement, and Regime Dynamics in Latin America* (Princeton, NJ: Princeton University Press, 1991).

UGTT, including its leadership, were national leaders, and the first postindependence government draws heavily from its ranks. The country's economic policies were shaped by pro-worker, pro-union, and pro-UGTT policies from the outset. Even those who suggest the UGTT's militancy came later still date the critical era to the 1970s and 1980s.[3]

Egypt, on the other hand, saw the military take the deciding role in the independence movement. Nasser's 1952 coup (eventually) drove the British out, reset regional balances of power, reorganized the economy, and overthrew the monarchy. He sought to organize and coopt sectors of potential resistance, starting with the military, and then capitalist enterprise and workers' organizations. The establishment of the ETUF in 1957 was at the largesse of the state. While the country also saw broad pro-worker policies implemented, it was at the beneficence of the state, not due to the power of the union or its organizational capacity. To borrow a religious metaphor, if the UGTT was "consubstantial" with the state and the national movement, the ETUF was "made" by the state.

These differences in the modes of labor incorporation are undeniable. A conversation with any trade unionist in either country, especially in Tunisia where "independence from birth" is a point of pride, will make it clear. Overattention to these facts, however, obscures more than it reveals. In the past decades, and especially since the 2010–11 revolutionary wave that has reset internal and external relationships in both countries, the differing outcomes in Egypt and Tunisia, especially with regards to their labor movements, have been rendered fait acomplis. In the eyes of many analysts, labor scholars, and even members of global labor, the UGTT is real, robust, independent, and original. The ETUF is fake, weak, captured, and state-created. This narrative is summed up in Alexander and Bassiouny's explicit contrast of the ETUF with the UGTT, stating that "fundamentally this was because, unlike the UGTT, which preceded and helped to create the post-independence Tunisian state, the ETUF was not a trade union but an extension of the state bureaucracy."[4] In this view, the latter's sycophancy to authoritarian politics was predestined in the 1950s,

[3] Keenan Wilder, "The Origins of Labour Autonomy in Authoritarian Tunisia," *Contemporary Social Science* 10, no. 4 (October 2, 2015): 349–63.
[4] Anne Alexander and Mostafa Bassiouny, *Bread, Freedom, Social Justice: Workers and the Egyptian Revolution* (Chicago, IL: Zed Books, 2014).

while the former's revolutionary bona fides meant its share of the 2015 Nobel Prize was more a "lifetime achievement" award than a recognition of real dynamism. This view is overly reductive. The ETUF's fate was not sealed in the 1950s, but in a long-running process born of the neoliberal reforms, and consolidated by its inability to forge robust internal links within Egypt, external links to global labor, or craft a successful narrative justifying its role as an independent force in the country. These multifaceted failures left a fractured trade union movement, largely unable to influence the transition that was coming.

Building on Collier and Collier's work, Caraway points to six factors for the continued dominance of a legacy union (in the instance of Egypt, the ETUF).[5] Three are inherited: membership, institutional connections, and legal structures. Three depend on the transition itself: economy, the nature of union competition, and partisan links. Caraway, however, is focused primarily on the ability of the legacy union to maintain its advantage over competitors. This analysis looks instead at the ability of the trade union movement as a whole to achieve its shared objectives in the transitional context. In this section I explore many of Caraway's proposed factors, but bring two new ones to the table: external linkages and legitimacy. When thinking about incorporation and legitimacy, however, it is important to recognize that it falls into both the "inherited" and "transition" groupings. Each union inherits its own prerevolutionary history, but also engages in an active process of reconstructing, packaging, and marketing that history to both external stakeholders and its own members. For the ETUF, this reconstructed history was distributional, focused on slowing down bad policies and occasionally bolstering good ones. This had been its legitimizing tactic since the 1990s. The position of the ETUF is best summed up in the words of former Minister of Manpower Aisha Abdel Hadi, who said in 2004, "[W]e have so little to work with. So few resources and labour is on the defensive. We need to talk to the government and we cannot negotiate with them if we are not on speaking terms."[6]

---

[5] Teri L. Caraway, "Explaining the Dominance of Legacy Unions in New Democracies Comparative Insights from Indonesia," *Comparative Political Studies* 41, no. 10 (October 1, 2008): 1371–97.

[6] "Aisha Abdel Hadi: A Labor of Love," available at http://webcache.googleusercontent.com/search?q=cache:http://weekly.ahram.org.eg/2001/532/profile.htm.

The ETUF prided itself on its ability to wring some concession from the government. As opposed to being a nonunion, it was a conventional, albeit coopted, one. The bottom-up forces within the union, to use another phrase from Collier and Collier, sought to slow down, redirect, and hamper elements of the reform package. Its legitimacy was based on its relationship to the regime. Both the ETUF and the new independent unions faced problems of legitimacy based on their incorporation. Caraway's discussion of incorporation is a key component in understanding pathways of labor displacement; however, for the purposes of analyzing Egypt, and later Tunisia, "incorporation" here means something different than Caraway intends. Caraway divides incorporation into two subtypes: transmission belt and exclusionary corporatist. She defines transmission belt unions as enjoying monopoly status and near universal membership. Exclusionary corporatist unions on the other hand served to exclude unions and have very low union density. Neither model captures the role of the ETUF. The union served different purposes at different times and was viewed differently by successive regimes. Neither captures the dynamics of collapsing corporatism under neoliberal reforms described earlier. I instead refer here to how incorporation constrains rhetorical options for unionists, not so much by dictating their structure, as truncating their appeals.

Attention to incorporation remains vital to understanding the trajectory of the ETUF following the uprising in Egypt. Invoking impressive past heroes, victories won, or members martyred activates cultural and religious tropes that can corral existing members, attract new ones, and dissuade disgruntled unionists from breaking away. For the ETUF, rhetorical appeals were particularly challenging. The ETUF was created by top-down decree, and strengthened by further regime-led nationalizations and unionization efforts. When challenged, the union had little to fall back on rhetorically, beyond its contentious connections to the Nasserist Era. Even these were challenged as Nasserist rhetoric was largely "owned" in the transition by the Nasserist Karama Party and other small political groups, most of whom were more closely aligned with the independent trade union movement. Any legacy of good will they had in pushing back on the *infitah* reforms of the Sadat era had been forgotten in their complicity in the crony capitalism that emerged under Mubarak. If these factors were not damning enough, its actions during the revolution confirmed the perception that the union worked for the regime and not for its members.

An assemblage of independent workers' organizations gathered in Tahrir Square on January 30, 2011. Only five days after the outbreak of what would come to be known as the January 25th Revolution and two days after "Angry Friday" a group of workers from several of the independent trade unions that had emerged in the late 2000s arrived in Tahrir Square to declare a new labor confederation, the Egyptian Federation of Independent Trade Unions (EFITU). Eleven days later, strikes broke out around the country. Some explicitly declared solidarity with the protests in Tahrir, while others simply pressed their advantage on issues that are more prosaic, including wages, contracts, and working conditions. Some reports suggest that tension spread to military production facilities, consistent with ongoing labor strife documented there by the CTUWS prior to the revolution. Regardless of the extent, the possibility of labor unrest added to the atmosphere of chaos in the country.

Even without it, the ETUF's efforts to contain the labor sector following January 25 gave a clear indication of its loyalties. Throughout the transition the organization claimed impartiality, attacking the leaders of independent trade unions as crass political opportunists. This rhetoric failed to capture the zeitgeist, in which all sectors of society, even those far removed from politics, had been politicized by the direct action of protest during the revolution.

The ETUF's competitors had a somewhat easier time, but faced their own challenges. The independent unionists had a recent, if powerful, rhetorical well to draw on in their recruitment efforts. The founding declaration in Tahrir Square was a deft political move, one reflected in Mohammed Morsi's decision to take the oath of office a second time in Tahrir Square. As time went on, the January 30 declaration became more prominent in the groups' narratives. The strike wave, stretching back to the mid-2000s was claimed as the start of the revolution, and labor was situated at the vanguard of the revolutionary movement. These new unions made the sharpest inroads in the places most neglected by the policies of the late Mubarak era. In addition to Abu Eita's ties to white collar workers harmed by lay offs and stagnant wages in the public sector, labor militancy was seen in SOEs and para-state bodies. The new industrial sectors, where the ETUF's control had been limited, also saw the formation of strike committees and, eventually, independent unions. The ETUF struggled against its challengers in part because the independent unions were able to claim a robust (if rather new) revolutionary legitimacy. The declaration of EFITU in Tahrir Square, the strike wave that preceded the revolution, the general strike called 48 hours before Mubarak's departure, all gave the independent unions a well to draw on in attracting new members, disciplining their present membership, and challenging the ETUF.

This promotion of revolutionary legitimacy was increasingly challenging to maintain in 2012 and 2013 as the conflict between secular forces, including the remainder of the coercive apparatus of the state, entered into open conflict with the Muslim Brotherhood. Ironically, the independent unions mirrored the make up of the anti-Brotherhood coalition, including leftist, liberal, and Salafi trade unionists. Despite this, as the legacy of the January 25th revolution was tarnished by the political infighting that followed it, the independent trade unionists also faltered. If the movement could have produced real changes for workers, or even maintained its internal unity, it may have been able to reconcile its pre-January 25 legitimacy with their efforts to oust Morsi in 2013, but the descent into infighting prevented this.

The actual street-based struggles of the Egyptian revolution have been discussed in various reports, ranging from the eye-witness to the theoretical. Citizens, under the banners of bread, freedom, and social justice, took to the streets, most notably in Tahrir Square in central Cairo, and called for a new government. They engaged in pitched battles with the security services, breaking the back of Egypt's coercive apparatus.[7] With the international community stepping back from its staunch support of Mubarak, and his relationship with his own levers of power increasingly untenable, Mubarak stepped down on February 11, 2011. Eighteen days after protests broke out, and two days after independent unionists called for a (symbolic but not widely adhered to) general strike, the regime had fallen.

The independent trade unions, unlike the ETUF, were empowered by the revolution. Some workers found that their colleagues shared similar views only by encountering them in Tahrir Square itself.[8]

---

[7] Neil Ketchley, *Egypt in a Time of Revolution: Contentious Politics and the Arab Spring*, Cambridge Studies in Contentious Politics (Cambridge: Cambridge University Press, 2017).

[8] Hani Al-Kas, Independent Transportation Union, interview with author, March 28, 2012.

Workers discussed a desire to unleash an anger "boiling" under the surface.[9] Independent unions sprouted throughout the country. While both Kamal Abbas and Kamal Abu Eita seeded them, many organizations were sui generis, reaching out to Abbas or Abu Eita (or both) only after starting discussions among themselves.[10] The flourishing of Egyptian civil society that included citizen councils, new NGOs, and political parties also impacted the labor sector.

While the long-running strike wave contributed a new repertoire of contention to the Egyptian people and set the groundwork for the revolution, the revolution also inspired workers. Many workers interviewed cited the revolution and the seizure of Tahrir Square as the inspiration for their own strikes and creation of independent unions. One strike leader cited the experience in Tahrir, which he had joined as an individual, as an inspiration for the massive transit strike in 2012. During an interview he presented a bullet and claimed security forces had fired it at him on January 28, 2011, changing his perception of the regime. His independent union was formed in April 2011.

It is here that we find another issue with the "incorporation" argument for the ETUF's continued path of cooptation and regime complicity. The ETUF enjoyed many of the benefits of legacy unions identified by Caraway and others. It had the power to directly deduct dues, significant financial resources, a legal apparatus, and ties to the bureaucracy even after the fall of the regime. These benefits, however, had not been converted into rhetorical support for the ETUF even internally to its own cadres. The most notable feature of interviews with independent trade unionists in 2011 and 2012 was not their dislike of the ETUF, but their claimed lack of knowledge of it. This is not to say that these workers were not fully informed of the ETUF's actions at an elite level, but a lack of knowledge that it even existed. Across dozens of interviews, workers who decided to join new independent unions claimed that they were shocked to learn they had even been members of a union. If estimates from the ETUF and independent unions in 2012–14 are to be believed, unions covered around 22 percent of workers in Egypt.[11] More conservative estimates place the number as

[9] Mohammed al-Amm, Independent Gas Union, interview with author, April 2012.

[10] Nehal al-Qadi, Activist, interview with author, April 2012.

[11] LO/FTF Council's Analytical Unit, "Labour Market Profile Egypt 2015" (Copenhagen, Denmark, 2015).

low as 12 percent.[12] Despite this, Arab Barometer data, along with interviews at the time, suggest that those who knew they were in a union might be even lower. The Wave IV of the Arab Barometer, the best public opinion data available for the period immediately following the revolution, shows that when asked "[A]re you a member of any organizations?" followed by a list that included not only unions but also religious and cultural organizations, farmer's groups, and sports clubs, only 10.9 percent said yes. Numbers provided by the union federations would place union membership at nearly a quarter of the workforce, and as much as 10 percent of the total adult population. When including the variety of other organizations included in the question, the number should be far higher. Rank-and-file members may have felt no real connection to the institution, and limited investment in its success or failure. When asked unprompted if they are a "member" of the organization they may say no, as the union has no real ties to their daily lives. In this way, the ETUF is quite different than the sort of "legacy" union we see in post-Soviet states. Regardless of their level of state subservience, these unions served as a commonly used vehicle to deliver real services to members who would be unlikely to be unaware of the institution and its leadership. The ETUF faced an uphill struggle in retaining its power not only because of the percentage of workers in the informal economy and uncovered by labor contracts, which has been estimated to be as high as 40 percent, but because of its relatively unknown status even to its own members. In this context, a new union promising a revolutionary change held great appeal.

For other new unionists, the decision to form an independent union came later, as EFITU gained traction in the media, and postrevolutionary governments put a spotlight on worker grievances. While prerevolutionary independent organizing encompassed both bureaucratic and industrial workers, postrevolutionary organizing expanded in new directions. While workers formed new unions outside the auspices of the ETUF, the ETUF faced an even greater threat to its eroding power: a military interregnum and increasingly powerful new domestic actors.

---

[12] Tarek Masoud, *Counting Islam: Religion, Class, and Elections in Egypt* (New York, NY: Cambridge University Press, 2014).

Internal Linkages

Prior to the revolution, the ETUF had one relationship to manage, its own to the regime. Following the revolution, the ETUF had several new relationships: that between itself and newly independent unions, the military regime, the state bureaucracy over which the military sat, business interests, and a variety of political forces, including Islamist, liberal, and conservative strains. How these relationships emerged (or failed to) helps explain the lingering dynamic of cooptation that gripped Egypt's labor sector. Instead of a simple cooptation of the ETUF by the regime, Egypt saw an emerging dynamic of "competitive cooptation" with efforts by a variety of actors to direct or corral labor discontent to various political ends. This dynamic only increased the weakening and fracture of the trade union movement, leaving it more vulnerable to predation and limiting its ability to push for real change.

The most pressing concern for labor was the new reality it faced in the form of a military dictatorship. After the revolution, the Supreme Council of the Armed Forces (SCAF) appointed a new government of national unity. On March 7, Field Marshall Tantawi swore in the interim cabinet, headed by Prime Minister Essam Sharaf. Unlike previous administrations that had drawn candidates for positions like minister of labor from the leadership ranks of the ETUF, Sharaf and the military establishment chose a candidate from the independent trade union movement.

Ahmed Hassan Al-Borai was a lawyer and longtime counselor to the International Labor Organization. Prior to being tapped to head the ministry of manpower, he served as a legal advisor to Kamal Abu Eita's Real Estate Tax Authority Union (RETA). Urbane and cosmopolitan, Al-Borai spent years in Europe and spoke fluent French. His close relationship with the ILO and other components of the international trade union movement made him unique in his position, which had usually been given to ETUF officials who were members of the NDP. The tension between the new leadership of the ministry of manpower and the ETUF was unprecedented. Al-Borai claims that the ETUF spent over 1 million Egyptian Pounds to remove him from office, joking that he would have left for half the price.[13] While the million pound figure may be an exaggeration, rhetoric against Al-Borai continued to pour

---

[13] Ahmed Hassan Al-Borai, former minister of manpower, interview with author, May 2012.

out of the ETUF even after his departure from the position, demonstrating a deep antagonism between them.

In March 2011, only days after being sworn in, Al-Borai announced at a labor conference the end of the ETUF's monopoly over trade unions. Sitting next to Abbas and Abu Eita, Al-Borai announced that trade unions could be formed with no government oversight, no affiliation with the ETUF, and no interference with their economic plans. The dramatic scene ended with Abbas declaring that the ETUF had fallen and encouraging attendees to start unions. This scene would be remembered in the coming years as the high point of the independent trade union movement.

Despite Al-Borai's declarations of trade union independence, the ETUF was still in power, and had massive resources in terms of both mobilization and facilities. Former ETUF Vice President Abdul Monem Al-Ghazzali listed them as including "child care, schools, beaches, vocational health and safety, and three hundred cultural centers."[14] These assets were in addition to the Worker's College system of educational institutions that had benefited from Solidarity Center support through 2003. With membership rolls numbering in the millions, and dues collected automatically through payroll deductions, the ETUF remained a force to be reckoned with.

Al-Borai took a juridical approach to dealing with his adversaries in the ETUF. His attempt was two pronged: starve the ETUF, and then decapitate it. In March, following his announcement of trade union freedom, he stopped government subsidies to the ETUF. He called for a new nonmandatory dues policy, though workers still reported dues being removed in 2013. Next, Al-Borai worked to change the ETUF board. In August a decree from the Prime Minister enforced a court ruling that the 2006 ETUF board elections had been fraudulent. While fraud in union elections and outright meddling from the regime had a long history, the 2006 elections were, by some reports, especially egregious.[15] This move shows obvious unease on the part of Al-Borai and the independent unions. New elections for the ETUF were only weeks away, but fear was rising that the tenacious old guard would manage to survive. Al-Borai was charged with replacing the liquidated

[14] Abdul Monem Al-Ghazzali, former ETUF Official, interview with author, April 2012.
[15] CTUWS, "Facts About the Trade Union Elections for the Term 2006–2011," 2006.

board, and he assembled a new board with "old people (ETUF officials), Muslim Brothers, youth, and technocrats."[16] The addition of
Muslim Brothers was a first for Egypt. Muslim Brotherhood members
had held a number of seats in parliament and had won union elections,
but had not for the duration of the Mubarak regime been appointed to
other political positions. Despite the more "balanced" nature of the
board, political infighting continued within the ETUF. The old guard,
still angry over the board dissolution, organized protests over the delay
of elections to 2012.

During Al-Borai's period as minister of manpower, eight general
conferences on amending the Egyptian trade union law (Law 35/1976)
were held in an attempt to build consensus on the issue. A variety of
drafts existed, including ones contributed by the Muslim Brotherhood,
the ETUF, and other Egyptian politicians. The draft that finally gained
support was colloquially referred to as "Borai's Law" and had the
benefit of having been approved by the ILO. The goal was to bring the
law into accordance with those international labor standards that Egypt
was a signatory of, and thus have its name removed from the ILO
blacklist. Despite gaining support from the Cabinet, SCAF shelved the
law. The deeply conservative streak among the Egyptian generals had
been established in the days after the revolution, when one of the first
acts SCAF undertook was to ban strikes. While the military leadership
seemed comfortable drawing support from the independent unions, and
even appointing their allies to top positions, the prospect of more unruly
unions being codified into the law seemed a bridge too far.

SCAF's removal of Mubarak left a political vacuum at the top that
it made clear the military would fill. The first constitutional proclamation, issued just days after Mubarak's departure from power, suspended the constitution and dissolved the parliament. It maintained the
government of Ahmed Shafik that had been appointed in Mubarak's
waning days. This government did not last long. Shafik stepped down
on March 3, 2011, and most of his cabinet was replaced soon after. On
the labor side, this would be the last time that a leading ETUF official
would be the natural choice for minister of manpower. The Shafik
cabinet had Ismael Ibrahim Fahmy in this role, who stepped down to
become ETUF acting president, a continuation of the revolving door

---

[16] Ahmed Hassan Al-Borai, Former Minister of Manpower, interview with author,
April 2012.

between the labor ministry and the official trade union that had lasted decades. The cabinet also included internationally minded technocrats, some of whom had worked at the ILO.

Despite this, the military's desire for stability trumped prospects for labor reform. Soon after acquiescing to demands to appoint a more independent union-friendly candidate, SCAF approved a law that sharply curtailed labor rights in the country. The law criminalized anything that "makes a stand or undertakes an activity that results in the prevention of, obstruction, or hindering a State's institution or a public authority or a public or private working organization from performing its work" or who "incites, invites or promotes [such activity]."[17] As the ILO noted at the time, such a restriction interpreted broadly would effectively outlaw all strikes against both public and private institutions in the country. Amazingly, this was actually a steeper restriction than what existed prior to the revolution. While strikes needed to be approved by the ETUF (a daunting process that was rarely successful), their legality was enshrined in law. By passing this declaration, SCAF attempted to blunt, if not eliminate, the strike weapon.

SCAF's hesitance to address labor issues can also be seen in its unwillingness to pass a rewritten trade union law for the country. Egypt's trade union law (Law 35/1976) had been roundly criticized since the 1980s for concentrating power in the hands of the ETUF. It was complimented by a labor law that enshrined flexibilization. While isolated voices had called for its replacement for decades, a broad front supporting a new trade union law coalesced in 2008, and included the CTUWS, the new independent unions, and a variety of leftist parties and activist groups. Several draft laws had been circulated, with some rough consensus emerging around a text written by Al-Borai. The Al-Borai text had the benefit of having won the support of the ILO, as well as the independent trade unionists. Despite presenting it to them with cabinet support, the draft suffered a "pocket veto" by SCAF. The message by April was clear. The military was using a tool from the Mubarak playbook: allowing limited governmental participation (in

---

[17] International Labor Organization, *Observation (CEACR) Adopted 2011, Published 101st ILC Session (2012)*, www.ilo.org/dyn/normlex/en/f?p=1000:13100:0::NO:13100:P13100_COMMENT_ID:3080829.

the form of Al-Borai receiving a ministry portfolio) while slowing the pace of actual change.

Protests grew as the spring dragged on with no timeline for new elections. Fears of indefinite military control grew. Labor protests also continued, as the emboldened independent trade unionists carried out strikes and protests throughout the country. Tensions came to a head on July 12, 2011. A sit-in calling for an end to military rule, among other goals, chose to block traffic in and out of Cairo's busy Tahrir Square. Essam Sharaf, whose resignation was also called for, showed little ability to calm the situation. SCAF took to the airwaves directly, sending Gen. Mohsen El-Fangary on national television to address the nation. El-Fangary's speech included both a scolding tone and literal finger wagging, as he cautioned the country against those who would seek to take over power or slow recovery.[18] The threat to striking workers was blatant. The economic priorities of the state still focused on stability, despite cosmetic changes to labor leadership.

Military interventions did not simply amount to rhetorical tongue-lashings. Throughout 2011 the army, often with direct force, broke strikes. By early 2012, tactics evolved to be less confrontational. In March 2012 Cairo's independent transit workers began a strike demanding to be incorporated into the transportation ministry.[19] The transportation sector in Cairo is extremely important, moving millions of workers every day. In addition to this, the sector has a long history of political activity and was vital to both establishing unions in the country, and supporting Nasser's regime. The strike proved politically sensitive, and SCAF used a new method of dealing with it by directly running busses under its own authority. Conscripts drove busses personally, replacing the striking workers. The decision to bring the military directly into the economic sector foreshadowed moves made by the later Sisi regime, which often sought to "militarize" key

---

[18] ‏2011 يوليو 12 الثلاثاء - بيان القوات المسلحة (A Statement from the Armed Forces, July 12, 2011). Available at: www.youtube.com/watch?v=CqpgsqPggH0&feature= youtube_gdata_player (accessed April 26, 2014).

[19] Sheikh Tariq, Activist, interview with author. March 28, 2012. While the issue at first sounds likes one of privatization, the workers are actually government employees. Not unlike Abu Eita's tax collector strike, the fight was one of governmental efficiency. The vice president of the independent union reported to the author that "ministerial decisions are faster," and that the workers wished to be moved from the auspices of the Cairo Governate to those of the federal government.

economic activities. While the process was not new in Egypt, doing so in such public-facing institutions was a change.

The battle over strikes and unions in the country had attracted the attention of several political forces in the country in addition to the SCAF. During his time as minister of manpower, Al-Borai appointed a new caretaker board of directors for the ETUF. Five of the new ETUF board members were Muslim Brothers, who held on to their positions throughout the power struggle that took place. Yosri Bayoumi, an MB parliamentarian and leader in the organization's labor sector, became the ETUF's treasurer, a powerful position with direct influence over the organization's substantial holdings. Bayoumi conveyed the Brotherhood's position in early 2012, stating his desire for one union only at each work site, claiming "if you have five unions, after a year you hold elections, every loser gets to have his own union."[20] This was a far cry from the support the Brotherhood showed for independent syndicates prior to the revolution, and a sign of its emerging institutional conservatism. Other members of the board reflected existing ETUF leadership, while some came from more militant local unions. This reconstruction of the board, however, did not succeed in changing the organization profoundly. Its creation was undemocratic and did not reflect or include the labor militancy taking place outside of the ETUF's structure. Struggles between Muslim Brotherhood members and other political currents grew, foreshadowing the larger conflict in the government.

Al-Borai's turbulent leadership of the ministry of manpower came to a quick end in December 2011 when, following protests, SCAF appointed Kemal Al-Ganzouri as the new prime minister. Fearing continued unrest in the labor sector, Ganzouri appointed Fathi Fekry, a professor with no previous connection to the labor movement to head the ministry. For the following 7 months, battles over labor would move to other territory. Fekry would be the last "neutral" administrator of the ministry of manpower, with future appointees once again coming from the ranks of the independent unions or the ETUF.

---

[20] Yosri Bayoumi, Former ETUF Treasurer interview with author, April 2012. Despite his position in favor of "one union per worksite," Bayoumi was clear in his opposition to the existing version of Law 35/1976 and called for its elimination in favor of a new trade union law.

Mohammed Morsi was elected the country's fourth president, and the first freely elected president in its history, on June 24, 2012. Morsi promised to be a president for all people, and resigned his position as head of the Muslim Brotherhood-affiliated Freedom and Justice Party. Unsurprisingly, however, the electoral victory increased the Brotherhood's involvement in union issues. Out of all cabinet positions, only five went to members of the Brotherhood's Freedom and Justice Party, but labor was among them. Khaled Azheri was appointed minister of manpower. Azheri had served as a member of parliament, sitting on the labor committee, and a member of the constituent assembly charged with drafting the constitution. The fight for trade union rights in the parliament raged just as it had under SCAF. The labor committee, which Azheri sat on, entertained multiple drafts of trade union freedom laws, including the FJP's own, which heavily favored the ETUF. Now the Muslim Brotherhood enjoyed the power that came with having seats on the ETUF board and controlling the ministry of manpower. Other political movements kept their political distance from labor.

Prior to the January 25th Revolution, Egypt functioned as a de facto single party state. The NDP controlled a vast patronage network that used both rural elites and urban masses. Opposition parties were formally legal, both for the benefits they provided the regime, and as a nod to international pressure for democracy. Some of these parties enjoyed long histories and their own dedicated constituencies. Despite this, they were weak, coopted, and constrained. The universe of legal parties did not reflect the true political commitments of the public. Parties that used a religious frame of reference were illegal, precluding the Muslim Brotherhood from fielding an official party.

Despite having been disbanded for years following Nasser's revolution, the party that claims the oldest legacy in Egypt is the Wafd. The original Wafd party was founded in 1919 and was a powerful nationalist, liberal party through 1952. Upon its reemergence under reforms carried out in the 1980s, the party resurrected its liberal party platform. In this instance, despite the almost thirty-year lag in official existence, the term "reemergence" is accurate. One study conducted at the time suggested almost a third of members had existing family ties to the old Wafd of the 1940s and 1950s.[21] Members interviewed after

---

[21] Raymond A. Hinnebusch, "Party Activists in Syria and Egypt: Political Participation in Authoritarian Modernizing States," _International Political Science Review / Revue Internationale de Science Politique_ 4, no. 1 (January 1, 1983): 84–93. Interestingly, Hinnebusch mentions a deep antipathy towards

the revolution emphasized this continuity as well.[22] Wafd membership consisted largely of upper-middle class, professional, and business elites. Unsurprisingly, their economic policies called for capitalist reforms. Despite the perhaps natural tension between a capitalist-oriented nationalist political party and organized workers under threat from capitalist reforms, authoritarianism made strange bedfellows in the 1980s. Wafd resisted the media blackout of the steel and rail strikes of the late 1980s and published dramatic photographs of security services crackdowns on labor activists.[23] In the words of labor organizer Saber Barakat, "Wafd would stand with workers against torture, but not on worker's rights."[24] Wafd also took a pragmatic stance with regards to elections, working with the Muslim Brotherhood in the 1980s to maximize electoral gains.[25]

After the emergence of the wave of labor unrest in the mid-2000s, Wafd took some small steps to engage with the issue, conscientious of the bounds placed on them by the regime. Wafd established a labor committee made up of members involved in the ETUF following a conference in 2005.[26] These close ETUF ties persisted after the revolution. Leaders working on labor issues explicitly rejected both trade union pluralism and any attempts to dissolve the ETUF. The Wafd also took the position that independent trade unions were illegal.[27] Said Googrey, one of the leaders of the Wafd Labor Committee stated a recurring fear among some labor activists regarding accountability. Technically, the ETUF was required to provide reports to the General Accounting Office, while due to the uncertain legal status the independent unions had no such responsibility.

With little hope of more militant trade unionists turning back neoliberal reforms, some modus vivendi with classically liberal political groups would be necessary to advance trade union goals. While their economic ideas may not match perfectly, the history of

Nasser during interviews conducted in the early 1980s. Interviews conducted in 2012 started with denunciations of Nasser as well.

[22] Said Googrey, Wafd Party, March 27, 2012.
[23] Saber Barakat, Activist, interview with author, April 2011.
[24] Ibid.
[25] Joshua A. Stacher, "Parties Over: The Demise of Egypt's Opposition Parties," *British Journal of Middle Eastern Studies* 31, no. 2 (November 1, 2004): 215–33.
[26] Tarek Al-Tohami, Wafd Leadership, interview with author, March 26, 2012.
[27] Ibid.

antiauthoritarian protests and shared progressive goals would be important in any possible compromise. In addition to this, the Wafd is a political survivor, and despite its long-standing support from the Mubarak regime as a "loyal opposition" party, its leadership carried enough political clout for it to exist even after the withdrawal of support. Its name and ideology survived over a quarter century in political exile, and the political turmoil of 2011. As a liberal standard-bearer, its support for the ETUF and rejection of the independent unions posed a serious challenge for reconsolidation.

If the Wafd is the standard-bearer legacy party for liberals, Tagammu was the standard-bearer legacy party for leftists. Originally established under Sadat's political liberalization plan, Tagammu subsumed regime-approved socialists, communists, and other left-leaning politicians of the 1970s. As such, Tagammu carried the hopes of progressive labor during the 1970s and 1980s, as strides were made toward greater autonomy for political parties. Labor leaders were often active Tagammu members, and Tagammu, to the extent it was allowed to, supported workers' demands.

As political parties became more constrained in the 1990s, Tagammu receded from the labor scene. The Mubarak regime worked hard to silence and marginalize parties that stepped outside the accepted boundaries it laid out for the opposition.[28] Tagammu was hesitant to engage with the emerging street politics of the mid- and late 2000s, refusing to be associated with upstart groups that challenged conventional opposition. Even after the revolution, a paranoid air gripped the organization, accusing foreigners of being spies, informed perhaps by a long history of penetration by the security services.[29] The Mubarak regime saw Tagammu as a useful opposition party, absorbing and containing the Egyptian left in an ineffectual institution. Leaders were provided with political patronage, securing seats in even the most rigged parliamentary elections.

Despite the resistance to engaging with new political activists likes the April 6th movement, some Tagammu members grew restless with the organization's historical ineffectiveness. Arguments broke out over willingness to run in the parliamentary elections in 2010, which Wafd and the

---

[28] Joshua A. Stacher, "Parties over: The Demise of Egypt's Opposition Parties," *British Journal of Middle Eastern Studies* 31, no. 2 (November 1, 2004): 215–33.

[29] Eric Trager, "Trapped and Untrapped: Mubarak's Opponents on the Eve of His Ouster," Ph.D. diss. (University of Pennsylvania, 2013), 64.

Muslim Brotherhood considered boycotting.[30] Some token support was also provided to the independent teachers' union formed in the wake of Abu Eita's successful organization of the independent tax collectors.[31]

Despite these tentative moves, Tagammu was seen as a largely exhausted vehicle for leftists following the revolution. Long-standing Tagammu apparatchiks like Abdul Ghaffar Shokr saw it as an opportunity to strike out and found new organizations.[32] Young leftists were drawn to less coopted and more militant organizations like the Revolutionary Socialists. Even among trade unionists, few saw a renewed position of power for Tagammu. Tagammu's political plan following the revolution showed the generic platitudes that allowed it to succeed under Mubarak. Flyers circulated that describe its political plan mention the death of five members during the revolution in an attempt to bolster legitimacy, but the political plan is vague. On workers' issues, it mentions little more than the establishment of minimum and maximum wages, a position even embraced by Wafd.[33] The first postrevolutionary parliamentary election saw Tagammu running in a coalition with other center-left parties, including the Social Democratic Party and the Free Egyptians Party, a coalition that barely survived the election itself. Tagammu barely improved upon its parliamentary successes under Mubarak, taking four seats.

Unlike the Wafd, whose ideological commitments, class composition, and ties to the ETUF precluded close collaboration with independent unionists, Tagammu was a victim of its own success under the previous institutional arrangement. While quiescence and accommodation were the keys to surviving under Mubarak, these qualities left the party unable to attract more militant youth and labor organizers. Even some of their old guard saw the party as unable to measure up to the new revolutionary situation.

---

[30] "Divisions within Al Tagammu Party Amplify Following Decision to Participate in Runoffs," *Daily News Egypt*, accessed May 16, 2014, www.dailynewsegypt.com/2010/12/05/divisions-within-al-tagammu-party-amplify-following-decision-to-participate-in-runoffs/.

[31] Abdul Hafeez Tayal, Independent Teacher's Union Founder, interview with author, April 21, 2012.

[32] Abdel Ghaffar Shokr, Founder of Socialist Popular Alliance, interview with author, November 22, 2012.

[33] "The National Progressive Unionist Party [Hizb Al-Tagammu']: Who Are We?," accessed May 16, 2014, www.tahrirdocuments.org/2011/08/the-national-progressive-union-party-hizb-al-tagammu-who-are-we/.

While parties that survived under Mubarak failed to recruit unionized workers en masse, new political actors also entered the field after the revolution. While only Tagammu and Wafd managed to secure more than one seat in the final parliament of the Mubarak era ten parties managed to do so in the first postrevolutionary parliament. The most seats by far went to the Freedom and Justice Party (FJP), formally affiliated with the Muslim Brotherhood. Not only across the political spectrum, but also in the trade union movement, the Brotherhood was increasingly interested in keeping its toehold on power.

Borai's addition of Muslim Brothers to the ETUF's oversight board was one of the more momentous decisions in labor politics in the postrevolutionary era. The infighting between the Brotherhood and more progressive and independent voices on the ETUF board prefigured the later cleavage in national politics that led to the military coup against Morsi. By placing the Brotherhood, and with it the FJP, firmly in the camp of supporting the preservation of the ETUF, the decision closed off one of the last avenues to political party support for the independent unionists.

Following the election of Mohammed Morsi, the FJP's position toward labor can be described as heel dragging and entrenchment. In the ETUF, the old guard feared a process of "Brotherhoodization" in the trade union movement. The threats of such a move were almost certainly overstated in 2012. Interviews conducted at the time saw the ETUF old guard referring to increasing Brotherhood involvement as a "cancer." Bayoumi's position as treasurer certainly gave him influence over the organization, and Brotherhood influence grew after independents and leftists appointed under Al-Borai left the ETUF board.

In the parliament, debate was reopened on a new trade union law. Instead of accepting the document commonly called Borai's Law following its rise to power, the FJP decided to consider alternatives to trade union pluralism. The ministry of manpower was one of only five turned over to a member of the FJP. Khaled Al-Azheri reopened discussions on the trade union law, stating that the basis for the new law would be noncompetition among trade unions at the work site. New elections would be held quickly, with the winner earning the right to represent workers. No competing unions would be permitted, and a losing union would have its assets liquidated. This proposed process ensured almost certain defeat for independent unions. Despite the longstanding success of unions like RETA, most independent unions were weak, fractured, and less than a year old in 2012. The likeliest winner would be the ETUF. Despite this apparent victory for the legacy union, concerns remained about the prospects of Brotherhood intervention in the elections through its strongholds in the ETUF board and manpower ministry.

While independent union elections were taking place under auspices separate from those of the ETUF, the long-term goal was to supplant the ETUF with a reformed national trade union system. Such a system would need to work under government-mandated rules, and both a Brotherhood-dominated movement and age restrictions on trade union members posed problems for the independent movement. In light of this, the independent unions took a firm stance against the changes to the trade union law, and while not exactly cooperating with the ETUF, held its own rallies and meetings to denounce it. Additionally, the independent trade unionists were angered that after years of calling for changes to the trade union law, months of meetings on Borai's Law, and Brotherhood foot-dragging on passing any version of the trade union freedom bill, the law had finally been changed in a one-sided way. The long-standing call for reform was threatened by Morsi's choice to unilaterally change the law while conceding almost none of the actual demands put forth by labor activists.

If the biggest political gains in the postrevolutionary period were made by the Muslim Brotherhood, the second biggest were made by the Salafi current. Most Salafi movements prior to the revolution explicitly rejected involvement in national politics. More assertive groups that framed their ideology as broadly "Salafi" like Gama'a Islamiyya (GI) had either been brought to heel by security services or undergone ideological shifts.[34] A *volta face* took place following the revolution with the emergence of the Salafi Nour Party. Nour has been widely seen as a political arm of an older Salafi organization, the Salafi Dawa (Call). Established in the 1980s, the organization faced the same repression as other Islamist groups during the 1990s. The Salafi Front, another umbrella coalition of Islamists, also fielded political parties, and an Islamic Bloc was formed, eventually emerging as the second highest vote-getting electoral bloc after the Democratic Front led by FJP. With a long-standing policy of not running in elections, Salafis

---

[34] Ewan Stein, "What Does the Gama'a Islamiyya Want Now?" *Middle East Report*, no. 254 (April 1, 2010): 40–44.

had the benefits and deficits of running with no real political platform. For the Nour Party, this was extremely successful, capturing the second greatest number of seats in the first postrevolutionary parliament after the FJP.

The organization's policies with regard to labor were limited. Independent unionists reported that some of their members were Salafi, but that the Salafi parties paid limited attention to worker issues, focusing instead of evangelization.[35] The economic policies of the Nour Party are a hodgepodge of notions, including the government providing jobs, capitalists investing in projects, and support for small and medium enterprises.[36]

Interestingly, the FJP's embrace of neoliberal economic policies left some room for maneuvering on the Islamist left. In the fall of 2012 a new Salafi party was announced by members of the Salafi Front called the "People's Party," which would focus specifically on workers and farmers. Despite this, at the time no Salafi groups or parties had reached out to the main trade union groups in the country, and the party seems to have largely fallen by the wayside by the following year. Salafi identity and trade union identity seem perfectly capable of coexisting, but neither the union movement nor the Salafi organizations have worked to build linkages between the two.[37]

By the end of 2012, Egypt's trade union movement was surprisingly stuck given the high hopes that followed the revolution. The ETUF managed to find an unexpected ally in the Muslim Brotherhood through its desire to control the organization *à la* the NDP. The independent unionists, fractured into two warring camps, continued to get their only real substantive support from the international community, which was increasingly fearful of crackdowns from the security services. Attempts to forge alliances with political parties almost entirely failed. The "new left" parties had fared poorly in all elections compared to the Islamist bloc. The old left of Tagammu was politically impotent. Liberal parties like the Wafd had ideological commitments incompatible with independent trade union work. The Salafi

---

[35] Fatma Ramada, interview with author, November 11, 2012.

[36] Al Nour Party Website, "Economic Program," archived at "Internet Archive Wayback Machine," July 10, 2011.

[37] In an interview, Elhamy Elmergany mentions that some prominent independent unionists were Salafi, including leaders of the militant Cleopatra Ceramic factory union and some regional union leaders in Suez.

organizations barely took up worker issues barring occasional personal interventions. With these failures to find a new political outlet for their aspirations, Egyptian workers were left with a largely unreconstructed labor regime. Its hallmarks were competition and diminished political support. Token appointments of notable independent figures failed to bring about substantive change on any of the key demands: increased wages, trade union pluralism, or a new relationship to capitalists.

In response to increasing fears of an Islamist power grab, a block of political parties in Egypt (numbering more than thirty) announced the formation of a National Salvation Front, including prominent politicians from across the political spectrum. Tagammu and socialist parties occupied the left wing of the group, the new Constitution Party took the centrist position, and former regime officials like Amr Moussa occupied the right wing. In addition to Amr Moussa, the group included Mohamed ElBaradei, the former Nobel Peace Prize winner and former head of the International Atomic Energy Agency. ElBaradei was popular with international figures, but had limited support domestically. The group was ideologically conflicted and focused only on retracting Morsi's constitutional declaration of November 2012, stopping the referendum of the new constitution, and drafting a new constituent assembly. These demands eventually grew to include Morsi's ouster. They did not, however, grow to include workers' demands.

The National Salvation Front was a continuation of Egypt's top-down, paternalistic politics with regard to workers. Amr Moussa, one of the Front's most outspoken leaders and a former presidential candidate, offered a strike moratorium, despite his lack of affiliation with any trade union movement.[38] The position of the newly organized opposition to the Muslim Brotherhood matched the Brotherhood's: instrumentalizing labor. Workers were a useful prop, an institution and segment of society to control, but not a power that needed to be reckoned with. Trade unions did, however, participate in some of the protests organized by the NSF. They did so without having a leadership role and an at-best indifferent orientation to their actual demands from the Front's leadership.

[38] Joel Beinin, "Workers, Trade Unions, and Egypt's Political Future," MER Online, January 18, 2013.

Egyptian labor's ties to political parties and movements were weak at best, and based on cooptation at worst. Labor had not shown the willingness or ability to forge a unified front and mobilize electorally or for industrial action in a way that made them an appealing base for a political party. The parties that did exist saw the labor movement in much the same way that the NDP had – a sector of potential unrest that needed to be managed, with its loyalties denied to competitors. Notably, the fracture of the trade union movement, between the ETUF and independent unions, and later between the independent unions themselves, was less driven by ideological linkages to domestic political parties, or even its history of incorporation and legitimacy, than it was by its engagement with international stakeholders.

External Linkages

When scholars discuss the domestic impact of international organizations, the usual suspects are the International Monetary Fund and the World Bank. More distributed forms of international institutions, such as transnational advocacy networks, can also diffuse norms and influence domestic policy. An under studied area of international influence is the network of organizations focused on labor and worker issues, "global labor." The components of global labor are not homogenous, but from the evidence presented, it appears that support (rhetorical and material) tends to move consistently.

Egypt, as a powerful Arab state, has had ties of labor activism since the earliest days of the ETUF and even before. The country joined the ILO (ILO) in 1936 and ratified its first ILO convention in 1940. Egyptian workers took solidarity strikes with workers in Indonesia and Palestine in the 1940s. In the heyday of pan-Arabism, Egypt was host to the International Confederation of Arab Trade Unions. Despite this, by the 1990s and 2000s, the Egyptian labor movement, and more specifically the ETUF, had become alienated from global labor.

During the 1990s and 2000s, the nature of global labor changed quickly. What had once been a divided global labor movement since liberal and capitalist states split from the World Trade Union Federation (WTUF) in 1949 was moving toward reunification. The fall of communism left two major international trade union confederations: the World Confederation of Labor (WCL) and the International Confederation of Free Trade Unions. By the early 2000s, efforts increased to bring the two major confederations together. This goal was achieved in 2006 with the formation of the International Trade Union Confederation (ITUC). The ITUC oversaw the rebranding of the International Trade Secretariats as "Global Union Federations" in 2006. This coincided with an increasingly international focus of the AFL-CIO in the United States.[39]

The AFL-CIO's international operations had been throughout the Cold War a supporter of anti-Communist US policy, often working directly with US intelligence to undermine Communist and Communist-leaning unions around the world.[40] In Egypt, these efforts were channeled through the African American Labor Center, which had been conducting training, meetings, and capacity-building exercises with the ETUF since the 1980s. Following the Cold War, however, the AFL-CIO under John Sweeney sought to transform its international efforts, creating the Solidarity Center in 1997 with a broad mandate to collaborate with unions around the world. The AFL-CIO was not the only national trade union to engage with international support and capacity building in Egypt. The Norwegian Confederation of Trade Unions (known by its Norwegian abbreviation LO for Landsorganisasjonen i Norge) had been active in Egyptian labor politics since the 1970s.[41] Other European labor activists were also frequent visitors to Cairo, offering training and support throughout the 1980s and 1990s.

The changes impacting the global labor movement were reflected as well in new priorities for the ILO. In 1998 the organization passed a resolution declaring a cluster of rights mandatory for all ILO members, whether they had ratified the relevant conventions or not. These rights, called the Fundamental Principles and Rights at Work, cover the "bare minimum" of labor rights countries are expected to uphold.[42] Egypt was a signatory of each of these conventions, many having been signed in the early Nasser era. The most relevant conventions include

[39] Joe Uehlein, "Using Labor's Trade Secretariats," *Labor Research Review* 1, no. 13 (1989): 7.

[40] Geert Van Goethem, Robert Anthony Waters Jr., and Palgrave Connect (Online service), *American Labor's Global Ambassadors: The International History of the AFL-CIO during the Cold War* (Basingstoke: Palgrave Macmillan, 2013).

[41] Øystein Jackwitz Rovde, "I solidaritetens navn: LOs forhold til Midt-Østenkonflikten 1947–2002," 2004, www.duo.uio.no/handle/10852/23436.

[42] International Labour Organization, *The International Labour Organization's Fundamental Conventions* (Geneva: International Labour Office, 2003).

Convention 87 and Convention 98, which cover the freedom to organize and the freedom to collectively bargain, respectively. These conventions include language that could be read as supporting either trade union pluralism (multiple trade unions within a country) or trade union unity (one trade union with in a country.) It has been the official policy of the ILO to not explicitly endorse one idea or another, as there are successful tripartite relationships in countries that follow each model. This opinion has been a topic of some consternation, however, with the ILO's Committees of Experts often calling for legal pluralism in a given country.[43] The ILO does not dictate other organizations' perceptions of trade union pluralism or unity, and each institution likely has its own view of the issue. It is, however, worth exploring how trade union pluralism became a dominant issue in Egypt, encouraging the many disgruntled trade unionists to break off and form their own union, often under international tutelage.

Global labor was actively supportive of trade union pluralism within Egypt in the early days of the revolutionary reconsolidation. One labor leader active in training other activists recalled, "[O]ur foundational conference had attendees who were British, German, Spain ... a European delegation, members of the Solidarity Center, and the ITUC all issued supporting statements and recognized us. International law is important ... as an independent labor movement our legitimacy is international, not local. We are waiting for a new (domestic) law to come through." International legitimacy as opposed to local would come up again in the Tunisian context, as will be explored later in the book.

Global labor helped the independent unions in Egypt in several ways. First, it provided a rights and legal-based framing for efforts to

---

[43] CEACR, "Observation (CEACR) – Adopted 1991, Published 78th ILC Session (1991) Freedom of Association and Protection of the Right to Organise Convention, 1948 (No. 87) – Russian Federation" (ILO, 1991), www.ilo.org/dyn/normlex/en/f?p=1000:13100:0::NO:13100:P13100_COMMENT_ID:2095925; CEACR, "Individual Case (CAS) – Discussion: 2006, Publication: 95th ILC Session (2006) Freedom of Association and Protection of the Right to Organise Convention, 1948 (No. 87) – Belarus" (ILO, 2006), http://ilo.org/dyn/normlex/en/f?p=NORMLEXPUB:13100:0::NO::P13100_COMMENT_ID:2556151; CEACR, "Observation (CEACR) – Adopted 1992, Published 79th ILC Session (1992) Freedom of Association and Protection of the Right to Organise Convention, 1948 (No. 87) – Ghana" (ILO, 1992), www.ilo.org/dyn/normlex/en/f?p=1000:13100:0::NO::P13100_COMMENT_ID,P13100_LANG_CODE:2106551,en:NO.

pressure the regime to allow trade union pluralism. Based on this it brought international pressure to bear at a time when the regime was particularly sensitive to perceived international legitimacy. It directly helped build capacity in the new federations, training and advising their leaders. Finally, and perhaps most importantly, it gave sums of money that were quite large in the local context. Both the framing device of pluralism and the prospect of funding incentivized the establishment of multiple federations and increased the capacity of these federations. But this help did not *create* the impetus for independent unions; it only stoked the flames already set. Global labor was reactive to events on the ground, funding first movers like Kamal Abbas and Kamal Abu Eita, among others. Here, we find the importance of legitimacy and narratives recreated around incorporation. While independent unions in Egypt could claim "international legitimacy" and "revolutionary legitimacy," the ETUF could claim neither.[44]

The Egyptian case suggests that when "global labor" focuses on trade union pluralism and freedom of association in a given country it can lower the costs of defecting from the established trade union federation, and give competing unionists a domestic and international discourse to latch on to. On the other hand, Tunisia suggests that a focus on capacity building and trade union cohesion, including continued international legitimacy, can raise the cost of defection, leaving more trade unionists affiliated with the majority union.

Each of these outcomes has serious policy implications that are thus far unknown to the components of global labor, who have underestimated their own capacity to make a difference, especially in quasi-authoritarian contexts. Trade union pluralism and the freedom of association may produce more internal democracy and the flourishing of new workers' organizations. It may also fracture the movement such that it cannot effectively advocate for its members. Union cohesion, capacity building, and international legitimacy may help sustain authoritarian unions that suppress workers. However, they may also allow unions the internal cohesion to seize new opportunities, initiate reforms, and weather national crises.

---

[44] Ian M. Hartshorn, "Global Labor and the Arab Uprisings: Picking Winners in Tunisia and Egypt," *Global Governance: A Review of Multilateralism and International Organizations* 24, no. 1 (January 1, 2018): 119–38.

While the concept of "democracy promotion" has become contentious in academic literature in recent years, it remains a touchstone of US and EU foreign policy.[45] Both rhetorical and material support that flowed from global labor into trade unions in Egypt and Tunisia came from funds earmarked for democracy promotion. As will be addressed herein, incentivizing trade union behavior can influence the transition to democracy, but not always in predictable ways. In addition to highlighting an important set of cases for scholars of global labor, Egypt and Tunisia may serve as cautionary tales for policy makers interested in using trade unionism as a mechanism for democratization.

Researchers have long debated the importance of international legal standards in empowering local activists. In addition to the classic example of the Helsinki Accords empowering local activists in Eastern Europe, researchers have explored human rights laws, environmental treaties, and labor conventions. Trade unionists in many countries have mobilized by using appeals to international law and international agreements to pressure their governments to respect labor rights, often by linking these rights to human and civil rights.[46]

While many have showed the import of these international legal standards, some have highlighted their particular effectiveness in democratic regimes.[47] The two cases under review here, Egypt and Tunisia, serve as interesting cases as they bring our attention to transitioning regimes before, during, and after revolutionary foment. During this critical juncture, regimes may be especially inclined to accept or reject international laws, norms, and agreements.[48]

---

[45] Lindsay Lloyd, "European Approaches to Democracy Promotion," *International Journal* 65, no. 3 (2010): 547–59; Dina Jadallah, "Democracy Promotion and Abstracted Sovereignty," *Arab Studies Quarterly* 34, no. 4 (Fall 2012): 205–29; Beate Jahn, "Rethinking Democracy Promotion," *Review of International Studies* 38, no. 4 (October 2012): 685–705; Jason Brownlee, *Democracy Prevention: The Politics of the U.S.-Egyptian Alliance* (Cambridge: Cambridge University Press, 2012).

[46] Susan L. Kang, *Human Rights and Labor Solidarity: Trade Unions in the Global Economy* (Philadelphia, PA: University of Pennsylvania Press, 2012).

[47] Eric Neumayer, "Do International Human Rights Treaties Improve Respect for Human Rights?" *Journal of Conflict Resolution* 49, no. 6 (December 1, 2005): 925–53.

[48] Orfeo Fioretos, "Historical Institutionalism in International Relations," *International Organization* 65, no. 2 (April 1, 2011): 367–99.

In addition to international legal standards empowering local activists *rhetorically*, institutions that promote these standards can support local activists *materially*. Turning again to the example of the Helsinki Accords, some have argued that the creation and maintenance of the Conference (later Organization) on Security and Co-operation in Europe was the driving force behind changes in Eastern Europe.[49] These institutions can have major impacts on the ground, directing funding and expertise. For instance, the AFL-CIO channeled more than $4 million to Poland's Solidarity Movement during the 1980s, aiding its ability to operate under government pressure.[50] For reasons still somewhat murky, global labor approached Tunisia and Egypt differently both rhetorically and materially.

As discussed earlier, independent trade unions failed to forge strong domestic political ties in the two years following the January 25th revolution. Their allies on the left were either unwilling or unable to further their goals, while liberals and Islamists were uninterested or committed to the ETUF. Despite this, the independent unions maintained their ties with international organizations and in some cases gained even more support following the revolution.

Global labor, which had pivoted away from the ETUF in the mid-2000s, benefited from making its support for the independent unions even more vocal and direct following the revolution. The ILO took the surprising step of removing Egypt from its blacklist when Al-Borai was appointed minister; even before substantive new trade union laws were introduced. While the Solidarity Center had ceased its program with the ETUF in 2004, and closed its regional office in the country in 2005, it directed funds to independent unionists via a grant from the National Endowment for Democracy, which was also involved with several other civil society initiatives in the country. The ITUC, which had rejected ETUF membership under Mubarak, increased its activities with independent trade unions as well, underwriting conferences and training throughout the transition. The ITUC was quick to issue a call for solidarity with the declaration made by EFITU in Tahrir Square on

---

[49] Kathrin Fahlenbrach, *The Establishment Responds: Power, Politics, and Protest Since 1945* (Basingstoke: Palgrave Macmillan, 2012).

[50] Eric Chenoweth, "AFL-CIO Support for Solidarity: Moral, Political, Financial," in *American Labor's Global Ambassadors*, ed. Geert Van Gaoethem, Robert Anthony Waters Jr., and Palgrave Connect. (Basingstoke: Palgrave MacMillan, 2013), 103–19.

January 31, 2011, and support for the general strike held several days later. ITUC posted an international trade union solidarity video on February 5, just a few days after the announcement of the new independent federation.[51]

Global labor was nearly unanimous in its praise for the openings following the revolution. Ahmed El-Genedy of the Friedrich Ebert Stiftung (FES), the international foundation of the German Social Democratic Party, said that the period after the revolution was "like heaven," in which international organizations were free to directly support the independent unions.[52] This support certainly included financial support, though recipients are cagey on the exact amount. Following the closing out of the Solidarity Center's USAID grant to work with the ETUF, the organization continued to support independent unions through their funding from the National Endowment for Democracy. FES also financed training and conferences in the newly liberalized atmosphere. Other organizations that had backed independent union organizations before the revolution, such as Oxfam-Novib, stepped up their efforts.

The liberal atmosphere did not last long. Security forces raided the offices of two US democracy-promoting organizations, the National Democratic Institute and the International Republican Institute, as well as the office of Konrad Adenauer Stiftung in December 2011. The organizations were accused of illegally operating and financing groups within Egypt. The discrepancy was largely a function of the poorly written NGO law passed in 2002, designed in part to prevent union organizing outside the ETUF. It stated that if groups who submitted paperwork for recognition from the government never received official notification regarding their application, they were assumed legal. The ambiguity was used against these institutions and dozens of their employees, both Egyptian and international, were arrested and tried either locally or in absentia. Organizations like FES were frightened of

---

[51] *Trade Union Solidarity with Egypt*, 2011, www.youtube.com/watch?v=bWqOKbYM1UI&feature=youtube_gdata_player. It is worth noting that both Sharan Burrow of the ITUC and Richard Trumka of the AFL-CIO specifically invoke their support for independent unions in Egypt, whereas other international unionists (including those from CLC Canada, COSATU in South Africa, and SOLIDARNOSC in Poland) made more general statements to the people of Egypt.

[52] Ahmed El-Genedy, Friedrich Ebert Stiftung Representative, interview with author, May 2, 2012.

the possibility of another raid and were largely isolated in their office. Solidarity Center did not reopen its permanent office in Cairo, and a planned permanent ITUC office never materialized. Building a base of power on international support was becoming more tenuous for the independent unions.

One of the few trade union organizations to maintain a continuous presence in Cairo was the ILO. The ILO's relationship with the ETUF soured in the mid-2000s. In 2010 the ILO representative was kicked out of the country for alienating the ETUF. Egypt's inclusion on the so-called ILO blacklist was a regular topic of discussion for trade union activists prior to the revolution. In reality, the ILO rejects the description of the tracking of labor violators as a "blacklist." The list reflects dozens of countries found to be out of compliance with labor conventions they have agreed to. In Egypt, this was most notably Convention 87 on the freedom of association and Convention 98 on the right to collectively bargain. In 2011, Egypt sent a delegation to the annual International Labor Conference of the ILO in Geneva that consisted of Al-Borai and representatives of both the ETUF and EFITU. The promise of a new trade union law, combined with Al-Borai's assertion of emerging trade union freedom in the country, convinced the ILO to remove Egypt from the blacklist, a perceived boon to international reputation. The actual inclusion on the blacklist seems to hold much more rhetorical value within the country than it does real influence internationally. The rulings by the ILO were used as a cudgel by which the independent trade unionists could club the government and the ETUF, and their removal was a feather in Al-Borai's cap as minister of manpower. The 100th session of the International Labor Conference also saw Kamal Abbas bitterly denouncing the corruption of the ETUF, an action for which he was later tried in absentia and sentenced to a six-month sentence. The sentence was later overturned.

The invocation of ILO Conventions 87 and 98 became common during the late 1990s and early 2000s during the corporatist collapse experienced by the Egyptian regime. During interviews in 2012, I asked dozens of trade unionists under what authority they had the right to form their own union. Almost all invoked these particular conventions, or, more generally, "international agreements" that allowed workers to organize. Egypt in the 2000s was rife with violations of Convention 87. Public authorities, including the security apparatus, regularly interfered with the election of union officers. But perhaps more problematic after the revolution was Article 1 of the convention, stating:

Workers and employers, without distinction whatsoever, shall have the right to establish and, subject only to the rules of the organisation concerned, to join organisations of their own choosing without previous authorisation.

By invoking Convention 87 and training workers in their rights under this convention, and encouraging the CTUWS, among others, to carry out further training on it, the ILO helped provide a rhetorical toolkit of trade union pluralism and freedom of association.

At first, representatives of ILO's ACTRAV (Worker's Bureau), long frustrated with ETUF stubbornness, embraced an alternative interlocutor with Egypt's workers. Within the regime itself, the ETUF wanted to be seen as a robust organization that could provide two services: quiescence and legitimacy. A large component of that legitimacy came from its relationship to outside organizations, namely the Solidarity Center prior to 2003 and the ILO prior to the growing tensions in 2010. Global labor's pivot to the independent union not only bolstered an alternative worker power base but it also weakened the ETUF vis-à-vis other regime organs.[53]

External linkages conditioned Egyptian labor in important ways before and during the transition. They continued the practice of bringing international pressure to bear on the government. This practice, however, was of diminished salience following the revolution. SCAF was more driven by internal security concerns than it was with maintaining the support of the international community, and was less hesitant to alienate American and European government. It is also possible that the SCAF had a more realistic assessment of the importance of labor policy in Europe and America. The ETUF in particular seemed to have an outsized notion of the political power of the AFL-CIO and European trade unions in driving their governments' perceptions of Egypt. SCAF, many of who enjoyed robust individual relationships with the American military complex, may have known better.

Global labor also worked to build the capacity of the independent trade union movement prior to and after the revolution. This training

---

[53] Mustapha Said, ILO Representative, interview with author, November 26, 2012.

largely focused on preparing for neoliberal reforms, striving for collective bargaining rights, and leadership training. It did not, necessarily, prepare trade unionists for pushing their prerogatives in a chaotic transitional process. Finally, global labor's offer of financial support coupled with a framing device of pluralism was perhaps the most significant factor in helping independent unionists strengthen their position against the ETUF prior to the revolution. These factors were poisonous to the prospects of a robust independent trade union movement following the revolution, helping to cultivate and exacerbate the divisions that were already evident in the nascent movement. Global labor had thrown its support behind a fractious movement, driving it apart even more.

By early 2012, the relationship between Abbas and Abu Eita had frayed. EFITU was organizing workers away from the CTUWS, which had started organizing its competing federation, the Egyptian Democratic Labor Congress (EDLC). Global labor was clear in its preference for a unified movement in light of the ETUF's entrenchment and newfound support from the Muslim Brotherhood. Several attempts at rapprochement were organized both within Egypt and outside it.[54] The efforts at reconciliation were rocky at best. Both organizations continued to draw support, including technical assistance, conference support, and perks like trips to Europe for meetings. The prospect of sharing the attention of the international trade union movement did not seem to appeal to either side. In addition to this, fundamental differences regarding who spoke for workers remained. Abbas claimed legitimacy through his extensive work with shop floor and industrial unionists. Abu Eita claimed his legitimacy through being a unionist himself. Abbas was hampered by the fact that he was not perceived to be "of the workers," while Abu Eita struggled with the fact that his organization mainly drew from white-collar unionists. A group of *éminences grises* attempted to paper over the differences in late 2012, with mixed results. The corrosive effects of direct funding were not lost on representatives of ACTRAV, one of whom reflected bitterly "[t]he ILO has made a mistake. Trips with 5-star hotels. This is a corrupting influence."

---

[54] Walid Hamdan, ILO Representative, interview with author, October 10, 2012.

Trade Union Position: Weak, Fractured, and Coopted

As 2012 continued without a new constitution and with an increasing conflict between President Morsi and the judicial system, political struggles had also gripped the independent trade union movement. While Abu Eita and Abbas had worked closely together in early 2011, a dispute emerged between them by the end of the year. Some point to traditional competition for control of the labor movement. Others suggest that their different origins, Abbas from the industrial sector and focused on organizing outside the union structure, and Abu Eita from the bureaucracy with long-standing union ties, explains the conflict.[55] Abbas himself endorsed the latter view, stating, "EFITU has no way to establish a union."[56] Others argued for some unrevealed personal conflict.[57]

The incentives to fracture, especially early on, were high. Both secular forces and the Muslim Brotherhood sought to coopt and influence the trade union movement. The ETUF showed signs of weakness, but continued to exist with its various structures and affiliated entities. Each of these would be a prize to any political movement that succeeded in the country. Robust party–labor linkages, such as those that have characterized the political economy in Western Europe, failed to emerge. International funders had both promoted trade union pluralism, and funded new union movements. The strategy of forming new confederations may have even had an appealing logic: If the defining dynamic on the political scene was cooptation, more federations could better withstand these assaults. Individual unions could selectively affiliate when and if a federation proved itself to be independent from pernicious political forces.

The first challenge to the ETUF–EFITU duopoly came from Abbas's CTUWS. It organized a competing labor organization parallel to EFITU, the EDLC. The EDLC concentrated its efforts in the traditional sites of the CTUWS, new industrial cities and manufacturing areas. While plans had been in the works throughout 2012, a founding congress was held in October of that year. While each group counted hundreds of unions in its structure, their divided efforts posed a

---

[55] Emad al Arabi, EFITU Representative, interview with author, April 2012.
[56] Kamal Abbas, CTUWS Founder, interview with author, November 2012.
[57] Trade Union Activists, interviews with author, November 2012.

challenge to the future of independent unionization. Workers were unsurprisingly disinterested in elite competition, and more concerned with prosaic concerns. Workers would coordinate with either EFITU or EDLC depending on who seemed most capable of getting work done. Even members of the EFITU board acknowledged that while hundreds of unions had been created following the revolution, most were only nominally connected to either federation, and existed largely beyond their control.[58] Eventually, another independent federation would form. Independent unions in Alexandria were removed from the main political struggles in Cairo. Their members were drawn from Alexandria's factories and shipping facilities, different industries than those that dominated EFITU and the EDLC. Eventually, these unions formed a "Permanent Conference of Alexandria Workers" focused on these local issues. By 2013 the independent union movement was riven by divisions that were personal, sectoral, and geographic. As the independent unions fractured, the possibility of a path of attrition, in which the ETUF would slowly cede members to the more activist independent unions, or a revolutionary collapse of the ETUF became less likely. In addition to the cleavages between secularists and the Muslim Brotherhood, and long-standing tensions between workers and the government, the movement faced the efforts of cooptation by new political movements.

The fracture weakened the trade union movement in several ways. While independent organizing could disseminate a message of trade union pluralism and the strength workers have when they use the strike weapon, they could not credibly or consistently call for strikes or call for strikes to stop. Despite the NSF's almost comical offer of strike abatement, it had no capacity to deliver this. Neither did any of the federations. This stands in sharp contrast to the UGTT in Tunisia, which could offer labor peace if its demands were met. Conversely, the UGTT could mobilize tens of thousands of workers qua unionists, not simply as the masses displeased with Islamist or any other rule. None of the Egyptian federations could do that. Egyptian unions did, however, agree on their increasing displeasure with Morsi. Morsi's heavy-handed tactics with trade unionists had driven the ETUF, EFITU, and EDLC closer together in principle if not in coordination.

---

[58] Fatma Ramadan, Trade Union Activist, interview with author, November 2012.

As the crisis deepened in 2012 and 2013, violence at protests increased. Labor demands were increasingly pushed off the front page, as secular versus Islamist fighting dominated the national discourse. The lingering threat of a military intervention persisted in early 2013, even after Morsi's consultations with his military chief, Abdel Fattah el-Sisi. The Tamarod (Rebel) Movement was launched in April 2013. The new group called for a signature gathering campaign, coupled with protests, to call on Morsi to resign the presidency. The origins of the group remain murky. Accusations have been leveled against it that it was in part directed by the national security services.[59] It is certain that many members of the old regime actively endorsed the movement and its call for protest and civil disobedience to oust Morsi. Following its success in July, Egyptian billionaire and sometimes-politician Naguib Sawiris took credit for the movement. While his financial support is not in doubt, his eagerness to take credit for the entire operation remains dubious. The Morsi government lost members throughout the spring, leading to an isolated and more reactionary mindset. He further alienated secular groups in the country by endorsing a Syrian solidarity rally that included calls for jihad in the country. The increasingly violent clashes between pro- and anti-Morsi protesters, and the spike of terrorist attacks in the country hardened the position of the secular forces that feared the emergence of a full-blown Islamist insurgency.

The Tamarod movement picked up speed during the spring and summer, announcing the success of its signature campaign to an extent that strains credulity. While the group claims 22 million signatures calling for Morsi's ouster, this would come close to the total number of people who voted in the hotly contested 2012 presidential election. Even without this exaggeration its efforts were impressive, though it did enjoy help. In a significant turn from their former animosity, all major trade union federations joined the Tamarod bandwagon, endorsing the campaign and encouraging and organizing for their members to sign. Many independent trade unionists joined the massive June 30 protests that led directly to the military intervention that removed Morsi from power.

---

[59] Charles Levinson and Matt Bradley, "In Egypt, the 'Deep State' Rises Again," *Wall Street Journal*, July 19, 2013, sec. World, www.wsj.com/articles/
SB10001424127887324425204578601700051224658.

Conclusion

The trade union movement in Egypt was founded in an era of strong government intervention in the economy. In the 1980s and 1990s it faced mounting pressure from the regime in the form of structural adjustment, labor flexibilization, and the loss of political power. The union reacted by doubling down on its ability to influence the regime, slowing down the most odious legislation and seeking to stymie the plans of the regime through elite persuasion. It allowed its rank-and-file structure to atrophy, unable to aggregate and advocate on behalf of its dwindling pool of members. More workers were outside labor protections, and those who were still dues-paying members may have had little knowledge of the union and little faith in its efforts. Militant unionists were driven from the official ETUF structure, eventually forming independent groups that served as "unions in waiting." The most militant managed to break away and begin to form independent unions during the unprecedented strike wave that began in 2006–7.

The revolution of 2011 gave the independent unionists the ability to step into a more public role. They pressed for their main demands: a new trade union law, better wages, and a say in the political and economic direction of their country. The military interregnum installed one of their staunchest allies as minister of manpower, who promptly declared the monopoly of the ETUF over. Independent unions used their newfound revolutionary legitimacy and the support of their strong linkages to global labor to recruit as many as a few million workers to their movement. Despite these initial strengths, they struggled due to an incentive structure that promoted factionalism. New political actors sought to coopt the movement, preserving the ETUF in the process. Instead of either a reformed legacy union or powerful unified replacement, the entire union movement was beset by infighting, scattered resources, and threats of cooptation. By 2013, the movement was increasingly mobilized to a resurgent anti-Islamist campaign with military backing.

4 | *Corporatist Collapse in Tunisia*

While the challenges that Egypt's trade unions have faced since the revolution have been noted as a failure, the success of Tunisia's trade unions, particularly the UGTT, has received global acclaim. Popular narratives, including those promoted by the UGTT itself, claim that the union has been lying-in-wait, tirelessly protecting its members from successive authoritarian regimes and waiting for its moment to defend civil society. This narrative elides the real efforts and contributions of trade unionists over the last 70 years to turn to the UGTT into a force within Tunisia.

Historical Corporatism

Trade union activity in Tunisia predates the emergence of the independent state. The first major labor national confederation, the Confédération générale des travailleurs tunisiens (CGTT), was formed in 1924, at a time of increased nationalist agitation under the leadership of the Destour Party. The CGTT largely supplanted a local affiliate of the French Confédération générale du travail (CGT). The local affiliate benefited little from the relationship.[1] The CGTT forged ties with the Destour Party during the 1920s more for political benefit than sincere ideological similarities. Despite this early alliance, the protectorate government managed to eliminate this union by the close of the 1920s after the Destour turned their back on them in the hopes of appearing moderate. Spurred by the Depression, new political leadership emerged within the Destour in the mid-1930s, including Habib Bourguiba. Part of Bourguiba's rise to power included cultivating ties with the working class, who were alienated by Destour abandonment

---

[1] Kenneth J. Perkins, *A History of Modern Tunisia* (New York, NY: Cambridge University Press, 2004), 90.

of them. Bourguiba was successful in wresting power from the Destour and creating his new party, the Neo-Destour in the mid-1930s.

Following World War II, nationalist sentiment grew in Tunisia as Tunisians suffered economically with the return of French colonists. The Neo-Destour became the dominant nationalist party. The local branch of the CGT, the Union départmentale des syndicats de Tunisie (UDST), evolved into a communist trade union known as the Union des syndicats des travailleurs Tunisiens (USTT). In opposition to this, a long-time activist named Farhat Heched created the UGTT in 1946. The UGTT was explicitly Tunisian, which caused friction with its communist-minded competitor, which welcomed French as well as Tunisian trade unionists. Both eventually joined the World Federation of Trade Unions, an international trade union organization with communist leadings, but Heched soon removed the UGTT from its ranks in favor of the International confederation of Free Trade Unions (ICFTU). The decision won him favor in American circles, leading to a trip for both Heched and Bourguiba to the United States in 1951 at the invitation of the American Federation of Labor.

Pressing their advantage following the announcement of imminent Libyan independence, Neo-Destour leaders pushed for Tunisian independence. The effort was backed by a UGTT general strike in 1952. The French colonial regime cracked down on the uprising, arresting thousands of UGTT members and Neo-Destour cadres. With Neo-Destour leadership arrested, Farhat Heched was symbolically, if not literally, the leader of the independence movement.

Heched was assassinated before the close of 1952 and is memorialized as a national martyr. Heched's death cast a shadow over both the nationalist and trade union movements. His photo continues to adorn trade union offices. Immediately following the assassination, violence increased dramatically in the country. Within three years, Tunisia achieved internal autonomy and earned full autonomy in 1956.

Collaboration between the UGTT and the dominant Neo-Destour party under President Bourguiba reached its high point in the mid-1960s, with the appointment of UGTT leader Habib Achour to the Political Bureau of the party in 1964. This close coordination between party and the union federation came with a policy of strike restraint. With new groups calling for greater political plurality, the government tightened the corporatist system by declaring the UGTT and the peak employer's association "social partners" in 1973.[2] There is little evidence that the strongly corporatist turn penetrated downward into the rank-and-file membership of the union.

The UGTT was the most intellectually diverse organization in Tunisia, and contained socialist, nationalist, and communist tendencies.[3] The 1970s also saw the inclusion of more professional, white-collar, and academic workers, which increased the organization's militancy. The corporatist bargain, like those before it, was struck mostly between the leadership and President Bourguiba himself.[4]

Despite these signs of regime cooptation, the system began to fall apart in the mid-1970s. The protests emerged in an era of apparent economic improvement, with GDP growing by over 7 percent, but also a perceived shift to a more liberalized and market-driven economy. The prime minister at the time, Hedi Nouira, projected an image of the competent technocrat, but focused on business liberalization as opposed to increasing the wellbeing of workers.[5] Starting in 1973 a series of crippling strikes broke out, most with no support from the UGTT leadership. The army was deployed to break the strikes and arrest the protesters, leading to even larger confrontations.[6] By 1976 over 90,000 workers had gone on strike during the wave of protests.

Despite this, the UGTT signed a "compact" with the government ensuring wage restraint, productivity increases, and a limit on militancy in return for an increase in base salary. Wildcat strikes continued throughout 1977, leading the UGTT leadership to follow its rank-and-file members into conflict with the regime, eventually demanding redress for the grievances of the workers in the fall of 1977. When

---

[2] Christopher Alexander, *Tunisia: Stability and Reform in the Modern Maghreb*, 1st edition (Routledge, 2010), 47.

[3] Eva Bellin, "Civil Society Emergent? State and Social Classes in Tunisia," Ph.D. diss. (Princeton University, 1993).

[4] Alexander Bates, "Between Accommodation and Confrontation: State, Labor, and Development in Algeria and Tunisia" (Duke University, 1996).

[5] Marvine Howe, "Tunisians See Gains in Economy As Dependent on Political Events," *The New York Times*, March 19, 1977, sec. Business & Finance.

[6] Nigel Disney, "The Working Class Revolt in Tunisia," *MERIP Reports*, no. 67 (May 1, 1978): 12–14.

the government dithered due to cabinet infighting, the UGTT called for a general strike on January 26, 1978.[7]

The general strike soon turned into a general revolt as thousands came into the street. Soon the government deployed the army, who wound up firing on its own citizens. Over 200 protesters died. Within days, Bourguiba turned on his former corporatist partners and had the UGTT leadership confined to house arrest.[8] Through severe repression, the uprising was quelled. The regime attempted to select a new UGTT leadership, but failed to do so successfully. The UGTT's most powerful leader, Habib Achour, remained under house arrest until 1981, when he was brought out of exile to run the union once again, in a further attempt at elite cooptation.[9] This late 1970s and early 1980s period of rapprochement between the regime and the UGTT was short lived. The regime hoped to once again obtain labor quiescence. Strikes had emerged in multiple sectors and it was hoped that a restored UGTT would be able to corral them in return for wage increases. The gambit failed spectacularly.

Bourguiba attempted a limited political opening in 1981. The Parti Communiste Tunisien (PCT) was legalized and elections were held. The growing popularity of Islamists in the form of the Mouvement de la Tendance Islamique (MTI) led to the legalization of more parties, including the Parti d'Unité Populaire (PUP) and the Mouvement des Démocrates Sociales (MDS). The partial political opening did little to quell reactions to economic realities. The regime lifted the subsidies for bread and semolina, threatening citizens with hunger. The price of bread went up 80–110 percent, producing a renewed wave of protests. Two weeks of protests broke out, forcing Bourguiba to restore subsidies.

Continued criticism for the more economically liberal turn in Tunisian economic thinking led to more confrontations between the regime and the UGTT. In an attempt to pressure the union, the government extended its largess to a competitor confederation called the Union

---

[7] "Strike By Tunisians Erupts in Violence: Protests against Bourguiba's Rule Leave One Dead and Many Hurt Police Attacked by Crowds," *The New York Times*, January 27, 1978.

[8] "Labor Leader's Arrest Is Disclosed by Tunisia," *The New York Times*, January 30, 1978.

[9] "Tunisian Regime, after Major Setbacks, Regains Vitality: 'Wanted to Do a Mini-Kabul' Anti-Unionists Removed Per Capita Income Has Risen Liberalization Issue Emerging," *The New York Times*, May 21, 1980.

nationale tunisienne du travail (UNTT) and imprisoned Achour once again in 1985.[10] Unlike in Egypt, divisions in the UGTT were more likely to produce breakaway groups vying for the opportunity to be even closer to the government, rather that striking a more militant line.

In 1986 trade union leaders were once again removed completely from their positions of power. Those loyal to Achour, who had worked to distance the union from the regime, were replaced with long-serving regime loyalists. Trade union organizing was banned on the shop floor, constraining the ability of the union to legitimately operate on behalf of its members.[11] The new leadership of the union, unelected and handpicked by the government, stopped giving official sanction to the strike wave that had barely abated since the bread riots of 1984. Bourguiba decided, as Mubarak would later decide in the 2000s, that the trade union movement was no longer beneficial to regime mainten-ance, and that it would need to be forced into quiescence if it could not be bought off. Due to the nature of the organization's incorporation (its anticolonial history and sterling republican credentials) it could not be liquidated, and the prospect of controlling the rank-and-file directly threatened more industrial unrest. Bourguiba opted instead for elite control, denying any would-be challengers, be they leftist or Islamist, an opportunity to find a base in the UGTT. While Mubarak opted to corrupt the elections with security services, Bourguiba simply "decapi-tated" the leadership and replaced it.[12]

Structural Adjustment and Renewed Crisis

A confluence of negative economic factors, including the drop in the price of oil, led to further economic trouble. The IMF and World Bank proposed structural adjustment in 1986, and economic plans were drafted to reflect that, securing additional financing. In addition to added economic pressure, the regime came into open conflict with the MTI. After arresting its leader, Rashid Ghannouchi, and putting him and his compatriots on trial, Bourguiba overturned the sentences

[10] Kenneth J. Perkins, *A History of Modern Tunisia* (New York, NY: Cambridge University Press, 2004), 173.
[11] Mohammed Trabelsi, ILO Representative, interview with author, October, 2012.
[12] Eva Bellin, *Stalled Democracy: Capital, Labor, and the Paradox of State-Sponsored Development*, 1st edition (Ithaca, NY: Cornell University Press, 2002), 112–14.

as too lenient and attempted to carry out capital punishment. Minister of the Interior Zine El Abbedine Ben Ali intervened fearing the blow-back from such a decision.[13] The following year Ben Ali, serving as prime minister but with deep ties to the security apparatus, organized a "medical coup" by having Bourguiba declared unfit for office. Ben Ali set about taking over the state apparatus, promising a kinder and gentler version of the old regime. UGTT leaders were released from house arrest along with Islamist leaders including Ghannouchi. The "presidency for life" was eliminated, and a general tone of pluralism and consultation became the hallmark of the new regime.[14] The Neo-Dostour Party, which Bourguiba had rechristened the Parti Socialiste Destourien (PSD), was renamed yet again as the Rassemblement Constitutionnel Démocratique (RCD).

Conflicts between the Bourguiba regime and the UGTT left the union in disarray. The intermittent jailing of leadership, the legacy of the 1978 crackdown, rendered the union weak. Ben Ali sought to rebuild the organization by holding new elections and reorganizing its upper echelons. He hoped to both bring the organization back from the brink and use it to support his new regime. These electoral openings afforded Islamists the opportunity to inject themselves in trade union politics, a realm where they held little influence. No doubt inspired by the success of their fellow Islamists in the Egyptian Muslim Brotherhood who had successfully leveraged their university bases to win control of professional unions, the MTI (now renamed Ennahda) sought to gain seats in the UGTT elections of 1988–89.[15] A combination of government repression and sincere differences on economic vision thwarted the attempt. Ennahda at this point did not enjoy a broad base of support, especially among the working class or trade unionists, and they claimed less than 10 percent of trade unionists by most estimates. Alexander claims that Ennahda sought to gain a toehold in the UGTT in the hopes of offering to abandon it in favor of having a recognized political party. Regardless, the reconsolidation of

---

[13] L. B. Ware, "Ben Ali's Constitutional Coup in Tunisia," *Middle East Journal* 42, no. 4 (October 1, 1988): 587–601.

[14] Dirk Vandewalle, "From the New State to the New Era: Toward a Second Republic in Tunisia," *Middle East Journal* 42, no. 4 (October 1, 1988): 602–20.

[15] Christopher Alexander, "Opportunities, Organizations, and Ideas: Islamists and Workers in Tunisia and Algeria," *International Journal of Middle East Studies* 32, no. 4 (November 1, 2000): 465–90.

Ben Ali's regime had no role for Islamists in it, and Ennahda was soon under direct repression.

The neoliberal reforms in Tunisia showed strong signs of "crony capitalism." While there was fear that Egyptian SOE's were being sold below market value, the benefits were flowing to politically connected oligarchs. Tunisia's ruling clique was even smaller, with benefits flowing to Ben Ali's immediate family. Both countries' neoliberal terms were characterized by a uniquely North African variant of neoliberalism that lacked the ideology's normal commitment to property rights. In Tunisia any property or wealth was subject to expropriation by the rapacious Ben Ali-Trabelsi clan.

The concepts of structural adjustment were incorporated into Tunisia's 7th five-year plan designed to cover the years 1986–91. The program had several parts and focused primarily on currency revaluation, wage restraint, and shrinking the government budget. The program did not initially call for flexibilization or vast privatization, distinguishing it in some ways from the ERSAP in Egypt. The documents from the World Bank are unusually tone deaf even for the time. The President's Report rightly notes that removing subsidies will be politically problematic, but specifically cites the country's recent "political cohesion" only half a year after a coup removed its long-standing leader and a standoff with the country's Islamist groups almost ended in the execution of its leader.[16]

The structural adjustment program as initially outlined contained three main parts: the removal of import restrictions, liberalizing the interest rates, and tax reform. As with Egypt (in practice, if not in planning), public enterprises were to be sold at a later time. This early wave of structural adjustment was not as dramatically detrimental to workers as later waves would be. The economy was growing, and low interest loans from multilateral institutions were put to use in liberalizing sectors of the economy.[17] The minimum wage grew, if slowly, during the initial years of structural adjustment.

---

[16] "Report and Recommendation of the President of the International Bank for Reconstruction and Development to the Executive Directors on a Proposed Structural Adjustment Loan in An Amount Equivalent to US$150 Million to The Republic of Tunisia," The World Bank, Report Number P-4808-TUN, May 20, 1988.

[17] Bradford Dillman, "The Political Economy of Structural Adjustment in Tunisia and Algeria," *The Journal of North African Studies* 3, no. 3 (September 1998): 1–24.

Despite this, the need for worker quiescence was obvious, and Ben Ali restructured the UGTT in part to ensure this. In 1998, Ismail Sahbani was chosen as the new secretary general of the UGTT. He was a regime loyalist and was on board for the economic reforms Ben Ali was carrying out. While the structural adjustment plan called for phasing out subsidies at a slow rate, based in part on global costs and exogenous shocks like drought, memories of failed sudden subsidy cuts in the past concerned the regime.[18] Despite its absence in official documents from the emergence of structural adjustment, the interplay of UGTT control, labor legislation, and market flexibilization soon emerged.

The repressive state apparatus of the Ben Ali regime was built in the late 1990s and early 2000s, part and parcel with the structural adjustment program. Inspired by the low-grade civil war carried out against Islamists in Egypt, and frightened by the more overt civil war in Algeria, Ben Ali built a coercive apparatus of police and internal security. This apparatus had conventional components, including powerful police, political prisoners, and censorship.[19] It also operated in subtle ways, including a type of authoritarianism described as "the political economy of repression" by Hibou. The regime intervened in the market at almost every turn, disciplining and steering enterprises. The relationship was reciprocal, with the state seeking more access to ensure control and tranquility, and enterprises seeking interventions to operate more successfully. An entire class of intermediaries, lodged between local businesses and state power, benefited from these intercessions. The number of individuals on the security payroll ballooned, and came to include taxi drivers and any number of anodyne informants who tracked citizens' activities. The extensive apparatus was put toward the developmental goals and capacities of the state, its main claim to legitimacy. The rhetoric of the Tunisian miracle made up a core component of Ben Ali's power.

[18] "Report and Recommendation of the President of the International Bank for Reconstruction and Development to the Executive Directors on a Proposed Structural Adjustment Loan in An Amount Equivalent to US$150 Million to The Republic of Tunisia," The World Bank, Report Number P-4808-TUN, May 20, 1988.

[19] "US Embassy Cables: Tunisia – A US Foreign Policy Conundrum," *The Guardian*, December 7, 2010, sec. World news, www.theguardian.com/world/us-embassy-cables-documents/217138.

This consistent appeal to "reformism" without actually letting up on the levers of power led to slow-downs in privatization schemes.[20] In the first four years of the privatization program, around $100 million dollars in assets were privatized.[21] This was a fraction of the total number of public sector companies. At the outset of privatization, the public sector employed around 10 percent of the population, and World Bank estimates placed the "redundancy" number at around 30,000.[22]

Activists in Tunisia claim that workers felt the effects of structural adjustment starting in 1995, as the orientation of the government shifted toward attracting foreign direct investment. One activist claimed, "[Tunisia] had the same process as elsewhere, the international institutions recommend cuts to social funds."[23] These reforms that frustrated labor activists were widely hailed as the most profound success story of all the Arab structural adjustment programs. By 1996, Tunisia had lowered inflation, raised the rate of GDP per capita, and raised the rate of growth in gross domestic investment. The country struggled, however, to raise exports to the levels imagined by the international institutions, and these export-oriented markets failed to solve excessive unemployment in the labor market.[24]

Flexibilization

In line with dominant thinking at the time, Tunisia also focused on flexibilizing its labor market. During the socialist era, Tunisia enacted an extensive set of proworker labor codes. These included provisions on the workweek, labor inspection, and a tripartite labor commission

---

[20] Béatrice Hibou, *The Force of Obedience: The Political Economy of Repression in Tunisia* (Cambridge; Malden, MA: Polity Press, 2011), 246.

[21] Jamal Saghir, "Cofinancing and Advisory Services (CFS)," *Privatization in Tunisia* (The World Bank, January 31, 1993), http://documents.worldbank.org/curated/en/1993/01/699149/privatization-tunisia.

[22] The redundancy figure is proportional to the one estimated in Egypt during the privatization process in the late 1990s, per total number of workers in the economy.

[23] Aouadhi Chaker, UGTT Official, July 25, 2013.

[24] Karen Pfeifer, "How Tunisia, Morocco, Jordan and Even Egypt Became IMF 'Success Stories' in the 1990s," *Middle East Report*, no. 210 (1999): 23–27.

to deal with individual labor disputes.[25] It also, however, limited strikes and required UGTT permission, in the same fashion as the ETUF in Egypt.[26] The 1970s saw the emergence of state-guided collective bargaining, in the form of the "convention collective cadre" with the goal of obtaining worker buy-in for early liberal reforms. This development did little to improve the position of workers with regard to strikes or the right to form new unions outside of UGTT control, but did allow it the possibility of negotiating wages.

The pressure for flexibilization of the labor code grew under structural adjustment. Employers were expected to be more competitive in international markets and sought greater flexibility in hiring and firing to achieve this. Though it had been mentioned since the outset, the international financial institutions, reacting in part to persistent unemployment, also called for greater labor flexibilization in the 1990s.[27] Drafts of the new labor code began circulating as early as 1987 calling specifically for short-term and temporary work, as desired by the business confederation. Union tunisienne de l'industrie, du Commerce et de l'artisanat (UTICA), a national business confederation, had grown in power during the 1980s and 1990s and was then in a position to directly engage with the UGTT, if not on an equal footing, at least on one that wielded influence over the business-minded Ben Ali regime.

The UGTT, for its part, walked a fine line in negotiating a new labor law. The newly installed UGTT leadership hoped to strengthen its position against business owners, while maintaining tight control over its own rank-and-file. Alexander describes this balancing act saying,

The power to authorize strikes gave these leaders a valuable tool in their effort to control the UGTT's rank and file. For their part, UTICA's leaders certainly had no complaint with a regulation that made it more difficult for

---

[25] "Summary," accessed June 3, 2014, www.jurisitetunisie.com/tunisie/codes/ct/menu-26.html.

[26] Christopher Alexander, "Labour Code Reform in Tunisia," *Mediterranean Politics* 6, no. 2 (2001): 104–25.

[27] "Completion Report: Economic and Financial Reforms Strengthening Programme (PRREF) Tunisia" (African Development Bank, January 1998); Edgar J. Ariza-Nino and Cheri Rassas, "Tunisia's Economic Adjustment Program: Impact on Lower Income Groups" (United States Agency for International Development, n.d.), http://pdf.usaid.gov/pdf_docs/PNAAZ504.pdf.

workers to strike. On this issue, then, the government and the UGTT and UTICA leaderships shared very similar positions.[28]

The UGTT would also benefit from a reorganized and centralized representation structure. The original labor code made it clear that the national confederation was legal, but was largely agnostic on how workplace unions were to be organized. This benefited UGTT leadership, and they hoped to reform workplace organizing to maintain central control.

Like in Egypt, negotiations between the "social partners" dragged out for several years with input from international bodies. The ILO report from the Committee of Experts in 1989 notes,

> In this context, the Committee wishes to recall that, while the proposed amendments to the provisions of the Labour Code ... tend towards a better application of the Convention, the proposed amendment whereby an absolute majority of the workers concerned is needed to call a strike should be modified so that the decision to have recourse to a strike may be taken by a simple majority of the voters in an enterprise (excluding workers not participating in the ballot). The Committee again draws the Government's attention to the need to amend section 389 of the Code in order to confine the authorities' power to requisition workers to cases in which a strike would affect essential services ... "[29]

Several topics were up for consideration in this raft of labor reforms: strike authorization; strike circumstances; flexibilization; and reorganization of shop floor representation. The only stakeholder legitimately interested in simplifying strike authorization was the ILO (barring perhaps rank-and-file members who were insufficiently represented at the decision-making level). This topic was largely ignored in the ensuing legislation. The new law did narrow when the government could ban a strike by limiting it, effectively, to issues of life and death in accordance with international standards. Another flexibilization article specified what constituted a "faute grave," or a dismissible offense. The list no doubt seemed extensive to the UGTT and included ill-defined concepts like "any deliberate act to impede the operation or normal activity of the company or to cause damage to its property,"

---

[28] Alexander, "Labour Code Reform in Tunisia."
[29] "Comments," accessed June 4, 2014, www.ilo.org/dyn/normlex/en/f?p= 1000:13100:0::NO:13100:P13100_COMMENT_ID:2078466.

which could open striking workers to firing. However, from the UTI-CA's perspective, the continued limitation on firing was not a victory.

While flexibilization in Egypt weakened the ETUF by giving it less control over workers, shorter worker tenure, and more turnover in workers, it operated differently in Tunisia. In Tunisia, the UGTT was intimately involved with managing the labor market. The union often served as a labor broker, assigning workers to different companies, moving workers from one location to another as needed. This gave the union not only the role as patron, but also tied it more intimately to the success of business. This role was eventually criticized for its perceived corruption and the collusion of UGTT officials in the Gafsa region. While the question for workers in Egypt might have been "Where is the union?" in Tunisia it was "Why is the union doing this?" as the UGTT had a direct role in deciding who got a job.

The reforms to the labor market ultimately took the form of the 1994 labor code. These labor code amendments were expanded in 1996. This process is still remembered by trade unionists within the country as the beginning of a "social disaster."[30] For many, the passage of the amendments marked the decisive shift to a market-oriented and labor-hostile era. The 1996 labor revisions established more flexibility in hiring workers under a raft of specific economic conditions. The net effect was to flexibilize hiring, while retaining some limits on firing. The biggest winner from the new labor laws was the government. It managed to reassert its indispensable role in maintaining social harmony. UTICA managed to win some concessions, but its increased strength in this period was more a function of the general pro-business orientation of the government. The labor legislation formalized some of the issues the UGTT had spent time scrambling to address in an ad hoc manner. It maintained its privileged position as the only labor confederation and the final arbiter of the strike weapon. The UGTT maintained its primary stronghold in government bureaucracy, with additional members in the oil and gas sector. The process of restricting government spending and the sale of SOEs meant an almost certain contraction of its membership numbers. The elite bargain struck between the UGTT, UTICA, and the regime bore some of the hallmarks of previous agreements. It was largely an elite bargain, struck in Tunis, which

[30] Sofienne Ben Hamida, Journalist, interview with author, April, 2012.

did not necessarily enjoy buy-in down through the ranks. With its emphasis on export and tourism, the entire structural adjustment scheme was shifting the balance of economic power even more drastically from the underdeveloped "interior" of the country to the wealthier coast. The UGTT's position at this point did little to stop the economic or regional alienation of its members.

Political Power Loss

During the 1990s, while the UGTT was largely quiescent, little independent organizing outside the UGTT structure took place in Tunisia. Tunisia's actual economic development during this period cannot be understated. From Ben Ali's rise to power to 2008, the GDP of the country quadrupled. Measuring by GNI per capita, wealth in the country doubled. Human development goals were also reached. Life expectancy went from 65.6 years in 1985 to 74.3 in 2010. Literacy went from 48 percent to 80 percent. The poverty headcount was approximately halved from 1990 to 2005, dropping to 3.8 percent. Compared to Morocco, this is a sharper decline with less than half the poverty. From 1996 to 2008, a period of continuing and renewed structural adjustment in Egypt, poverty was static and may have even increased. By macroeconomic indicators, Tunisia's liberalization in the 1990s and 2000s yielded impressive results, but deep structural flaws remained, beyond even the repressive apparatus that had emerged to protect it.

Persistent unemployment continued to hamper the economy. Given the rapidly changing social and economic indicators from the 1990s and early 2000s, the persistence of unemployment is impressive. Unemployment in Tunisia in 1991, the first year for which ILO data is available, was 15 percent of the total workforce. In 2010, the year the revolution started, it was 13 percent. The Tunisian economy was producing jobs, as indicated by the steady unemployment numbers despite an increase in the proportion of the population aged 15–64 from 57–70 percent at that time. It simply was not producing enough to substantively draw down the reserve of unemployed people in the country. Unemployment was concentrated both regionally and demographically. Unemployment for young people hovered near 30 percent for most of the 2000s. Numbers are even starker in the labor force participation rate, which dropped from near 56 percent for young men in the late 1980s, to 40 percent by 2010. Early data suggests this figure was as high as 70 percent in 1980.[31]

Unemployment was most notable in the less-developed interior of the country. These parts of the country included agricultural land and the phosphate-mining region of Gafsa. Estimates have placed unemployment in this region at double the national average. Across almost all metrics, the interior suffered in comparison to the coast. While almost 100 percent of births were attended in Tunis, the capital in 2000, less than 50 percent were in Kesserine, in the interior.[32] Despite major national drops, poverty rates were constant in the south throughout the 1990s.[33]

Unemployment among educated professionals may have been even more politically destabilizing than poverty in the long run. A joint Government of Tunisia–World Bank study published in 2008 shows the troubling dynamics among young, educated workers. While Tunisia did not have a guaranteed work scheme for university graduates as Egypt did, the public sector was the largest employer of university graduates. The expectation was that this would continue contra structural adjustment's budget constraints. The picture in the mid-2000s was grim. The World Bank study showed general unemployment for young graduates in excess of 47 percent, with the highest concentration among graduates with degrees in business and law. Much of this unemployment proved to be persistent, lasting over two years. When university graduates did find work, it was often in government ministries far removed from their own interests and abilities, contributing to bureaucratic inefficiency.[34]

In addition to poverty for the rural poor and idleness for the university-educated middle class, Tunisia's reforms in the 2000s

[31] "World Development Indicators I Data I The World Bank DataBank – Create Widgets or Advanced Reports and Share," accessed June 5, 2014, http://databank.worldbank.org/data/views/reports/tableview.aspx#.

[32] "Tunisia National Report on Millenium Development Goals" (United Nations, May 2004), www.undp.org/content/dam/undp/library/MDG/english/MDG%20Country%20Reports/Tunisia/Tunisia%202.pdf.

[33] "Poverty Profile Executive Summary Republic of Tunisia" (Japan Bank for International Cooperation, February 2001), www.jica.go.jp/activities/issues/poverty/profile/pdf/tunisia_e.pdf.

[34] "Dynamique de L'emploi et Adequation de La Formation Parmi Les Diplomes Universitaires" (World Bank and Ministere de l'Emploi et de l'Insertion Professionnelle des Jeunes, July 2009), http://siteresources.worldbank.org/INTTUNISIAINFRENCH/Resources/Dynamique.de.lemploi.pdf.

challenged industrial workers. Tunisia had been a beneficiary of the
Multi-Fibre Agreement (MFA), a global quota system that limited the
amount of clothing exports underdeveloped countries were permitted
to produce. This agreement helped Tunisia capture a share of the
European Union textile and clothing market, which became a growth
sector in the country. At the expiration of the MFA in 2005, the textile
and clothing (T&C) sector employed over 200,000 Tunisian workers.
The first year of the liberalized T&C market saw Tunisia lose 5.8
percent of its exports to the EU. A World Bank study suggests that
net job loss was around 1 percent, though reports from the UGTT say
as many as 50,000 workers lost or changed jobs during this period.[35]
The churn in the industrial sector also deepened problems between
UGTT leadership and their rank-and-file. Wildcat strikes were
reported during this period.[36]

Persistent unemployment had several effects. Masses of young, educated citizens were unable to find work, or worked in positions below
their education level. The frustration over such a situation remains
palpable in the country. The perception that friends and family of Ben
Ali were profiting from structural adjustment only highlighted the
problem. Furthermore, removing young people from the economy also
helped to remove them from the political economy of repression that
undergirded the Ben Ali regime. In addition to the disciplinary benefits
of daily work, especially in a country where many companies are
closely tied to the regime, being outside of a standard wage or salaried
position meant that greater proportions than ever were outside the
UGTT. UGTT membership is an incredibly difficult thing to determine.
After the revolution, the UGTT claimed numbers in excess of
750,000.[37] Some news outlets claimed over 800,000.[38] The UGTT
has every incentive to inflate these numbers. A more realistic number

---

[35] "Morocco, Tunisia, Egypt and Jordan after the End of the Multi-Fiber
Agreement" (World Bank, 2006), http://doc.abhatoo.net.ma/doc/IMG/pdf/
morocco_tunisa_egypt_jordan_end_agreement.pdf; "Wikileaks Cable: Tunisia's
Textile Sector Bounces Back" (Embassy Tunis [Tunisia]: Wikileaks, September
24, 2007), www.cablegatesearch.net/cable.php?id=07TUNIS1299.

[36] "Cable: 06TUNIS2465_a," accessed June 6, 2014, www.wikileaks.org/plusd/
cables/06TUNIS2465_a.html.

[37] UGTT Official, interview with author, July, 2013.

[38] "Tunisia's Islamists Resist Proposal to Step down | Reuters," accessed
June 5, 2014, http://uk.reuters.com/article/2013/09/23/uk-tunisia-crisis-
idUKBRE98M0K220130923.

for the final years of the 2000s is somewhere around 500,000 members. With a labor force participation rate of just over 2.2 million, this would give Tunisia a union density comparable to the more generous estimates of Egypt's.[39] While the regime exerted strong control over the UGTT in the 1990s and 2000s, the organization's influence eroded simply as a function of decreased labor force participation and chronic unemployment. Like in Egypt, a main prop of the regime was losing its grip on those it was supposed to keep quiet.

Nothing about the situation described here leads automatically to revolution. The UGTT had been alienated before. A growing gap between the rank-and-file and the leadership of the institution was not new either. The UGTT never enjoyed a massive union density on the order of communist unions, so the growing number of unemployed and militant activists did not automatically mean that workers would be put to new revolutionary purposes. Despite this, and in accordance with the situation in Egypt, leaders emerged in sectors that had slipped from central union control. These new leaders spoke out for workers who were laid off, never hired, alienated, and generally disgruntled by the state's policies. The labor unrest that emerged in 2008 served as a dry run for the protests of 2010.

Cracks appeared in the UGTT in the 2000s. Notably, the General Secretary of the UGTT, Ismail Sahbani was sacked in 2000 under government pressure, and eventually tried for embezzlement. While this was far from unprecedented in UGTT history, usually exiled UGTT leaders would be rehabilitated and returned to the fold under government sponsorship at some point. This happened with leaders in the Bourguiba era like Achour, and also under Ben Ali. In the 2000s, this "recycling and rehabilitation" system seems to have broken down, and while Sahbani was unable to rally his supporters in a structure outside the UGTT in the way of Abu Eita or Abbas in Egypt, he did maintain loyalty outside the structure, and formed a competing

---

[39] One outlier in the attempts to estimate UGTT membership comes in the form of a leaked classified cable from the Labor Office of the US Embassy in Tunis. In it the officer puts the number of UGTT members at a rather startling 1 million, a number never mentioned to the author in interviews with either the UGTT or other activists in Tunisia. Internal politics of the US State Department may be at play, or simply faulty information in the run up to the UGTT elections in 2006. "Cable: 06TUNIS2887_a," accessed June 5, 2014, www.wikileaks.org/plusd/cables/06TUNIS2887_a.html.

confederation after the revolution. Stefen Erdle describes the process of "recycling" as the "presidentialization of recruitment," and explains it thusly,

Elite members continuously circle the regime core; usually without being "in" too long, but also without being "out" forever. Sooner or later, first circle members will be sent for some time into political "exile" (which can be an embassy, an international organization or a public enterprise), while particularly promising second circle elements will take over their posts. However, this calculated "disgrace" is mostly a transitory situation, followed by the pardoning of "culprit" and his re-integration into the "circuit" ...[40]

The recycling system of presidential recruitment was breaking down, and having both elite "outsiders" and masses of politically disconnected citizens was the perfect storm that helped bring down the regime.

An extraordinary congress of the UGTT was held to elect new leadership, which was surprisingly competitive for the union's history. Competing lists, including those tied to Sahbani, ran against one another. Abdessalem Jerad was elected despite his close ties to Sahbani. Ali Romdhane, leader of a competing strain of UGTT members was also elected to the executive board, creating a diversity of opinion in the leadership. While the reconsolidation of leadership with Romdhane's supporters and Jerad's old guard steadied the UGTT's ship for a brief period, it did leave some activists interested in more substantive reforms in the cold. The UGTT was more alienated from its rank and file than ever and now real cracks had appeared in the executive board. Sahbani's removal was a stark reminder that the organization's leadership served at the pleasure of Ben Ali.[41]

The UGTT's 2006 elections were almost as contentious as the ETUF elections of the same year. The elections were called months early: possibly to preclude real competition from unionists angry about the direction the leadership had taken.[42] A series of issues including the relationship between the UGTT and the regime alienated independent-

---

[40] Steffen Erdle, *Ben Ali's "New Tunisia" (1987–2009): A Case Study of Authoritarian Modernization in the Arab World* (Berlin: Klaus Schwarz, 2010).
[41] Ibid.
[42] Cable: 06TUNIS2887_a accessed June 6, 2014, www.wikileaks.org/plusd/cables/06TUNIS2465_a.html.

minded unionists. Notable among them was Habib Guiza, a long-time UGTT official who that year began to prepare the foundations of a new labor confederation. Guiza claims that a large fraction of his support was drawn from young members, who went on to make up 80 percent of his new confederation after the revolution.[43] Like CTUWS in Egypt, Guiza began to work with private-sector employees who had less faith in the UGTT's ability to protect their interests. At the time, Guiza met with Kamal Abbas and the CTUWS and followed some of their organizing models.

While the government took pains to keep UGTT leaders in check, much like in Egypt, these leaders lost their position as a legitimate aggregator of the demands of their workers. Instead of diffusing or transmitting these demands, cleavages began to form between elites and rank and file. Some in the leadership were also openly questioning the government's dual role, as both an employer of an enormous number of UGTT workers, and as the mediator of labor–business negotiations.[44] The union had also gained some distance from the government by hosting protests regarding the invasion of Iraq, which helped to reinvigorate its position as a geographical site of contestation.[45] These simmering tensions exploded in a wave of labor militancy in 2008 that in many ways paralleled the one that emerged in Egypt in 2006 and 2007. Both were centered on regions at some distance from the capital that were perceived to be economically neglected despite serving as engines of the national economy. For Tunisia, this region was Gafsa in the country's south.

Corporatist Collapse and the New Repertoire of Contention

Like Egypt, Tunisia's labor unrest had both sectorial and regional components. The Gafsa region is home to Tunisia's phosphate industry. Phosphate is the backbone of the global fertilizer market, and Tunisia's phosphate regions are among the world's most profitable. The phosphate industry began in the late 1900s and is directed by a national corporation, the Compagnie des phosphates de Gafsa (CPG). Several organizations were merged in 1976 to create the company. It

---

[43] Habib Guiza, CGTT Leader, interview with author, July 2013.
[44] "Cable: 05TUNIS768_a," accessed June 5, 2014, www.wikileaks.org/plusd/cables/05TUNIS768_a.html.
[45] Habib Guiza, CGTT Leader, interview with author, July 2013.

has been a national asset since that time. To say the region has historically been restive is an understatement. In 1980, a group of armed commandos attacked the region and called for a revolution against Bourguiba. While international opinion pinned the operation on Gadhafi's Libya, the rebels were all Tunisian, and their actions enjoyed at least some support among certain disaffected portions of the local community.[46] The decision to hold the operation in Gafsa should not be understated.

As an industrial region, the phosphate mining and production companies are the largest source of employment. The company itself claims it employs approximately 4,300 individuals.[47] Despite this, the region had a major unemployment problem in the mid-2000s. Some reports place the total number of unemployed as high as 30 percent, which was, at the time, more than double the national average. In 2008, which saw a major outbreak of civil unrest in the Southwest, which includes Gafsa, the National Statistics Bureau reports that the governates of Gafsa, Tozeur, and Kebili had a population of 581,600 and over 64,000 registered job seekers.[48] Many more were likely underemployed or experiencing conditions of precarity. Mechanization in the extraction process limited employment in the industry.[49] While jobs may have shrunk in the mid-2000s, the value of the phosphate

[46] James Rupert, "Tunisia: Testing America's Third World Diplomacy," *World Policy Journal* 4, no. 1 (December 1, 1986): 137–57.

[47] "CPG-GCT: TUNISIAN PHOSPHATE INDUSTRY – INDUSTRIE PHOSPHATIERE TUNISIENNE," accessed June 9, 2014, www.gct.com.tn/english/wgct.htm; the number may have grown dramatically following the revolution, as more recent quotes put the total employees closer to 7,000. "Tunisia: New CEO of GCT and CPG Confident Despite Difficulties," *Tunis Afrique Presse*, January 23, 2013, http://allafrica.com/stories/201301240660.html.

[48] No doubt for political reasons, finding unemployment by governate in Tunisia is challenging. Despite that, the gap between population and formal job seekers is one of the largest in the country. All figures drawn from *ANNUAIRE STATISTIQUE DE LA TUNISIE 2008* (République Tunisienne Ministère du Développement et de la Coopération Internationale, 2008).

[49] An article by Eric Gobe quotes a figure provided by the Tunisian Communist Party claiming a decrease from 14,000 to 5,000 employees from 1980 to the late 2000s, but this is hard to confirm. National statistics show a growth from 15,307 job seekers in the South West region in 1995 to more than 34,000 in 2008, suggesting an erosion of jobs that exceeds that percentage increase in working-age population. Eric Gobe, "The Gafsa Mining Basin between Riots and a Social Movement: Meaning and Significance of a Protest Movement in Ben Ali's Tunisia," 2010, http://halshs.archives-ouvertes.fr/halshs-00557826/;

industry was increasing. As reported by the Central Bank of Tunisia, the value of phosphates went from $71 a ton in 2007 to a high of $430 a ton in 2008.[50] The increased wealth for the company did not trickle down to the permanent or sub-contracted workers. The unemployed, disconnected from both jobs and the oppressive RCD-UGTT relationship, were able to agitate for a better position in the regional economy.

Unemployed workers in 2006 formed a Union for Unemployed Graduates (Union des Diplômés Chômeurs or UDC) under an activist named Hassen Ben Abdellah. Like the ETUF in Egypt, the UGTT had ceased to speak in any way for the working classes, and had retreated to only defending its own members. While in Egypt this left an opportunity for independent organizing among unrepresented or underrepresented workers in the industrial and public sectors, in Tunisia it meant unemployed workers. Local residents had good reason for being suspicious of the local UGTT, which was closely tied to the RCD and business leaders themselves. For unemployed workers, the prospects of gaining meaningful employment in the local industry were slipping away in the mid-2000s despite record profits and its role as a public company.[51]

The job placement program in Tunisia contributed to the frustration. The local UGTT boss, Amara Abbassi, also owned the recruitment subcontractor that provided workers to the industry. The 2008 hiring round was perceived as particularly nepotistic and sparked a round of protests that linked unemployed workers, discontented employees, the banned communist party, and rank-and-file UGTT members alienated from the leadership's perceived sycophancy vis-à-vis the RCD. The protests, starting in Redeyef, soon spread throughout the region. Much like increasingly emboldened protests in Egypt, the complaints voiced by protesters extended from more prosaic concerns on wages to more fundamental complaints on uneven development and corruption.[52] The complaints on development struck to the very of

---

"Annual Report 2001" (Ministère du Développement et de la Coopération Internationale, 2001).
[50] "Annual Report" (Central Bank of Tunisia, n.d.), June 2009.
[51] Laryssa Chomiak, "Architecture of Resistance in Tunisia," in Lina Khatib and Ellen Lust (eds.), *Taking to the Streets: The Transformation of Arab Activism* (Baltimore, MD: Johns Hopkins University Press, 2014).
[52] "Cable: 08TUNIS131_a," accessed June 9, 2014, http://search.wikileaks.org/plusd/cables/08TUNIS131_a.html.

the Ben Ali regime's supposed legitimacy. Observers noticed the limited response from the Government of Tunisia early in the protests. The delay in response may have been due to hubris, regime officials not taking seriously a marginalized part of the country, or to a sincere inability to rhetorically combat the assertion that the "Tunisian miracle" was distributed unevenly across class, region, and social network.

The Union of Unemployed Graduates joined protesting workers. Many of the members had ties to other opposition groups and helped disseminate new tactics. Whereas the April 6th Movement in Egypt, which took its name from a planned labor strike, were intermittently decried as freeloaders and newcomers to the labor issue, the plight of unemployed graduates and unemployed workers in the phosphate mining region were closer to one another. The protest also included members of the UGTT.

While the UGTT's local leadership was closely allied with the RCD, the union itself contained strong leftist and independent currents.[53] Frustration with union leadership ran deep and included anger over the perceived corruption of Ismail Sahbani, the UGTT's former leader, and the perception that the local union stood more with the CPG than workers. The original protest cycle started in January 2008, and continued on a near-constant basis throughout February and March. By April, repressive actions had increased. Leaders of the protest movement were arrested, but this failed to end the movement. Ben Ali's National Guard carried out a massive crackdown in June, leading to the death of one protester, injuries to dozens more, and the arrest of hundreds.

The protest wave that swept the mining regions in central Tunisia during this period produced some disturbing contentious tactics. While international attention went to the immolation of Mohammed Bouazizi in December 2010, he was actually following in the footsteps of several other protesters. Chokri Selmani committed suicide during a protest on May 27, 2008, and Hichem Aleimi refused to release power lines despite warnings from security forces that they were turning them on, resulting in his death on May 6, 2008.[54] While these acts may not have directly inspired Bouazizi's self-immolation in 2010, they speak to

[53] Adnen Hajji, UGTT Activist/MP, interview with author, July 26, 2013.
[54] "Cable: 08TUNIS596_a," accessed June 9, 2014, http://search.wikileaks.org/plusd/cables/08TUNIS596_a.html.

the willingness of disaffected youth to take radical actions to draw attention to their plight.

The increasingly violent protest cycle and the participation of militant local members like Adnen Hajji forced the UGTT to move toward supporting protesters. In July, with a deadline for wage negotiation with UTICA looming, the UGTT called for a release of those arrested and a dialogue on the situation.[55] The situation also began to draw international support and attention to the protesters. With the arrest of trade unionists, the regional and international trade union movement took up the issue. Algerian and Moroccan unions issued statements of solidarity.[56] As the crisis dragged on, the CTUWS in Egypt held conferences in support of imprisoned workers.[57] Domestic support also poured in. While the legal parties were hesitant to throw their support behind the protesters, more militant and independent groups provided coordination support, including the Tunisian Human Rights League (Ligue tunisienne des droits l'homme or LTDH). The LTDH's history mirrored that of the UGTT's with successive waves of militancy or quiescence in relation to the government. Their support for the protests provided both some legitimacy for the activity and more linkages between inland activists and coastal elites. The LTDH's involvement also helped drag the UGTT further toward the side of protesters. The two organizations had been working together for a number of years, and the LTDH used UGTT facilities for conferences and meetings after their own facilities became a regular target for coercive actions by the security services.[58]

Outside the Gafsa crisis, the UGTT continued its role as central negotiating partner with the government. Broad agreement was reached with UTICA on overarching issues in the spring of 2008, with bargaining moving to the sectorial level. The UGTT, as it had in 2005, refused to accept seats in the country's "Chamber of Advisors," an upper house of the national assembly created in a round of reforms in 2005. A number of seats were reserved for the UGTT, but they were

---

[55] "Cable: 08TUNIS761_a," accessed June 10, 2014, http://search.wikileaks.org/plusd/cables/08TUNIS761_a.html.

[56] Adnen Hajji, UGTT Activist/MP interview with author, July 26, 2013.

[57] "Press Release: Seminar Calling to Release Imprisoned Tunisian Workers – CTUWS," accessed June 10, 2014, www.ctuws.com/programs/press/?item=359.

[58] Tunisia 2006 Country Reports on Human Rights Practices, Bureau of Democracy, Human Rights, and Labor, US Department of State, March 6, 2007.

not permitted to select which members attended and had refused to take their seats. In 2008 Ben Ali directly appointed Mohamed Chandoul, the Deputy Secretary General of the UGTT. The decision led to complaints from rank-and-file members as another sign of elite cooptation.[59] In a move to limit any potential victory for the UGTT, and in the hopes of blunting the criticisms emerging from Gafsa, the regime increased the minimum wage in the country prior to the issue being negotiated in the social dialogue. Both actions were a reminder to rank-and-file members that the UGTT's support for the RCD bought it little. Wage increases did little to address the concerns of those who had been pushed out of the formal mechanisms of interest aggregation: the unemployed graduates, rural poor, and laid off. While it might seem odd to call an increase in wages a strategic loss for the UGTT, the decision of the regime to preempt the social dialogue by intervening directly shows the loss of political power the union once enjoyed.

Reports of Ben Ali's inner circle stealing, expropriating, and scamming their way into obscene wealth were well known to the business and professional community. Ben Ali's wife, Leila Trabelsi, was known as having a particularly perfidious family. The Trabelsi clan was involved in a number of high-profile scandals in the years preceding the revolution.[60] The exact nature of their influence over Ben Ali, or his decision-making process, is opaque. While at first glance it seems that Tunisia has a more competent, technocratic bureaucracy than its Egyptian counterpart, this does not suggest it is any more transparent. It was in the 2000s, as a leaked diplomatic cable said, as clear as mud.[61] Whoever did have influence over the political system, it was neither the UGTT nor its leadership. While the organization was able to directly influence and even set policy during the socialist period of Bourguiba's rule, and maintained the capacity to at least disrupt the system in the 1970s and 1980s, it showed no such capacity in the 2000s. When and where militancy remained, it did so at the rank-and-file level and only in certain regions of the country. Even during the 2008 round of social dialogue, where the Gafsa protests were already

[59] "Cable: 08TUNIS1015_a," accessed June 10, 2014, https://wikileaks.org/plusd/cables/08TUNIS1015_a.html.

[60] "Cable Viewer," accessed February 25, 2015, http://wikileaks.org/cable/2008/06/08TUNIS679.html.

[61] "Cable: 08TUNIS63_a," 63, accessed February 26, 2015, https://wikileaks.org/plusd/cables/08TUNIS63_a.html.

raging, the UGTT confined itself to narrow concerns, focusing on the protection of trade union leadership and guaranteeing working hours and a four-year limit to flexible contracts (both goals already enshrined in Tunisian law). A diplomatic cable sums up the opinion of one UTICA representative by stating,

"It's clear," he said, "Djilani (UTICA head) wants to see how little he can give up. Jerad (UGTT head) wants to see how much he can get." Khanfir exclaimed that the whole process was for appearances' sake and we should not expect to see anything significant come out of this.

While the security crackdown in Gafsa limited protests there in 2009, it's after effects were felt in the trade union movement. In addition to rank and file vs. leadership debates over supporting demonstrators and taking seats in the upper house, internal divisions also broke out regarding supporting Ben Ali's presidential campaign in 2009. While there was no likely alternative to Ben Ali and elections were largely shams, the symbolic support of the UGTT remained important to the regime. While most legal opposition parties endorsed Ben Ali, the leader of the Forum démocratique pour le travail et les libertés (known by its French acronym FTDL or Ettakatol in its Franco-Arabic transliteration), Mustapha Ben Jaafar, attempted to run, but met with little success.[62] Regional and sectorial unions protested the decision to endorse Ben Ali, though details are scarce. Statements by activists suggest that medical professionals and teachers were some of the most active in resisting support for Ben Ali. Teacher union militancy is a hallmark of union activity around the world, and especially in the Arab world. Teachers' unions were also particularly militant in Egypt.

Both Egypt's and Tunisia's corporatist structures were designed to control and channel labor. Under neoliberal reforms, flexibilization, and diminished political influence, it failed spectacularly in these goals in the 1990s and 2000s. The regime's reliance on the heavy hand of the security apparatus instead produced workers and worker advocates hardened by strikes, arrests, and police brutality into militant cadres ready to be put to new purposes. Already roiling in a multi-year strike wave that neither threat nor concession could control, Egyptian

---

[62] "Tunisie: l'opposant Mustapha Ben Jaafar candidat à la présidentielle," Le Monde.fr, accessed June 11, 2014, www.lemonde.fr/afrique/article/2009/09/25/tunisie-l-opposant-mustapha-ben-jaafar-candidat-a-la-presidentielle_1245376_3212.html.

workers were inspired by the example of Tunisian unionists who had already gained major concession in their own unions. Independent workers' activists joined the protests in Tahrir, and soon called for a general strike. The ETUF showed its loyalty by calling for worker quiescence. Its leadership helped lead the counterrevolution. The trade unionists and unaffiliated yet disgruntled workers who pushed for change to the Egyptian system reached their zenith in Tahrir Square. Victory appeared to be at hand with the departure of Mubarak after days of difficult protest and pitched battle with the security apparatus. Unfortunately, this victory would be elusive, and the process of reconsolidating a new regime in the country would leave alliances rent, workers coopted, and trade unions with little impact on the new governments.

The Tunisian case contains the same outcome as its counterpart in Egypt, corporatist collapse. The main variables, including neoliberal policies, flexibilization, and withdrawal of political influence, remain the same, though the context changes on some dimensions. First, the neoliberal policies of the Ben Ali regime were both more successful and more important to the regime's control than they ever were to Mubarak's in Egypt. While Mubarak often held himself up as the father of the country who would cool the capitalist excesses of his technocratic cabinet, Ben Ali's rule was rhetorically defined by its economic modernization and advanced capitalist development. In some ways, this made him even more vulnerable to cracks in the system.

Labor flexibilization started earlier in Tunisia, with the labor law being reformed in the 1990s as opposed to the 2000s in Egypt. The types and kinds of labor reform produced a specific pattern of worker alienation. Unemployment was highest in the interior of the country and most notable among young people. Both were necessary but not sufficient conditions for the 2010–11 revolution.

The loss of influence the UGTT experienced in Tunisia is also different from that experienced by the ETUF in Egypt. Egypt's attempt at cooptation and control of the ETUF went down through the ranks of the organization, as evidenced by the decision to directly intervene in shop-floor elections in the 2000s. Militant workers were not allowed to take on a role in the management of the union even at the most local level. In Tunisia militant workers were able to take up these positions in the regional divisions of the union, while the regime maintained strict control of the union leadership. Union leaders were subject to the same process of reshuffling and exile followed by return to the political elite as other cabinet ministers and close officials of the regime. This leadership was increasingly alienated from its rank-and-file, showing little ability or willingness to grapple with the insurgency brewing in the interior of the country or the increasingly challenging position of its members.

Finally, the structure of the Tunisian and Egyptian labor systems meant a different level of influence for each union. The ETUF was barely able to budge policies that would influence all workers, including minimum wages. Collective bargaining agreements were often ignored and national bargaining barely existed. Tunisia on the other hand saw national collective bargaining with extension agreements that covered as much as 80 percent of the country's workers. The collapse of corporatism in Tunisia followed a slightly different path than Egypt, but the driving factors were the same. The fact that the UGTT's political influence affected so many more workers only made the collapse of corporatist bargaining be felt all the more keenly.

In 2010, the year the Tunisian revolution began, the UGTT was pulled in competing directions. Its militant local cadres had backed the Gafsa protesters despite its close ties to the phosphate industry. Ben Ali had succeeded in undercutting its bargaining position by increasing the minimum wage and sewing elite dissention by appointing one of its leaders to his rubber-stamp upper cabinet. It had weathered at least two attempts at independent organizing, and Adnen Hajji, its most vocal critic in Gafsa, had turned down the route of Kamal Abu Eita and Kamal Abbas in Tunisia by steadfastly remaining within the UGTT structure. Its ability to serve as an interest aggregator and diffuser of tensions for the working classes was hampered not only by its limited leverage over the regime, but its own internal strife, and lack of influence over masses of unemployed citizens. Despite this, the fact that the UGTT could still claim in 2010 to be the sole representative of trade unionists is a testament both to its own enduring hold on revolutionary legitimacy and Ben Ali's continued belief in its utility as a means of social control. That utility changed drastically by the end of the year, with ramifications not only for Tunisia but for Egypt as well.

On December 17, 2010, Mohammed Bouazizi, a 26-year-old fruit seller, immolated himself outside the government offices after an altercation with a police officer. The initial interaction was one that was common in Tunisia: the anodyne functioning of a bureaucratic police state and its underemployed youth. Bouazizi was not the first young person to commit suicide in protest at the political and economic conditions in the country, but he did get the most attention for it. Part of the reason the story gained national attention was that, gruesomely, Bouazizi did not die on the 17th of December. Despite serious injury, he survived until January 4, 2011, almost long enough to see the results of the protest wave that was reinvigorated by his action. By January 10 even the defanged and docile social and political actors in the country had followed the youth, sometimes unwillingly, into the protests. Even the UGTT, whose leadership had resisted taking a firm stand in Gafsa, could not ignore the revolutionary wave and moved to support their local cadres who had joined the protests.

Protests spread throughout the interior of the country in the two weeks following Bouazizi's act. Unsurprisingly, some took place in Gafsa. No doubt to the regime's frustration, UGTT offices had taken on the role of "free speech" squares in the country, where not only the activities of the trade union were carried out but also played host to the LTDH as well as regime-backed protests against the Iraq War and Gaza incursion of 2009. The UGTT regional offices once again played host to demonstrations regarding the situation in Sidi Bouzid.[63] Like in Egypt, the UGTT was far from the sole actor in these protests. Young unemployed activists from the coastal cities, including Tunis, attended the protests. Bloggers and online activists began to organize. The website Nawaat played host to a trove of Wikileaks documents, cited repeatedly in this chapter, which brought to light the internal machinations of the RCD regime in an unflinching tone. Videos of protests and the police reactions to them circulated, connecting areas that were geographically and administratively separated. Many of the young bloggers had taken active roles providing rhetorical support and critical outlets for the 2008 protests in Gafsa and were attuned to the situation in the interior. Slim Amamou, known by his handle Slim 404, travelled to the region to blog about the nascent uprising.[64] Artists also carried a critical message, notably El General, a rapper famed for his song "Rais Lebled" (President of the Country), released as protests

---

[63] *Gafsa Manifestation UGTT 28/12/2010/ Tunisie*, 2011, www.youtube.com/watch?v=0CF6oZlCwBk&feature=youtube_gdata_player.

[64] Alcinda Manuel Honwana, *Youth and Revolution in Tunisia* (London: Zed Books), 2013, 56.

spread in December. The song offered a blistering critique of Ben Ali, stating that Tunisians were "living like animals" and critiquing money promised for infrastructure that went instead to corruption. The song was a dramatic example of the collapsing wall of fear that protected Ben Ali and led to El General's arrest in early January during a roundup of perceived revolutionary agitators throughout the country.

The crisis of the revolution was a crisis of the two modes of legitimacy the UGTT claimed. Rank-and-file unionists, far from the central union administration, embraced a street-based revolutionary politics in solidarity with the unemployed, members of Bouazizi's extended family, and the activists of the interior of the country. The Executive Board of the union continued to try to play the role of mediator, moderating and streamlining the demands of the rank-and-file into something more manageable. The Secretary General of the UGTT, Abdelsalam Jerad, even decried chants against Ben Ali in the early days of the protest. The most comprehensive analysis of the decision making during this time is offered by Hèla Yousfi in her book *Trade Unions and Arab Revolutions: The Tunisian Case of UGTT*. In it, Yousfi argues that during the early days of the revolution, the intermediate and regional bodies of the union forced the Executive Bureau into militancy. Here, the revolutionary and militant legitimacy of the UGTT triumphed over the ideas of negotiating and extracting concessions from the government, a power long hobbled by neoliberal reforms.[65]

Conclusion

Tunisia's path to corporatist collapse closely follows that of Egypt's. Both countries embraced structural adjustment on the advice of international financial institutions without a full recognition of the political instability the decision could make. As with the ETUF, Tunisia's regime sought to ensure labor quiescence by corrupting the elections of the UGTT's leadership, limiting their ability to aggregate the demands of their members and advocate on their behalf. Flexibilization limited the number of full-time jobs, reducing union membership and the connections workers felt to their unions. The UGTT also faced a

---

[65] Hèla Yousfi, *Trade Unions and Arab Revolutions: The Tunisian Case of UGTT*, (New York: Routledge, 2018).

loss of political power as the Ben Ali regime became more outwardly focused and oriented toward capital. The result was an alienated and militant interior of the country. Like in Egypt, this interior launched an unprecedented challenge to the regime, as militant unionists joined forces with unemployed graduates in an unprecedented strike and protest wave. In many ways, the protests were as much against the leadership of the UGTT as they were against the regime. Workers also sought redress for their grievances in new and alternative structure, posing challenges for the UGTT from within and without.

5 | *Tunisia's Struggle to Reconsolidate*

Ten days into a protest movement sparked by the self-immolation of Bouazizi, Tunisians encountered a rare sight: their president summoned to speak by the people. On December 28, Ben Ali appeared on television criticizing protesters and threatening them. Photographs were also released of Ben Ali visiting Bouazizi's bedside with his family. The fruit seller who couldn't get the local government official to hear his complaint had summoned the most powerful man in the country to his hospital room. The lawyers' union joined protests rallying not only in interior cities but also in Tunis. Their protests eventually turned into a general strike on January 6, effectively blocking the ability of the regime's courts to function while security forces were rounding up large numbers of protesters charged with various offenses. Despite the massive protests and the activities of local cadres in supporting protesters, the UGTT did not call for a general strike until January 14.

By the 14th, the repressive forces of the regime spilled enough blood to catapult a regional crisis into a national one. From January 8–12 protests spread to the interior city of Kesserine. Kesserine was one of the poorest and least developed regions of the country. Unemployment was high, and smuggling with Algeria was a common activity for young men, leading to frequent confrontations with the security services. Violence cycled through the region in January following clashes between security forces and mourners at funerals from the last wave of clashes. Reports escaped from the city of security services using snipers on the roofs to shoot anyone filming protests. Later military reports confirmed this story, with evidence of protesters shot from behind with high-powered, high-accuracy rifles.[1] The Kesserine violence revealed the regime's control to be a mile wide and an inch deep, especially in

---

[1] "Tunisia: The Case of Amin Alkarami Reveals the Identity of an Army Sniper," *Nawaat*, accessed June 12, 2014, http://nawaat.org/portail/2012/09/01/tunisia-the-case-of-amin-alkarami-reveals-the-identity-of-an-army-sniper/.

regions like Kesserine and Gafsa with different relationships to the littoral power centers and the outside world. The regime's inability to use the "political economy of obedience" in these regions left it no fallback position besides naked oppression, something that had not been a hallmark of Tunisian politics to this point. The deaths in Kesserine were the overreaching of a desperate regime that was about to lose even more of its levers of power as its formerly quiescent interlocutors joined the revolution.

Incorporation and Legitimacy

Like its counterpart in Egypt, the UGTT brought its own baggage to the revolutionary process. Before assessing its actions immediately after the departure of Ben Ali, it is worth looking at how the organization had justified its legitimacy to this point. To use Collier and Collier's language, was the institution shaped more by "constant causes" or "historical causes?" The founding of the union, explicitly Tunisian and independent, working for the independence of the country is often highlighted but is hardly the only episode to point to in the institution's long history.

The narrative of the UGTT is recounted well by someone who has served as a leader of the organization and a political opponent of it at different stages of his career. Mustapha Ben Jaffar, leader of the Ettakatol Party, President of the National Constituent Assembly, and long-time democracy activist, describes the organization by saying,

... the UGTT has history in the national life of Tunisia, from the independence from France. Farhat Heched is both a symbol, and in reality was a national leader while Bourguiba was in prison ... after independence the UGTT was the counterbalance to the one-party system ... it worked to implement social stability ... it was the umbrella for freedom.[2]

The UGTT, in a deft move of historical revisionism, mobilizes multiple types of legitimacy. First, it rightly highlights its role in the anticolonial struggle. The organization predates the emergence of an independent Tunisia. It was authentically a nationalist group, banning the membership of non-Arabs. Its cadres were at the vanguard of independence,

---

[2] Mustapha Ben Jaffar, Former President of the National Constitutent Assembly, interview with author, August 3, 2015.

and many, including their early leader Farhat Heched, paid with their lives. The revisionism enters the UGTT discourse when it claims to have resisted neoliberal policies during the general strike of 1978 and food riots of 1984. The UGTT cites both as examples of its willingness to stand up for the working class, conveniently forgetting that in both cases rank-and-file members dragged the organization into the conflict. Furthermore, the idea that the UGTT of the preindependence era is the same as that which existed following 1978 or following Ben Ali's purge of the late 1980s is a stretch. It is true that in each instance elements of the UGTT stood against oppression, but the organization was also crushed in dramatic fashion in each instance.

The union also draws legitimacy from the idea of being an "umbrella" for different political currents during the days of dictatorship. Sami Tahri, a former UGTT deputy secretary general, describes it as follows "The UGTT gathered the political parties which existed in the absence of political life."[3] Like the narrative of "independence since birth," this idea holds a kernel of truth. After Bourguiba's (and later Ben Ali's) crackdowns on political pluralism, the UGTT had currents of leftist, social democratic, and centrist opinion within itself. A constrained political current, within a union structure whose leadership was coopted, however, had limited ability to direct the course of political events within the country.

The idea of an "independent since birth" UGTT does not hold up to scrutiny. The UGTT held influence in the early Bourguiba regime, but was also influenced by it. A Bourguibist group took over the leadership of the organization in the 1960s, and its independence was strongly debated not only by unionists within the country, but by international organizations concerned with "free labor." Its leadership was chosen by the regime, and when those leaders did not sufficiently genuflect to the regime's leadership, they were removed from office. What the UGTT did benefit from, however, was a strong narrative around the idea of legitimacy that activists throughout the 1990s and 2000s worked from the bottom up to build. The UGTT prides itself on the role it played during the Ben Ali era. In its own narrative, it was the only venue in which individuals from different political affiliations were able to express their preferences. While this may be true, these

---

[3] Sami Tahri, UGTT Deputy Secretary General, interview with author, July 23, 2015.

political opinions could not be aggregated up to national political life, which was strangled by the Ben Ali regime. Instead, activists, including those in the Gafsa region, argued that the militancy of the union was its strength. This counter-narrative suggests that the militancy shown by the UGTT in the 1970s and 1980s was a demonstration of real power, and one that should be emulated. These independent and militant unionists were allowed to rise to positions of leadership in regional unions. Their militancy likely would have prevented them from joining the union's executive bureau. This, coupled with international factors addressed in this chapter, helped set up a militant rank-and-file versus union leadership split that differed greatly from the federation versus federation split found in Egypt.

The relative independence of the rank-and-file and regional union structures reflects their entry into the labor union movement in the 1970s and 1980s, periods of expansion of the UGTT.[4] These more militant members were not permitted to take leadership roles in the organization, especially after the expulsion of Sahbani and general restrictions on the executive board of the union following Ben Ali's rise to power.[5] The union's history of militancy and the relative ability of the regional unions and rank-and-file to continue to engage in militancy gave the leadership a powerful rhetorical tool. This tool was most commonly used to discipline potentially wayward members. The pre-state existence of the union, its decision to come to the defense of "the nation" at times of crisis, and the commitment to militancy were used to convince potentially wayward members to support the UGTT. The idea of union cohesion became hegemonic. Activists in the 1990s and 2000s retained some confidence in the union maintaining militancy, even when it seemed unwilling to do so. Adnen Hajji, perhaps the most notable UGTT dissident, when asked why he did not strike out to form his own union, maintained his belief in the UGTT as an entity, even if the union leadership had gone astray.

The narrative of "revolutionary since birth" elides the challenging work done by regional and rank-and-file membership of the UGTT during the 1990s and 2000s. This work is often described as a push for trade union democracy. Hamma Hammami, leader of the Tunisian

---

[4] Keenan Wilder, "The Origins of Labour Autonomy in Authoritarian Tunisia," *Contemporary Social Science* 10, no. 4 (October 2, 2015): 349–63.

[5] Wilder also suggests that changing state–military relations may have limited Ben Ali's appetite for using the military to prevent dissent at the local level.

Worker's Party and a long-time activist, describes it as "a movement of the syndicate base against dictatorship, capitalists, corruption, from inside the UGTT."[6] Mahdi Abdaljawad, who went on to be a leader of Nidaa Tounes and later Machrouu Tounes, similarly dates the movement for trade union freedom to 2001, and a pressure to change the UGTT constitution to be more democratic.[7]

By the UGTT leadership's narrative, the revolution sprung from the union's breast. In reality its militant cadres, local offices, and a reluctant recognition that the revolution would define its legitimacy dragged it into it. The UGTT general strike was called for January 14, but was secondary to regional strikes going on throughout the country. It also only joined a strike by the lawyer's union that had brought to heel a key component of the regime, the legal system. The UGTT's central office's call for a strike came just in time to be on the right side of history. Like in Egypt later in the year, the final decision played out behind the closed doors of the Presidential palace, with the military eventually withdrawing support from the President. The strikes, now systemic and with UGTT endorsement, helped seal the President's fate. On the 14th, Ben Ali and his family boarded a plane (loaded down with gold from the national treasury if one is to believe a popular though dubious story) and took off for points unknown. After apparently being turned away from France, the family took refuge in Saudi Arabia, which had previously played host to deposed leaders like Idi Amin and Nawaz Sharif. Mohammed Ghannouchi claimed the title of President, but the constitutional court declared that Fouad Mebazaa, the president of the lower house of the legislature, was actually the rightful president. Mebazaa appointed Ghannouchi prime minister and charged him with forming a government of national unity.

Perhaps unsurprisingly, despite the decapitation of the regime, its functions survived. Mebazaa was an RCD member and had been in office since the 1990s. Ghannouchi was Ben Ali's prime minister for over a decade. The "government of national unity" drew on components of the defanged, legalized opposition groups in the country, notably the UGTT. The leader of the Progressive Democratic Party was named minister of regional development, perhaps in recognition of

---

[6] Hamma Hammami, General Secretary of the Worker's Party, interview with author, August 4, 2015.
[7] Mahdi Abdeljawad, Nidaa Tounes Politician, interview with author, June 27, 2015.

its support for Gafsa strikers in the previous years. Mustafa Ben Jaafar of Ettakatol was named health minister. Ahmed Ibrahim of Ettajdid was given the portfolio of higher education. Three UGTT leaders were given appointments. Houssine Dimassi was given the portfolio of the ministry of vocational training and employment. Abdeljelil Bedoui was named minister without portfolio. Anouar Ben Gueddour was named minister of transport. A simmering dispute between UGTT leadership and its rank-and-file exploded into a full-blown crisis. Ben Ali had a twenty-five-minister cabinet following the 2009 reshuffle. The new government had six "opposition" ministers, all from legal opposition groups. Even among those groups, only centrist, pragmatic, and potentially coopted ministers were chosen. Ben Gueddour, Bedoui, and Dimassi were all technocrats, not militant labor leaders. Ben Jaafar had successfully played the RCD game for over a decade. The rest of the ministries would almost certainly be turned over to RCD stalwarts, with occasional positions for, largely elderly, remnants of the Bourguiba regime. An exception was the unexpected appointment of blogger Slim Amamou, "Slim 404," as the minister of youth, a token position with limited political power. For a movement that saw itself as a youth revolution against RCD leadership, to have a new government that consisted of RCD stalwarts, token opposition, and not one major leader under the age of 60 was a tragedy.

The new government fell almost immediately. All three UGTT ministers quit after a day under massive protest from regional UGTT offices and ongoing street protests. Despite efforts by Ghannouchi and Mebazaa, such as quitting the RCD, the withdrawals, combined with that of Ben Jaafar, brought the government down. On January 18, the UGTT National Council, which consisted of the national, sectorial, and region secretaries general, passed a resolution stating in part,

Considering that the coalition government does not correspond to our ideas, that it does not express the demands we have put forward and that it does not represent the aspirations of the people and workers, [the UGTT] decides to withdraw our representatives from the coalition government; to have our elected union officials resign from the National Assembly, from the Assembly of the Council, and from the local councils; and to suspend the participation of the UGTT in the Economic and Social Council.[8]

---

[8] "Tunisia: Interview with UGTT Deputy Secretary General Hacine El Abassi – Newsocialist.org," accessed June 11, 2014, www.newsocialist.org/index.php/blog/352-tunisia-interview-with-ugtt-deputy-secretary-general-hacine-el-abassi.

The full withdrawal of the UGTT from all aspects of state management assured its downfall. The rump part of the RCD's attempt to work with a limited set of defanged opposition groups was untenable. While Ben Ali had fled several days before, only now was the regime teetering on collapse.

With a power vacuum forming in Tunis, popular committees began to spring up throughout the country. These groups sought to fill the security vacuum while also organizing further protests against the RCD and the regime, which still contained the hated interior minister who had overseen the police abuses and violence both in Gafsa and in the first days of the revolution. Protester killings were ongoing despite Ben Ali's removal. Militant members of the UGTT were among the leaders of these committees, as well as a challenge to the organization's conventional leadership structure. The organization was also about to receive its first official challenge since the early days of the Bourguiba regime.

On January 24, as the revolutionary contagion began to shift Egypt, Tunisian protesters formed a "caravan" to the capital calling on the fall of the entire government. The flow of people now reversed. Whereas, at first, Tunisian activists travelled to the interior to spread word of the protests, now young people from the interior travelled to the capital to finish off the regime. In a preview of what would happen in Egypt, security services began to collapse, as police joined the protests. The army, a small professional force, had already refused to fire on demonstrators and was now left as the main security force in the country. Another cabinet shuffle followed the "freedom caravans" but it failed to win support. On January 30, Rashid Ghannouchi, the exiled leader of the Ennahda Party, returned to Tunis for the first time in 20 years, rallying his supporters.[9]

Recognizing that the UGTT regional offices were continuing to serve as centers of protest in the governates, the interim government cut a deal with the UGTT on whom to appoint as governors throughout the country. The entire cadre of governors was replaced with non-RCD members. The UGTT was now in the role of endorsing or withdrawing support for governments and consulting on the appointment of

---

[9] " راشد الغنوشي زعيم حركة النهضة يعود إلى تونس اليوم بعد 20 عاما في المنفى, أخـــــبـــار " (Rashid Ghannouchi Leader of the Ennahda Movement Arrives in Tunis Today after Twenty Years in Exile)" accessed June 12, 2014, http://aawsat.com/details.asp?section=4&issueno=11751&article=606016&feature=#.U5m6Y_ldWSo.

regional governments. Both were new developments for the union, and prefigured its emergence as a supraconstitutional force in the country's reconsolidation. The UGTT during this period seems to have lost some of its coherence in the upper echelon. Decisions were being taken not by the Executive Board, its traditional leadership body, but by the National Council, which included regional and sectorial secretaries general, many of who sided with the more militant strand of the union.

The decision of the UGTT to operate under the National Council, instead of the Executive Board, was one of the most important and underexplored moments of the Tunisian Revolution. Shifting to a larger and more inclusive governing body during the crisis brought more militant regional members into the decision-making process, heading off the chance of fracturing the union. The more militant regional leadership, which had seen up close the uneven development of the Ben Ali years, had tangled with the devastating unemployment, and had seen the protest movement that grew following Gafsa in the 2000s, was more willing to take direct action in support of the revolution.

While the UGTT moved through this immediate revolutionary crisis more successfully than its counterparts in Egypt, the process was tenuous at every step. Leadership cadres of the organization were keen to preserve some elements of the status quo, as evidenced by their willingness to cooperate with former RCD members in the first transitional government. The most hagiographic accounts will suggest that the UGTT decisions during this time were a fait acompli, and that something about its origin or history predestined it to take a progressive and pro-revolutionary stance. Like the counterpart narrative of an irredeemably quiescent ETUF, the idea of a permanently revolutionary UGTT is also reductionist.

The idea that the UGTT "always" stands with the oppressed working classes was reinforced by the organization's telling of the Tunisian revolution. While rank-and-file members were vital to the success of the revolution, the organization rarely mentions its complicity in the excesses of the Ben Ali era. The strike wave that gripped Gafsa and other impoverished regions was as much against the UGTT as it was of the UGTT. Despite this, for rhetorical purposes the organization can claim its participation from the first days of the revolution. This claim is truer today than it was in 2011, as many of the rank-and-file members who forced the institutions have taken positions of legitimate authority within the organization, giving it a much more militant bend.

This renewed revolutionary legitimacy, and the decision to embrace the revolution taken by the leadership in late 2010 and 2011 would be used to great effect during future competitions in 2012. This ideological cudgel had two targets: internal and external. Internally, it was used to keep unionists from defecting to upstart unions or thinking of striking out on their own. Externally, it was used to push aside the insistence, usually coming from Islamists, that the UGTT should stick to economic and worker concerns as opposed to taking on broader political and social issues. While this revolutionary legitimacy was based in part on the UGTT's actions during the 2010 uprising, the rhetoric more commonly calls on the union's founding prior to state independence, and its key role in obtaining freedom from the French. Even prior to the opening of the trade union conference in December 2011, Abdessalem Jerad took the opportunity to assert that the UGTT's role was not limited to "un contexte particulier."[10] The sentiment was echoed by Samir Cheffi in 2012, saying "We know perfectly well what our role is, and have done since our foundation in 1946."[11] The veneration of Farhat Heched, both rhetorically in speeches and visually in every office, reminded members of the union's origins, legitimacy, and sacrifice in defense not only of workers, but the nation itself. This synthesis confirms the victory of the militant regional wings of the party that argued that the real strength of the organization was in its militancy and those periods when it took to the streets, rather than its ties to the regime or internal pluralism.

The UGTT had internal divisions to rectify following the surge of revolutionary activism. Grass roots, militant, young, and geographically isolated trade unionists had made their voices heard in the months following the ouster of Ben Ali, and the shift of power within the organization began to be reflected in the leadership. The 22nd Congress of the UGTT was held in the northwestern coastal city of Tabarka in December 2011. The organization was already under pressure from the transitional government. Prior to the meeting, the

[10] "L'UGTT Continuera À Agir Sur La Scène Politique (A.Jrad)," ShemsFm.net, accessed October 6, 2014, www.shemsfm.net/fr/actualite/l-ugtt-continuera-a-agir-sur-la-scene-politique-a-jrad-6888.

[11] Hèla Yousfi, "Political Islam After the Arab Spring; Tunisia's New Opposition," Le Monde Diplomatique, English Ed., Paris, November 2012.

new president, Moncef Marzouki, announced that continued strikes would constitute "collective suicide." Marzouki sought a moratorium on strikes, but unlike his military counterparts in Egypt, lacked the political power to enforce it. The Tabarka conference would determine who his negotiating partners would be. A long-serving trade union activist, Hacine Abbassi, was appointed as the new secretary general. The union staked out a more aggressive line through a number of resolutions denouncing privatization, international loans, and corruption. The leadership team assembled during the conference tilted leftist, reflecting the more militant proclivities of formerly repressed trade unionists. While it would later be decried as politicized and far-left, the executive board was a consensus choice that tended toward the center-left rather than the far left. Activists from the Parti Communiste des ouvriers de Tunisie (PCOT) were actually excluded from the committee.[12] While this conference solidified a center-left, militant, and regional wing of the UGTT in the leadership, it did not quell all internal strife. A group of aggrieved Islamist trade unionists resigned en masse, foreshadowing later conflicts with Islamists in the country. The fact that the UGTT managed to successfully hold its national congress at all demonstrates its organizational capacity. In addition to breakaway federations, the UGTT faced down disaffected workers on its doorstep in Tabarka.[13] Political parties in Tunisia were still organizing themselves, and the National Constituent Assembly had barely begun its work.

Internal Linkages

Succumbing to street pressure, Mohammed Ghannouchi stepped down as prime minister on February 27, 2011. Acting President Mebazaa appointed Beji Caid Essebsi as the new prime minister. Essebsi was one of the closest things Tunisia had to an elder statesman, having served as a minister of defense and interior under Bourguiba in the 1960s. While he held a position early in Ben Ali's regime, he had left politics in 1991, leaving him relatively free of the taint of the former regime. Essebsi managed to stabilize the political climate, appointing a technocratic government without ties to the former regime. Under

[12] Hamma Hammami, General Secretary of the Worker's Party, interview with author, August 4, 2015.

[13] Lassaad Abid, OTT General Secretary, interview with author, June 30, 2015.

him, the formation of a national constituent assembly (NCA) was announced. The assembly would be chosen by an election to be held in the summer. Essebsi also gathered several ad hoc and governmental reform commissions into one High Commission (called Haute instance pour la réalisation des objectifs de la révolution, de la réforme politique et de la transition démocratique in French), which served to end some in-fighting at the time. As the organization grew, it also came to include the UGTT, Ennahda, and other political parties. As a hybrid of de jure and revolutionary politics, the organization helped shape the political environment in the months before the election of the NCA. The NCA would be charged with not only writing a new constitution but also with extending the term of the government or creating a new one. The organization would be the de facto legislature of the country during the proposed transition.

Membership in the NCA was based on a vote held on October 23, 2011. The elections themselves were de-corporatized unlike Egypt's. No seats were reserved for political, religious, class, or other organizations. Official quotas were reserved only for women, as party lists were required to alternate male and female candidates, and a special set of nineteen representatives for Tunisians living abroad. Altogether, 117 parties ran in the election for 199 seats on the new assembly.

Ennahda took eighty-nine seats or 37 percent of the vote. Its closest competitors included a long-outlawed center-left party led by dissident Moncef Marzouki, the Congress for the Republic (Congrès our la République, CPR) with twenty-nine. Third place went to the populist Popular Petition for Freedom, Justice, and Development (commonly called Al-Aridah) with twenty-six seats. Al-Aridah was led by businessman Hechmi Hamdi, who advocated populist politics with an emphasis on the neglected southern regions of the country. Fourth place went to Mustapha Ben Jaffar's Ettakatol, a center-left party that won twenty seats. Ennahda forged a coalition government with CPR and Ettakatol, for a center-left/Islamist block that came to be called the Troika. Prior to the first meeting of the NCA, the three parties agreed to split the executive offices of the state, with Marzouki becoming president of the republic, Ben Jaffar becoming president of the NCA, and after a month of wrangling, an Ennahda leader named Hamadi Jebali became prime minister.

Having already brought down the first government made up of RCDists, and having forced its way into consultation on the appointment of regional governors in 2011, the UGTT was poised to influence policy under the Troika as well. No secular or leftist party managed to capture the majority of non-Islamist voters, and even within the NCA members were resigning from one party to form others with alarming speed. 2012 saw the emergence of several new parties, most of which claimed the left-liberal position, but few of which had the organization to compete with Ennahda. Over the course of 2012, the UGTT was increasingly called upon to serve as a counterweight to the Islamists. Ironically, it was a role built largely on an authoritarian legacy from the Ben Ali years. While the UGTT's role had eroded under Ben Ali's leadership, the organization had already managed to solve internal contradictions. When Ben Ali's brief flirtation with political opening ended in the early 1990s, the UGTT managed to subsume several existing political trends and parties-in-waiting. Among its cadres were socialists, nationalists, and communists.

The capacity to contain different political streams within itself and the lack of incentive to form competing federations greatly enhanced the UGTT's unity during the political transition. This unity has been key to its political success and expanded national role. Through 2012 it grew in stature as it maintained internal unity and friendly relations with all non-Islamist political parties. The political parties themselves failed to unify and present a challenge to Ennahda for leadership. Party splits took place throughout 2012. Notably, the CPR, one of the troika parties, saw a major split in May 2012 that left it down 12 NCA members when its former secretary general broke away to form a new party. Al Aridah lost more than a dozen members over 2012 and 2013. Ettakatol also lost more than half of its members to new political parties or declarations of independence.

The most important political party to emerge from the wave of defections was Nidaa Tounes (Call of Tunis). Led by Beji Caid Essebsi, the former Bourguiba and Ben Ali official who served as interim prime minister after the revolution, the party was formed in the summer of 2012 and occupies a center-left position. The party attracted many former supporters of the old regime, but also included a sizable contingent of disaffected members of center-left parties that emerged after the revolution. While the UGTT and Nidaa Tounes have never officially affiliated with one another, there is broad overlap in identity. Like the UGTT's post-2011 leadership, Nidaa Tounes includes a coterie of center-left and ex-regime apparatchiks. The affinities between the union and the party were clear, with Beji Caid Essebsi having been affiliated with the UGTT for years. Despite this, the UGTT did not formally endorse Nidaa Tounes, preferring to remain independent. The UGTT's decisions cannot be overstated here. The choices made in 2012, to remain a union and not directly enter politics as a party, to maintain loose ties to political parties instead of a formal alliance, and, eventually, to convene a national dialogue, are vital to understanding the UGTT's emergence as a powerful force in national politics. By avoiding the Scylla and Charybdis of division and cooptation, the union managed to obtain far more for its members than its counterpart in Egypt. It did, however, face competing unions, many of which pressed their advantage in the transition period.

In Egypt, alienated workers in industrial cities and bureaucratic offices turned to alternative proto-unions like Kamal Abbas's CTUWS or Abu Eita's independent strike committees. In Tunisia, they still turned to the UGTT, but to more populist and aggressive local rank-and-file leaders. The turn helped broaden the base of the UGTT in the revolutionary process. The organization had spent the past two years dealing not only with its own members but also with unemployed workers making demands of it. The pivot helped the union's self-conception as a broader, national actor. This role would be vital to the union's power following the revolution. The decision to include the regional leadership in decision making, as well as to step into work with the government on the appointment of new regional governors, brought this militancy into the leadership.

Habib Guiza's CGTT was the best organized of the independent unions. Having planned to launch a rival federation for years, Guiza announced the creation of the CGTT, and claimed 30,000 members. Guiza focused his criticisms on the UGTT's long-standing relationship with Ben Ali and his undemocratic nature. He claimed the right to trade union pluralism as enshrined in domestic and international agreements. Guiza drew inspiration from the CTUWS in Egypt and sought to compete with the UGTT for membership. Unlike his counterparts in Egypt, Guiza found relatively few takers, and limited domestic and international stakeholders or funders. It is worth mentioning that the strength of narratives of legitimacy reaching back to incorporation can also be found in the CGTT.

Disgraced former UGTT leader Ismail Sahbani faced a similar experience in attempting to craft the UTT as another counterpoint to the UGTT. Despite his ejection from corruption under the former regime, Sahbani's organization invoked the Ben Ali line, criticizing the politicization of the UGTT. The UTT claimed a narrower set of trade union preferences, focused on worker issues alone, as opposed to the increasingly expansive social program of the UGTT. Despite this, the UTT gained little traction in its effort to displace the UGTT. The organization claimed 150,000 members, a number disputed by both the UGTT and the CGTT. It has taken the step of reaching out internationally, to the WFTU, the collection of formerly socialist trade union organizations not affiliated with the ITUC. Ironically, the WFTU has also worked closely with the ETUF after its falling-out with the international trade union movement. Sahbani also touts his long-standing ties to the AFL-CIO, mentioning his "seven visits" and time studying in Ithaca (presumably at the AFL-CIO affiliated training programs at Cornell University's School of Industrial and Labor Relations).[14] What once might have been a powerful connection was inert following the revolution and global labor's embrace of the UGTT.

The importance of creating and recreating history is evident in the naming of both the CGTT and the UTT. Both seek to invoke older legitimacy going back to a mythologized incorporation. CGTT took its name from the radical union active in Tunisian politics in the 1920s that broke from the French-dominated CGT. The banners, website, and official materials of the CGTT state its founding date as 1924.[15] The UTT has also borrowed its name from an older trade union. The older UTT was the result of a short-lived breach within the UGTT during the consolidation of Bourguiba's rule in the late 1950s. l'Organisation tunisienne du travail (OTT), the newest and weakest challenger to the dominance of the UGTT, has not focused on long-standing claims to national importance. Instead it uses Islamist solidarity rhetoric.

Workers in both countries continued to struggle with cost of living and job insecurity. High unemployment meant continued protests, while little progress in Egypt meant continued wildcat strikes. The UGTT's increased role in Tunisia meant that it was left to attend to both political and economic grievances. Another point of continuity

---

[14] Ismael Sahbani, Secretary General of UTT, interview with author, July 28, 2015.
[15] "الجامعة العامة التونسية للشغل," Confédération générale des travailleurs tunisiens, accessed February 23, 2015, www.facebook.com/CGTT.tunisie.

was the role of global labor in bolstering the UGTT. Lassâad Abid, who led one of the dissident strains at the 2011 UGTT conference, organized a "front" within the federation in 2012. Abid later announced the formation of a competing trade union, the OTT. The OTT was accused from the start of being an Islamist front, emerging at a time of heightened conflict between the UGTT and Ennahda. This perception was furthered by media reports that OTT meetings began with Qur'an recitations and statements of solidarity with Muslim Brotherhood protesters killed in the Egyptian coup.[16] Abid has sought international attention along a parallel trajectory to independent unions in Egypt prior to the revolution, invoking ILO conventions and seeking support from global labor, including filing a still-classified complaint of a violation of freedom of association.[17]

Despite this, no breathless press releases have poured from the Solidarity Center or the ILO in support of the OTT. As in the past, global labor has treated competitors to the UGTT as a threat to trade union effectiveness instead of a flowering of pluralism. The pattern is unlikely to change. If the OTT can draw on internal ties of the Islamist movement, it may be able to sustain itself; however, disgruntled unionists, especially those not ideologically aligned with Islamism, are unlikely to see the group as a venue for their frustrations.

Unlike in Egypt, Tunisia's independent unions received no support from the ruling Troika of CPR, Ettakatol, and Ennahda. Despite the simmering conflict between Ennahda and the UGTT, the Islamists found no more fertile ground in the UTT or CGTT. The OTT did not receive extensive support from Ennahda, despite its Islamist rhetoric. In interviews, Ennahda leadership supported the idea of trade union pluralism and broadening social dialogue to include more actors, but stopped short of calling for the replacement or usurpation of the historical role of the UGTT. The structure of interest aggregation in Tunis also reduced the power of "prized roles" like the ministry of

[16] "Un Syndicat Islamiste Pour Contrer l'UGTT?" *Al Huffington Post*, accessed February 16, 2015, www.huffpostmaghreb.com/2013/08/26/lassaad-abid_n_3816101.html.

[17] "L'OTT Dépose Une Plainte Contre Le Gouvernement Tunisien, Selon Lassaâd Abid | Directinfo," accessed February 16, 2015, http://directinfo.webmanagercenter.com/2014/06/18/lott-depose-une-plainte-contre-le-gouvernement-tunisien-selon-lassaad-abid/; "FOA Cases," accessed February 16, 2015, www.ilo.org/dyn/normlex/en/f?p=NORMLEXPUB:50001:0::NO:: P50001_COMPLAINT_FILE_ID:3183574.

labor in Egypt. The Tunisian cabinet had been largely disempowered, and the ruling government was at best a temporary power with day-to-day managerial functions, while real decisions would be made in the NCA. Decisions about the future of trade union politics within the country would play out in this venue, with occasional interventions in the street.

The immediate postrevolutionary period saw an expansion of UGTT membership. Exact numbers are hard to obtain, though some sources suggest as many as 200,000 new members. Some of these new members were similar in profile to previous members. The policies of flexibilization introduced in the 1990s and 2000s led to many traditional union jobs being replaced by short-term contract work. The UGTT, riding the wave of revolutionary success, was able to convert many of these jobs over to permanent contracts, and render these workers eligible for union membership. Some sectors drew on the organizing skills of GUFs to get more members as well.[18] Other growth may have come from formalization of contracts not just in the private sector but in the public sector as well. World Bank data suggests that as many as 90,000 new or formalized employees were added in the public sector in 2011 and 2012, almost all of whom would have been eligible for UGTT membership.[19]

The expansion of the UGTT was a source of consternation for some who feared creeping Islamization. Some of the new UGTT workers came specifically from the private sector, a growing part of the economy under the liberalization of the Ben years. The private sector was also perceived to be a stronghold of Islamists. Several reasons fed into this belief, some of which were accurate, while others are more tenuous. Ennahda's predecessor organization the MTI drew much of its strength in the 1980s from young, college-educated students and professionals in the sciences. Furthermore, Islamists in particular may have felt more comfortable in the private sector due to pervasive hostility

---

[18] "Tunisia Textile and Garment Unions Seeing Growth," December 15, 2016, www.just-style.com/news/tunisia-textile-and-garment-unions-seeing-growth_id129553.aspx.

[19] Anne Brockmeyer, Maha Khatrouch, and Gael Raballand, "Public Sector Size and Performance Management: A Case-Study of Post-Revolution Tunisia" (The World Bank, January 1, 2015), http://documents.worldbank.org/curated/en/574821468166165145/Public-sector-size-and-performance-management-a-case-study-of-post-revolution-Tunisia.

toward them from the government. In Ben Ali's police state, Islamist affiliation was a major threat to one's career, if not to one's life and liberty. The surge of private sector workers into the UGTT stoked fears of a takeover by these now mid-career individuals.

The fears were largely misplaced. Existing UGTT laws insisted on a minimum of several years of trade union activism, ensuring that only existing cadres could become leaders at the 2011 Tabarka conference. Instead, a center-left leadership team that included militant rank-and-file members from regions around the country, and old members of the central union organization took leadership positions. No outside influencer, like Ben Ali in the late 1980s or an empowered labor minister in Egypt, could force an opening in the trade union structure. Older, regime-affiliated unionists were also free to incorporate leftist and rank-and-file members in a new governing coalition, unlike in 1989. The new leadership, however, left some stakeholders unhappy. Global labor, which had supported the UGTT after the revolution, was vocally upset with the fact that no women were elected to positions of power. Despite this, few steps were made to reduce global labor's consistent support for the UGTT.

Municipal unions, a major component of the UGTT membership and those working most closely with the Troika government, had been agitating for better working conditions and wages since the revolution. A deal struck in 2011 to limit outsourcing had not succeeded in stopping the practice. Politically, the UGTT's more militant regional leadership was eager to flex their considerable postrevolutionary muscle on a new issue. The UGTT leadership, still aware of the threat of emergent challengers, sought both to placate their base (public sector workers) and expand the field (new private sector workers). On February 20, a strike was launched. It was scheduled for four days, and attracted adherence from every region of the country. The ruling Troika parties had made clear their thoughts on industrial actions during the transition. Marzouki had already called them a suicide pact, and Ennahda had been outspoken on their undesirability as well.

The situation escalated quickly. Garbage collectors were on strike and the cities soon filled with trash. In reaction, some party deposited garbage bags on the doorsteps of UGTT offices around the country. The UGTT blamed Ennahda. Ennahda denied having taken the action. Perhaps fearing an overreach by its own partisans, Ennahda leadership decried the dumping, claiming that an attack on the UGTT was an attack on Ennahda. It is unlikely that Ennahda's membership felt the same way. Ennahda cadres reacted to the strike by organizing their own garbage collection throughout the country.

Following the strike by bureaucratic workers and the resulting attacks on UGTT offices, the union escalated its pressure on Ennahda. The slow pace of the NCA, continued economic difficulty (tied to both strikes and stagnant wages), and rhetorical missteps by Ennahda all aided the UGTT's campaign. A sense of government paralysis set in and mixed with growing fears of Islamist governance. Mohammed Morsi's surprising win in the first round of Egyptian Presidential elections focused the attention of those who feared an Islamist wave in the region. On June 17, just a week before Morsi was declared winner in Egypt's election, the UGTT announced a national dialogue to come to a democratic consensus on lingering political concerns. The decision stoked hopes, and fears among some, that the UGTT would follow the path of Solidarity in Poland and convert from a national trade union confederation to a political party. While it may have been considered by some of the union's leadership, the decision was taken to stay the course in civil society, while taking the vanguard position.[20] The decision greatly benefited Essebsi's Nidaa Tounes. The party also benefited from the UGTT's decision to welcome them into the national dialogue despite the objections of the CPR who considered Nidaa Tounes to be dominated by Ben Ali loyalists. The union's imprimatur effectively gave the party cover and revolutionary legitimacy that it otherwise could not obtain due to its creation after elections to the NCA. Giving Nidaa Tounes a seat at the table helped cement the union's role as political arbiter; in return, the party maintained its loose ties to the union and helped advance some of its agenda. Nidaa Tounes also strengthened its ties to the UGTT following the death of Lofti Naghd.

Naghd was a Nidaa Tounes leader as well as an activist with the local Union of Agriculture and Fisheries (Union tunisienne de l'agriculture et de la pêche or UTAP in French) in the southern city of Tataouine. Naghd died following a clash between members of the local "League for the Protection of the Revolution," self-organized groups

---

[20] "Hassine Abbassi: 'l'UGTT Ne Se Présentera Pas Aux Prochaines Élections Présidentielles et Législatives'," ShemsFm.net, accessed October 6, 2014, www.shemsfm.net/fr/actualite/hassine-abbassi-l-ugtt-ne-se-presentera-pas-aux-prochaines-elections-presidentielles-et-legislatives-19198.

that emerged from the revolution and had taken on an increasingly Islamist bend throughout 2012. Naghd's death was politicized from the start. Beji Caid Essebsi, whose party was just emerging, referred to it as the first political assassination after the revolution.[21] The death was denounced by the UGTT, UTAP, and the CGTT. It drew outrage not only from Nidaa Tounes, but from other sections of the secular, centrist camp, including Al-Massar and the new Republican Party.[22] While rapidly politicized, the death was controversial. The interior ministry and eventually the coroner's report both indicated that Naghd died from a heart attack, not from any violence during the fight between the revolutionary committees and their opponents. Despite this, several individuals were eventually held and charged with murder. While the UGTT did not use the strike weapon over this death, the crisis was a dry run for later incidents of political violence.

Trade union cohesion over trade union pluralism was embraced by secular elements in the country, especially over fears that new unions would have an Islamist orientation. The most notable Salafist organization in Tunisia is called Ansar Al-Sharia, a group active in street politics, morality "policing," and occasional clashes with secular political parties. While Ennahda's politics had grown distant from these groups, its vision of big-tent Islamist politics made them slow to react to the groups' provocations. Worrisome to unionists, Ansar Al-Sharia called for a new Islamist trade union at its conference in May 2012. While no Islamist trade union existed in Tunisia, such groups were active in Morocco and Algeria. Ansar Al-Sharia also challenged Ennahda's role as national Islamist movement, dragging it in a more conservative direction, even as other factors, including debates in the NCA, pushed it toward compromise.

The UGTT's relationship with the non-Ennahda political parties grew stronger, and the struggle between Islamists and secular parties intensified. Whether the UGTT could muster protesters enough to change policy would be challenged in December when it called for a national strike. The decision followed increasing clashes between

---

[21] "Tunisie: Nida Tounès Parle D'"assassinat Politique' après La Mort D'un de Ses Représentants," JEUNEAFRIQUE.COM, accessed October 13, 2014, www.jeuneafrique.com/Article/ARTJAWEB20121019165658/.

[22] "La Presse de Tunisie – La-Goutte-Deau-Qui-a-Fait-Deborder-Le-Vase | 57073 | 13102014," accessed October 13, 2014, www.lapresse.tn/13102014/57073/la-goutte-deau-qui-a-fait-deborder-le-vase.html.

union and secular party activists and Islamist youth who had organized themselves as "committees to protect the revolution." While the committees were originally emergent political groups founded for mutual defense during the transition, they took on an Islamist political element in 2012 and began running street battles with their political opponents. The conflict reached a crisis in December, when clashes near the UGTT headquarters left several injured.

The UGTT had not called for a national general strike since the near-civil war in 1978 and bread riots of 1984. The prospects of open civil unrest were high. The precipitating event saw an attack on the UGTT's headquarters, just a few blocks from Habib Bourguiba Avenue, the site of Tunis's largest protests during the revolution. The square in front of the UGTT office in downtown Tunis had served as a sort of de facto "free speech zone" even under Ben Ali, analogous to the steps of the Journalist's Syndicate in Cairo. While Ennahda officially denounced the attacks, as they it had the "garbage attacks" earlier in the year, it did little to calm the UGTT. The organization's call for a general strike, however, came more out of indignation than strategic thought. The general strike had no conventional economic goals; instead it was designed to demonstrate the UGTT's growing power and frustration with Ennahda's (in)action. The threat of a strike had some of its desired actions. First, it attracted the attention of the government. Abbassi, the UGTT secretary general, met with President Marzouki, and back-channel negotiations with Ennahda were held, despite their its official boycott of the UGTT's national dialogue. Second, it solidified their its position as sole union confederation. Their Its main competitor, the CGTT, was forced to join, likely to avoid the appearance of their members joining the national strike without the leadership's consent.[23] One of the few voices of dissent came from Adnen Hajji, leader of the social movement in the Gafsa region. This break was notable for its rarity. Finally, the UGTT rallied the support of the emerging opposition, including the centrists of Nidaa Tounes, who rallied outside their its headquarters and whose founder, Essebsi, made a statement of support. In contrast to a secular alliance in Egypt seeking to coopt and offer up labor quiescence as a token concession, secular forces in Tunisia had to line up to support the trade union.

---

[23] Habib Guiza, CGTT Leader, interview with author, July 25, 2015.

In the run up to the strike, a draft agreement that outlined four key points between the government and the UGTT was leaked. The document acknowledged the union's important position and denounced violence in general. It called for continued government–UGTT dialogue. It condemned the specific violence committed against the UGTT headquarters on December 4, 2012. Finally, it called for the formation of a joint commission to investigate the issue, mentioning specifically the role of the revolutionary committees, and called for a report within ten days. While far from an acknowledgment of the UGTT's claim that Ennahda was behind the attack, specifically identifying the revolutionary committees as a source of violence was an important talking point for the UGTT, as the groups' Islamization was well known.

The strike was called off almost as quickly as it was called. With no economic driver, and the government having capitulated as much as it was likely to, the strike threat had reached its natural limitations. The strike would also strain the central versus regional union divide, as conflicts around the country had centered on UGTT offices, but only an attack on the central office warranted a national strike. The decision to call it off came from both weakness and strength. For the cadres that were eager for a national strike, the opportunity would come far sooner than any imagined.

The post-"strike" lull in December and January allowed a social pact, in the works since 2011, to be completed. The history of social pacts in Tunisia was grim. The most prominent in the country's history was signed in 1977, in which the UGTT offered social peace in return for wage increases. The pact did not prevent (and in fact helped to provoke) the massive uprising in 1978. The 1990s and 2000s saw no large-scale social pacts, as the leadership of both the national employer's union (UTICA) and the UGTT were largely coopted by the regime. A standard tripartite negotiation, which covered multiple collective bargaining agreements, took place every three years and, through extensions, covered the vast majority of Tunisia's formal sector workers. With the tripartite arrangement in a state of postrevolutionary flux, the UGTT hoped to both reaffirm its role as sole labor social dialogue partner and press its advantage on issues like wages and labor flexibility. UTICA desired social peace and wage restraint in the wake of economic recession after the revolution.

While achieving a social pact was a goal of both the UGTT and UTICA, it was elusive during 2012. The Belgian government eventually provided the good offices and international support necessary to bring the tripartite pact to conclusion. The social pact of 2013 was sparse on details. The entire document is only six pages long, the first of which is devoted to identifying the social partners, praising the revolution, and reaffirming trade union and economic freedom. The substantive sections identify five areas of action: Economic Growth and Regional Development, Employment and Vocational Training, Labor Relations and Work Insecurity, Social Protection, and Institutionalizing Tripartite Social Dialogue. The regional development section, while loaded with platitudes about "decent work," is notable for its focus on the largely neglected interior of the country where the revolution began. The inclusion of this as the first article demonstrates at least a rhetorical shift in the UGTT's focus, reflecting the greater inclusion of the discontented rank and file and regional unionists in the organization's leadership. The second section called for a thorough reformation of the education system in the country to bring skills in line with actual economic needs. The most notable sections of the document were a call for a new social security scheme to be administered by the social dialogue partners and a new permanent national council for social dialogue that would bring all three members into a continuous conversation. The new national council was given a remarkably broad scope including the economy, labor issues, and governmental policy.[24]

The social pact was signed by the prime minister, secretary general of the UGTT, and president of UTICA at the NCA on January 13. It was witnessed by members of the NCA, its president, Ben Jafar, as well as the secretary general of the ILO, Guy Rider, and the Belgian labor minister, Monica De Connick, who had hosted the negotiations. The event was heralded by members of the international trade union movement as the first fruits of the Arab Uprisings, a much-needed dose of good news for workers who had been marginalized in Tunisia and Bahrain and were of relatively little concern in the ongoing fighting in

---

[24] Author's translation of full text document provided by Leaders.com.tn website available at: "Exclusif: Tout Sur Le Nouveau Contrat Social Tunisien," *Leaders*, accessed October 10, 2014, www.leaders.com.tn/article/exclusif-tout-sur-le-nouveau-contrat-social-tunisien. In focusing on goals as opposed to concrete mechanisms, the pact resembles the Tunisian Constitution of 2014 and may have served as a model for it.

Libya and Syria. The pact also solidified both the UGTT's role as sole interlocutor for labor, a point not missed by the CGTT, which denounced the compact, and the main recipient of international labor support and solidarity. While apparently a high point for labor in the country, despite the relative vagueness of its sections and the serious challenge of implementing its lofty goals, the celebration was short lived. In just over two weeks Tunisia was plunged into its most dangerous political situation since the revolution, which provided a chance for the UGTT to demonstrate what role it would play in the new Tunisia.[25]

On the morning of February 6, Chokri Belaid was assassinated outside his home just north of Tunis. Belaid was a leftist politician, a long-time activist, and outspoken critic of both Islamists and the former regime. His party, the Democratic Patriots' Movement, was part of the leftist Popular Front. Belaid was shot four times and died in a hospital nearby. His assassination sparked immediate and autonomous protests in Tunisia's capital even before any organized groups could call for it. Belaid's death confirmed the worst fears of the secularist camp that the street violence and small-scale clashes that had taken place throughout 2012 would explode into more extreme acts. No group claimed responsibility for the attack.

The UGTT's executive committee was called into session. President Marzouki returned early from an international trip to deal with the crisis. The UGTT's role became even more central when media reports emerged that Belaid was on his way to the UGTT headquarters in downtown Tunis for meetings as part of the national dialogue. The majority of the opposition, including Nidaa Tounes and other centrist political parties, announced the suspension of their participation in the NCA. Belaid's funeral was scheduled for Friday, February 8. The UGTT announced a general national strike in memory of Belaid, and called on citizens and its own cadres to join the funeral procession in the capital. The ministry of interior estimated that over 40,000 people joined the procession, impressive in a city of 700,000. Protests also raged in the Gafsa region, where Belaid was remembered for defending striking workers and protesters in 2008.

---

[25] Samir Taieb, General Secretary of Al-Masar Party, interview with author, July 24, 2015.

The UGTT's call for a strike, and its successful implementation, strengthened its position markedly.[26] Contemporaneous reports suggest widespread adherence to the strike call throughout the country. Also beneficial was the perceived responsibility of the strike. The UGTT called for the continued operation of hospitals and other care facilities, as well as bakeries, markets, and pharmacies. Members were also enjoined to protest peacefully.[27] While not all followed this direction, no major clashes emerged. The rhetoric, however, did change, with calls for the fall of the regime in the style of the January 2011 protests, as well as accusations that Rashid Ghannouchi, leader of Ennahda, was responsible for the murder. Ennahda denied the accusations.

The UGTT's leadership following Belaid's assassination demonstrated its ability to speak for the range of its internal constituencies. The violent act confirmed the worst suspicions of the non–Ennahda-supporting populace. As a direct attack on a leftist icon, the socialist and communist UGTT members felt particularly at risk. While it was disputed whether Lofti Naghd's death was a murder in October 2012, Belaid's death was certainly a political assassination. The left now had its own postrevolutionary martyr, and the government bore the responsibility and the blame as it had with Naghd. As the national organization that included both leftist and centrist camps, the UGTT emerged as the country's true opposition. It served as an authentic interest aggregator, even if the demand of the time was the fall of Ennahda's government. It was also able to nationalize the particular concerns of the Gafsa region both in the national pact and following Belaid's assassination.

While the UGTT had spent much of 2011 and 2012 growing from organized interest to indispensable national powerbroker, Ennahda had been the model of consistency. Unlike other political parties, which saw multiple schisms, Ennahda lost almost no NCA members to other political parties or independence. It generally spoke with a unified voice, focusing on its electoral legitimacy. Belaid's death revealed the first crack in Ennahda's united front. The prime minister, Hamadi

---

[26] "UGTT-Les Directives Pour La Grève Générale Du Vendredi 8 Février 2013," ShemsFm.net, accessed October 9, 2014, www.shemsfm.net/fr/actualite/ugtt-les-directives-pour-la-greve-generale-du-vendredi-8-fevrier-2013-36198.

[27] "UGTT-Les Directives Pour La Grève Générale Du Vendredi 8 Février 2013."

Jebali, a senior Ennahda official first appointed as part of the troika arrangement in 2011, offered to sack his cabinet and create a technocratic government. While Jebali had not previously been considered a "soft-liner," his actions ran contrary to the wishes of the Ennahda leadership, which rejected the change of government. The prospect of a politician-free cabinet was unacceptable to Ennahda. The crisis stretched on for two weeks, and finally Jebali resigned. The UGTT welcomed the resignation, but continued to call for a technocratic, and thus Islamist-free, government for the country. The threat of a total breakdown of the political system, including the NCA and government, emerged for the first time since the emergence of the troika. Appointing a non-Ennahda prime minister would violate the troika bargain and threatened to be rejected as illegitimate by Ennahda. Appointing another Ennahda prime minister threatened to enrage the secular and leftist camp, including the UGTT. Marzouki, whose own position depended on the troika arrangement, appointed another Ennahda member as prime minister, Ali Larayedh.

While the elite status quo was maintained by the decision, the UGTT still desired more dramatic action in the wake of Belaid's death. The commission charged with investigating the attacks on the UGTT headquarters in December issued and inconclusive report in April. The political polarization slowed work in the NCA even more. The continued stalemate resulted in a further decrease in the country's credit rating by Moody's from Ba1 to Ba2. The report specifically cited Belaid's death, the political instability, and the inability to forge consensus in the NCA on issues of new election timetables.

The question of legitimacy emerged again in mid-2013 just as it did in Egypt. In both cases, the government (consisting of the troika in Tunisia and the FJP in Egypt) claimed electoral legitimacy. In both cases this was true; Ennahda had a commanding lead in the October 2011 polls, and the FJP had won every election it participated in. Despite this, much had changed in the following 18 months. Many of the political parties Ennahda ran against no longer existed due to schisms and recombination. New challengers in the country, like Nidaa Tounes and other political parties, could not claim electoral or revolutionary legitimacy, which helps to explain the canonization of Naghd and Belaid as revolutionary martyrs. A third martyr was added to this roster in July 2013, and the UGTT took its final step toward supraconstitutional power broker.

Mohammed Brahmi was an outspoken leftist leader whose small People's Movement held two seats in the NCA and was a member of the larger Popular Front leftist coalition. Brahmi held one of the party's NCA seats, and was elected to it from Sidi Bouzid, his hometown, also the hometown of Mohammed Bouazizi, whose self-immolation became a focal point of the revolution. While from a different strain of leftist Arab Nationalism than Belaid, both were outspoken critics of Islamism and leading figures of left-wing politics in the country. Much like the other political trends in the country, the left was wrought by schisms and divisions, and in early July Brahmi had announced a new political movement, leaving the People's Movement he had helped found. Brahmi accused the leftist camp of having Islamist interlopers. On the morning of July 25, Brahmi was shot fourteen times outside his home in the Ariana neighborhood in Tunis, in front of his family. His murderers rode off on motorcycles, in the same style as Belaid's assailants five months earlier.[28]

The reaction to Brahmi's death was almost reflexive rather than organized. Within hours protestors gathered on Avenue Habib Bourguiba near the Interior Ministry, and at the offices of the UGTT a few blocks away. They held signs calling for the fall of "Muslim Brotherhood government," echoing similar calls in Egypt, where a successful mass mobilization and military coup had removed President Morsi just a few weeks earlier. Others accused Ennahda leaders of being murderers. Brahmi's origin in Sidi Bouzid connected him not only to the origin of the revolution, but the longer story of the underdeveloped internal portions of the country, which had been in turmoil for several years. His leadership of the secular left camp galvanized those sectors of society already roiled by Belaid's death. The Interior Ministry's announcement that not only was the modus operandi of the assailants the same in both assassinations, but in fact that the same weapon was used, gave credence to the perception that an Islamist conspiracy was executing the Ennahda's critics. Brahmi also had enemies in the centrist camp, having fiercely denounced Nidaa Tounes as "recycled" members of Ben Ali's RCD. Brahmi was a firebrand of the Nasserist school, having made enemies left, right, and center. Ironically, his death would galvanize many of the groups and individuals he antagonized in life.

---

[28] Mbarka Brahmi, Popular Front Leader and Widow of Mohammed Brahmi, interview with author, July 30, 2015.

The UGTT reacted swiftly to Brahmi's death, calling for a national strike. The union barely needed to organize protests, which emerged organically within hours of the announcement over the radio of Brahmi's assassination. The general strike was called for the same day as the state funeral organized for Brahmi by President Marzouki. On the day of the strike, the UGTT office was a hive of activity. Activists from across the country traveled to Tunis for the funeral and internment. The national airline ceased air traffic for the day. The NCA cancelled its meetings. Brahmi was laid to rest next to Belaid. The national strike had in excess of 80 percent participation in the capital, and reports of protests and attacks on Ennahda offices around the country suggest similar foment around the country.

The UGTT was supported in its decision by a new coordinating body made up of political parties. This group borrowed its name from an anti-Islamist bloc in Egypt and called itself the National Salvation Front (NSF). The NSF was made up mostly of parties already affiliated with the Popular Front or the Union for Tunisia, which included both the Republican Party and Nidaa Tounes. This center-left coalition called for the fall of the troika government and protests in support of the martyrs. The announcement also put the blame for any violence during the strike on Ennahda while calling for a strike on the NCA. At different points as many as sixty-five opposition members joined a sit-in in the Bardo neighborhood of Tunis outside the offices of the NCA. The protest was matched by a pro-Ennahda encampment that echoed the FJP in its calls for "electoral legitimacy" and rejection of a coup.

The situation in the summer of 2013 was superficially similar in Egypt and Tunisia. Both had seen violence enter the political arena. Both had a stalled constitutional process. Both had Islamist governance that had lost the support of much of the political establishment. During this period though, the National Salvation Front established in Tunisia would be forced to yield to the process dictated by the UGTT. The National Salvation Front established in Egypt would seek to coopt and largely ignore the demands of the country's labor movement. The UGTT was able to accomplish their its impressive pivot to dialogue partner for the Islamist forces in the country because of its decision to heal its internal conflicts, its ability to mobilize street protests, and the strong script of internal legitimacy it used against potentially dissident members. This within-country legitimacy was greatly bolstered by the position of global labor, which sought to promote global trade union cohesion, and dealt directly and consistently with the UGTT rather than its independent competitors.

External Linkages

Tunisia was an active and long-standing member of the International Labor Organization, having joined in 1956 just after independence. The country was a signatory of all fundamental conventions and dozens more as well. The UGTT had been a founding member of the ICFTU. It is worth noting that the ICFTU was historically agnostic on trade union pluralism, admitting both the American Federation of Labor and the Congress of Industrial Organizations from the United States at its founding. Despite this, the organization and its successor ITUC primarily supported the UGTT. This is particularly noteworthy as the organization faced a real dilemma as the UGTT became increasingly intertwined with the Bourguiba regime in the 1960s.[29]

The UGTT also had a strong working relationship in the 1950s and 1960s with the US labor movement. Heched toured the United States prior to independence at the invitation of the AFL, and later AFL-CIO officials were regular visitors to the UGTT. This relationship continued throughout the Bourguiba and Ben Ali regimes. In the run-up to the revolution, the Solidarity Center of the AFL-CIO had a technical assistance program active in the country, and the US government recognized the close relationship between the two movements, even when Tunisian public opinion and the UGTT were sharply critical of the US-led war in Iraq.[30]

Global labor, which took on the mantle of defender of trade union pluralism in Egypt, focused more on trade union cohesion in Tunisia. This is perhaps most evident in the views expressed by Sami Adouani, the director of the Friedrich Ebert Stiftung's operations in Tunisia from

---

[29] Anthony Carew, "Free Trade Unionism in the International Context," in *Communication Présentée À La Conférence "International Labour Movement on the Threshold of Two Centuries,"* Swedish Labour Movement Archives and Library, Stockholm, vol. 24, 2002.

[30] Cable: WikileaksRef: 07TUNIS83, "Cablegate: Labor Programming Needs in Tunisia – Scoop News," accessed February 24, 2018, www.scoop.co.nz/stories/WL0701/S01287/cablegate-labor-programming-needs-in-tunisia.htm.

2007–14. In a report written in 2017, Adouani shows the consensus view of the UGTT and any divisions to it:

The presence of several political currents at the heart of the organisation is handled by the fundamental principle of making the trade union identity the common denominator, regardless of political identity, with a view to maintaining trade union solidarity and thus maintaining the UGTT as a unitary trade union. Internal tensions run high when this principle is not respected by one of the members of the trade union movement, for instance, when one of them defines its trade union actions as a function of the political strategy of their respective political party. These tensions are regulated by internal dialogue, recourse to executive bodies and to the election of these bodies when the divergence is too deep. The organisational culture of trade union unity is largely fed by the collective trade union struggle and freedom of expression which characterises the members of the organisation. For the UGTT, this characteristic led to its developing a strong skill in managing conflict and bringing together different interests around a common mission.[31]

The description encapsulates global labor's view of the UGTT. Dissent was assumed to be politicized, or based on non-trade union loyalties. The report also refers to the UGTT as a monopoly. Other groups follow a similar tone. When asked about the UGTT, one ITUC official described them as "undeniably the vanguard." Training directed at the UGTT was focused almost entirely on empowering regional unions, or encouraging increased recruitment of youth and women into the cadres of the organization. Missing were the assertive narratives of trade union pluralism found in Egypt.

The view of the UGTT being a positive force for trade unionism and worthy of solidarity and support was nearly as universal among elements of global labor, as was the perception that the ETUF was irrevocably tainted by the Egyptian regime. GUFs that were militant in Egypt stood by their local affiliates in Tunisia. Education International, which had given tactical advice on how teachers could secure an independent union, supported UGTT-affiliated activists throughout Tunisia. Public Service International (PSI), which had supported Abu Eita's creation of RETA and the Health Workers' Union and sent

---

[31] Sami Adouani and Said Ben Sedrin, "Trade Union Power and Democratic Transition in Tunisia The UGTT: A Unique Story, an Unprecedented Experience" (Friedrich Ebert Stiftung, April 2017).

observers to Abbas's founding convention of the EDLC, stood by their UGTT affiliates in Tunisia. The framing of union cohesion was a constant, from NGOs to GUFs.

When asked to describe the relationship with the ITUC, one official spoke of the UGTT's important role in the international trade union movement. Little reference was made of its long deference to the Ben Ali regime, complicity in the corrupt situation in the Gafsa region, or irregularities in leadership under Ben Ali's reign. When speaking to breakaway unionists few invoked ILO conventions or made appeals to international solidarity. No large sums of money flowed to independent unions, nor were they flown to Europe for conferences and special training. Those luxuries were reserved for the UGTT itself. Left-wing political parties that wanted to stand in solidarity with trade unionism and its representatives often directly supported and called for solidarity with small left-wing parties in the country, especially after the assassinations of Belaid and Brahimi.[32]

Beyond the run up to the revolution, global labor stood by the UGTT and trade union cohesion during the transition itself. Even when the UGTT was at its most threatened political moment, during its early conflicts with Ennahda, including street battles in 2012, global labor backed the union with a multi-pronged campaign supporting them. An example can be found in the statement of the European Trade Union Confederation (ETUC):

The ETUC has consistently supported the UGTT in its activities, before, during and since the revolution, recognising its central importance for democratic development and the preservation of basic human rights including gender equality.[33]

The AFL-CIO Solidarity Center matched the tone, stating:

Following the attacks, thousands of union members and supporters, including Solidarity Center staff, gathered in the city center and marched to Hached's tomb to stand in solidarity with those injured and to denounce

---

[32] Mbarka Brahmi mentioned solidarity statements coming in from left-wing groups, including PODEMOS, SYRIZA, and the Worker's Party in Turkey.

[33] "Tunisia: Democratic Transition in Danger – UGTT under Attack | ETUC," European Trade Union Confederation, accessed March 1, 2018, www.etuc.org/documents/tunisia-democratic-transition-danger-%E2%80%93-ugtt-under-attack#.WphfkiOZPOQ.

violence in a democratic society that respects values of equality and social justice.[34]

The small competitor unions that emerged to challenge the UGTT told a very different story than their counterparts in EFITU and later EDLC. Habib Guiza of the CGTT stated that there was pressure on him to not work with the Solidarity Center. The CGTT filed an ILO complaint in 2012, calling on the UGTT to respect trade union pluralism. The complaint specifically cited the process of dialogue that took place prior to the signing of the Social Pact in 2013 as exclusionary.[35] Sahbani, the former UGTT leader turned founder of the UTT, touted his extensive ties to the AFL-CIO and other international organizations, but when pressed on timelines, almost all of these relationships languished after his imprisonment. Foreign relations for the UTT seemed to exist primarily with other upstart Arab federations.[36] When asked if they received support from these international linkages, the secretary general of the OTT simply stated that they had "no problems."[37] Competitor unions also seemed to believe Sahbani's rhetoric about his close ties to the United States, with the OTT secretary general claiming "Sahbani kept all the ties to the Americans." The ILO reports from Tunisia are notable in their lack of invocation of trade union pluralism. While the Committee of Experts requests specific information from the government, and issues recommendations that legal strikes need to be respected, it remains agnostic on the issue of pluralism. This is sharply contrasted with a similar Freedom of Association case launched by EFITU in Egypt. In this case, the committee's recommendations mention trade union pluralism several times, as a goal that should be implemented in accordance with new laws in the country.[38]

---

[34] "10 Injured in Violent Attack on Tunisian Trade Union | Solidarity Center," Solidarity Center, December 4, 2012, www.solidaritycenter.org/10-injured-in-violent-attack-on-tunisian-trade-union/.

[35] Habib Guiza, CGTT Leader, interview with author, July 2015. Committee of Experts, "Interim Report – Report No 370, October 2013 Case No 2994 (Tunisia)," Interim Report (International Labour Organization, June 4, 2012), www.ilo.org/dyn/normlex/en/f?p=1000:50002:0::NO:50002:P50002_COMPLAINT_TEXT_ID:3144119.

[36] Sahbani, Secretary General of UTT, interview with author, July 28, 2015.

[37] Lassaad Abid, OTT General Secretary, interview with author, June 30, 2015.

[38] Committee of Experts, "Definitive Report – Report No 375, June 2015 Case No 305 (Egypt)" (International Labour Organization, May 17, 2013), www.ilo.org/dyn/normlex/en/f?p=1000:50002:0::NO:50002:P50002_COMPLAINT_TEXT_ID:3241132.

When asked why the UGTT and ETUF were treated differently, international actors say the UGTT was authentically representative of its members' desires. A similar argument was being made about the ETUF until the mid-2000s.[39] The UGTT had not successfully negotiated any of its demands in the years prior to the revolution. It lost members to unemployment, privatization, and flexibilization. Its central leadership had not drifted from the direct influence of the RCD since Ben Ali's consolidation in the early 1990s. Members of the international trade union movement were either naive or in denial about these developments, or found them insufficiently concerning to cut ties.

In Egypt, disgruntled unionists moved out of the official structure of the ETUF and set up groups, non-profits, and eventually competing unions to aggregate their demands. Despite frustrations with the UGTT, disgruntled Tunisian unionists were unable to develop the same base as Abbas or Abu Eita, and the most successful independent confederation did not achieve official recognition until 2011. Habib Guiza claims that he received early support from the Solidarity Center, as well as token support from other members of the global labor movement, including the ITUC, but this support does not seem to have matched the extensive strategic and tactical support offered in Egypt. The money itself may have done more harm than good. When asked about the CGTT in the summer of 2015, one former Nidaa Tounes leader dismissed the confederation saying, "[A]fter the revolution Guiza took some money from some Europeans and started a union replicating the work of the UGTT."[40] Despite its close ties to the regime, the international community stood behind the UGTT, and, perhaps more troubling for Guiza, so did many of its most aggrieved members.

Guiza was not the only upstart unionist seeking to organize outside of the UGTT. The UGTT structure is different from other union confederations in neighboring countries in that it allows professional associations, not just working-class unions. Despite this, no journalists' union existed in the country. Press freedoms under Ben Ali were extremely limited, and while some independent newspapers were

[39] Agnieszka Paczynska, *State, Labor, and the Transition to a Market Economy Egypt, Poland, Mexico, and the Czech Republic* (University Park, PA: Pennsylvania State University Press, 2009).
[40] Nidaa Tounes Leader, interview with author, July 27, 2015.

allowed to be printed, their circulation was severely curtailed. Like the rest of the region, the introduction and spread of satellite TV changed news reporting in the country. Al-Jazeera's local correspondent in Tunis, Lotfi Hajji, was the impetus behind a drive for journalist unionization in the mid-2000s. Hajji's union was called the Tunisian Journalists' Syndicate (SJT) . The organization came under harassment, surveillance, and abuse from the security forces. Hajji was more successful than Guiza in obtaining international support. The international Committee to Protect Journalists publicized his activities starting in 2005.[41] The security services went on to disrupt his first attempt at a national congress for the organization in the fall of 2005, but, despite the setback, Hajji attracted the attention of the Solidarity Center. Records from the National Endowment for Democracy show a $99,026 grant distributed to the SJT via solidarity in 2006 to "build the capacity of the SJT to function as an independent labor union."[42] Despite the intentions of international backers, in 2006 Hajji began talks for his SJT union to officially join the UGTT. In the past, rehabilitation and cooptation of competitors was one of the UGTT's specialties, but as seen with the inability to reincorporate Sahbani and the discontent with Guiza, this had grown to be more challenging in the 2000s. Despite Hajji's apparent willingness to compromise and join the UGTT, the road was not easy. At least in part the UGTT's decision to include SJT in the fold was a result of ILO pressure. Generally, with legitimacy based more on its ability to be part of the "development" program of the regime than international recognition, the UGTT was less sensitive to international pressure, but the SJT may have become too high profile to ignore. In 2007, bowing to regime pressure, the UGTT instead recognized a competing journalists' union, the Tunisian National Journalists Union (SNJT). Despite its apparent creation as a regime puppet, the SNJT showed real independence in 2008 and 2009. Prefiguring later actions, the organization soon faced a rank-and-file versus elite fight, which the government intervened in heavily.[43]

---

[41] "TUNISIA – Committee to Protect Journalists," accessed June 6, 2014, http://cpj.org/2005/08/tunisia-1.php#more.

[42] "Tunisia | National Endowment for Democracy," accessed June 6, 2014, www.ned.org/publications/annual-reports/2006-annual-report/middle-east-and-northern-africa/description-of-2006-13.

[43] "Cable: 08TUNIS126_a," 8, accessed June 6, 2014, www.wikileaks.org/plusd/cables/08TUNIS126_a.html.

Taking a page from the Mubarak playbook on defiant organizations, the government sponsored a breakaway pro-regime faction, which eventually succeeded in displacing the SNJT leadership, bringing the organization to heel.[44]

In Egypt, global labor supported independent union organizing both rhetorically, through rights-based frames to use against their regime, and tactically through advice and financing. The absence of both types of support can be felt in Tunisia. In the case of SNJT, we see the lack of day-by-day tactical support like that enjoyed by Egyptian independent unions. Leadership of the upstart union was sidelined, coopted, or silenced by the UGTT. Independent trade unionists in Tunisia generally invoke their own laws and constitution rhetorically in their discussion of the right to form a union, rather than the international agreements, statutes, and conventions used in Egypt. Their rhetorical touchstones rely more on Tunisian history (such as the use of the names UTT and CGTT, both referencing early confederations) than international legitimacy. Economically, too, the independent union effort suffered. Generally unable to take dues directly from members' pay checks, they were forced to rely on voluntary contributions. The limited funding that did come in from international sources did not go nearly as far in Tunis as it did in Cairo. Interestingly, even with the high level of support the UGTT enjoys, Tunisians are equally unlikely to state they are a member of a union when polled. Arab Barometer data from 2013 states that only 2.7 percent of 1,199 surveyed Tunisians said they were a member of a professional association or trade union, an even smaller number than Egyptians who were polled on a related question.[45] Setting aside the possibility that Tunisians are less likely to answer the question honestly than their Egyptian counterparts, it is interesting to note that at very low levels of knowledge, it is possible that disgruntled workers were even less likely than in Egypt to defect. If one goal of international programs were to increase individuals' knowledge of their

---

[44] "Spotlight Interview with Nejiba Hamrouni (Tunisia-SNJT) – International Trade Union Confederation," accessed June 6, 2014, www.ituc-csi.org/spotlight-interview-with-nejiba?lang=en.

[45] Mark Tessler et al., "Arab Barometer: Public Opinion Survey Conducted in Algeria, Egypt, Iraq, Jordan, Kuwait, Lebanon, Libya, Morocco, Palestine, Sudan, Tunisia, and Yemen, 2012–2014" (Ann Arbor, Mich: Inter-university Consortium for Political and Social Research, 2015.)

rights in regard to forming trade unions, Tunisians may have been even less knowledgeable than Egyptians in this regard.

If any political power was going to support trade union pluralism, it would be the Ennahda movement, which found in the UGTT a consistent and powerful opponent. This accusation has been leveled against Ennahda several times, citing the Islamist bend of the OTT and consistent attacks on the UGTT's legitimacy in the press. However, Ennahda was hesitant to endorse this. In an interview, former prime minister Ali Laarayedh stated, "In Tunisia the culture refuses syndical pluralism even when it accepts it [pluralism] in politics ... even when we were in government every time we did something with another syndicate the UGTT would go mad."[46]

The external linkages enjoyed by the UGTT supported and reinforced its own internal narrative of trade union cohesion. Invoking its own revolutionary history served to dissuade global labor from backing independent upstarts, and the international support for the UGTT was used to further dissuade more divisions. Revolutionary legitimacy and narratives built around incorporation attracted international support, and that international support helped bolster the union even more. A virtuous cycle developed that strengthened the UGTT's grip on the trade union movement. When independent movements did form, the UGTT was skilled at bringing them to heel. Global labor abandoned the idea of trade union pluralism in Tunisia just as it was building it up in Egypt. The reality did not go unnoticed by UGTT leadership. In an interview former deputy secretary of the UGTT Belgacem Ayari stated, "The CGTT recently complained about representation. The ILO sent a commission to see the problem, and found they were wrong ... they didn't meet the requirements for representation."[47] While perhaps an oversimplification of the Committee of Experts report, Ayari effectively conveys the spirit of the international reaction to independent unions in Tunisia: support the UGTT to advance.

There is no question that representatives of global labor, be they European and American trade unionists, specialists at the ILO, leaders of the GUFs, or activists on the ground, sought to do their best to help the trade union movement (as they saw it) succeed in

---

[46] Ali Laarayedh, Former Prime Minister from Ennahda, interview with author, July 29, 2015.

[47] Belgacem Ayari, UGTT Deputy General, interview with author, July 30, 2015.

Egypt and Tunisia. They did this on a dubious, though sincerely held, view that the UGTT was the best vehicle for doing so in Tunisia, and that some alternative trade union confederation (be it EFITU, EDLC, or some idealized independent confederation that was never created) would be the best at doing so in Egypt. It is challenging to imagine the counterfactuals for each case. What if global labor had backed independent union organizing as vigorously in Tunisia as it had in Egypt? Would the CGTT be challenging the UGTT for supremacy? What if it had promoted internal reform and trade union cohesion for the ETUF as opposed to offering rhetorical and financial support to Abu Eita and Abbas? It is not the goal of this analysis to suggest that the UGTT would have been unsuccessful in obtaining its goals if facing more robust competitor federations, or that the ETUF would have been more successful if facing a rank-and-file versus central leadership split. These cases do, however, suggest that some fractures within the trade union movement are easier to heal than others, and that when combined with a strong narrative of incorporation and legitimacy, and non-exploitative links to emergent political parties, the trade union movement can secure some of its demands.

Trade Union Position: Strong, Cohesive, Reestablishing Corporatist Bargaining

Before looking at the role of trade union politics in the text of the constitution, and the different relationships of the trade union movement to Islamists in both Egypt and Tunisia, understanding the position of the UGTT during the transition process is important. As addressed previously, Tunisia benefited from a largely healed rank-and-file versus union leadership split. This split allowed the union to wield a legitimate strike weapon during the critical transition phase. In comparison to Egypt, where a federation versus federation split hobbled any hopes of common cause, Tunisia's main trade union cleavage was contained within the UGTT. The UGTT's long-standing history of revolutionary legitimacy, starting with its incorporation as a part of the anticolonial movement, and renewed by its involvement with the 2010 revolution, strengthened it functionally and rhetorically. The absence of global labor support for independent unions made these competing federations weaker and removed the incentive for disgruntled unionists to break away from the UGTT and go it alone. The decision to form flexible links on its own terms with new political parties kept the UGTT above the fray. Having dealt with multiple competing streams of political thought within its own membership, the organization was capable of finding issues of common ground with multiple political parties without throwing its lot in with one particular party or being coopted by any nascent movement.

The UGTT managed to wield a very credible threat to derail the transition process despite not having a high level of union density. Its cohesion was its greatest asset. The UGTT managed to threaten a strike once and successfully hold a general strike on another occasion. It also acted as the street-power for NCA members who chose to strike over clauses of the constitution. While the public came to expect the NCA to be plodding and ineffective, the prospect of the country shutting down because of a crippling UGTT strike was real. On the other hand, the decision to sign a social pact with UTICA demonstrated that the union could be trusted to also *halt* industrial action if it needed to, a capacity that none of the squabbling trade union federations in Egypt could ever muster.

Through the revolutionary and transition process, the UGTT masterfully used one facet of its strength to enhance others. It built street power by reminding militant members of their long history, while actively creating a narrative around its own independence. It used those militant street activists to win concessions and support from political parties. It leveraged its international connections to bolster its legitimacy, and to drive both rhetorical and material support away from competitors and to itself.

In addition to overcoming its own internal divisions, the UGTT was remarkably successful at delivering for its members. While its list of demands entering the revolutionary moment was vaguer than its Egyptian counterparts, it delivered on those demands much more effectively. It negotiated public sector and private sector wages. It converted short-term contracts into long-term contracts. It increased hiring in the public sector. It had its role as the sole voice of labor codified with international imprimatur in the social pact signed during the transition that promised to establish a national council for social dialogue, potentially reasserting the union's position as an influencer over the political economy of the country in a form that had not existed since the 1970s.

Conclusion

Tunisia's trade union movement predates the existence of an independent Tunisia. While the UGTT has often claimed a special status as a uniquely militant and independent union, its actual history is punctuated with periods of complicity with authoritarian politics. In the 1980s it was subject to the same structural adjustment pressures as many labor movements around the world. Hiring and firing were liberalized to flexibilize the labor market. The union saw its power and influence over the national government erode, especially after the coup d'état that brought to power President Ben Ali. Despite this, militant rank-and-file unionists in the UGTT's regional structure pushed back, calling first for union democracy and later resistance against the regime's political economy.

Tunisia experienced an unprecedented strike wave and insurgency in the late 2000s in its interior. Unequal development, corruption in the UGTT's role in hiring workers, and an unemployment crisis for young people led to strikes, protests, and a violent crackdown from the regime. Like in Egypt, the UGTT was unable to stem the rising tide of discontent, and lost its ability to aggregate and advocate for its members. Despite this, at the critical moments following the self-immolation of Mohamed Bouazizi in 2010, the UGTT was reluctantly dragged into revolutionary mobilization by the same militant rank-and-file. During the crisis, it expanded its leadership to include more militant regional members, and eventually included more activist leadership in 2011 in its executive bureau. The union managed to heal some of its major divisions, outmaneuvering its competitors and healing its rank-and-file versus central leadership divide.

This chapter has argued that internal linkages, external linkages, and the rhetorical power of incorporation explain the fate of the Egyptian and Tunisian trade union movements during the postrevolutionary transition. Tunisian trade unions' ability to link to parties through the institution of the national dialogue gave them major influence, while Egypt's inability left them open to cooptation. Independent unionists in Egypt's links to global labor provided them with rhetorical and material support for union pluralism, while Tunisia's external linkages focused on strengthening the UGTT. Tunisian trade unions had a deep well of historical and revolutionary legitimacy to draw on, while Egyptian trade unions were on a more level playing field of regime-derived legitimacy. The next chapter will explain how the cleavages these variables produced, federation versus federation in Egypt and rank-and-file versus elite in Tunisia, played out in the arena of constitutional design and when confronting ascendant Islamist forces in each country.

6 | Constitutional Crises and Islamist Competition

Corporatist collapse combined with internal linkages, external linkages, and the role of global labor to produce unique pathways for Egypt and Tunisia. Both saw cleavages and divisions within the trade union movement. Tunisia's trade union movement fractured primarily because rank-and-file unionists were pitted against the central leadership. This battle unfolded in multiple contexts. Rank-and-file unionists revolted against the coopted UGTT leadership in the earliest days of the revolution. They revolted again when the leadership sided with Mohammed Ghannouchi's attempt to create a new government with left-over members of the RCD. They finally won power by demonstrating their willingness to take the streets and hold general strikes. That power was enshrined internally with a new board in 2011 and the shift toward a more militant and unified footing in 2012.

Egypt's trade union movement fractured primarily because federations were pitted against federations. The ETUF faced new challenges from the EFITU. In 2012, EFITU itself split into warring camps behind Abu Eita and Abbas, the latter of who formed the EDLC. Eventually, even more region-based independent unions were formed. The weak internal linkages and continuing support for trade union pluralism left the trade unions extremely divided in 2012 and 2013, leaving them open to cooptation first by the Muslim Brotherhood and later by the military.

This chapter extends beyond the revolutionary reconsolidation to the establishment of the first new regimes in each country, those of Mohammed Morsi and Abdel Fattah El-Sisi in Egypt and the Troika and successive coalition governments in Tunisia. In this period, we see the codification of the new realities in the form of constituent processes in each country, where the UGTT was vital in Tunisia, and all trade union confederations were sidelined in Egypt. I will explore how militancy continued despite repression and what advances were made on labor laws and salary negotiations. I will specifically focus on trade

162

union movements' reactions to a new context: constitutional assemblies and a new competitor – empowered Islamist parties.

Islamism and Unionism

The relationship between trade unions and Islamist parties in Egypt and Tunisia is one of the most interesting and overlooked stories of the revolution. In the differing trajectories we see signs of a paradox: The more "alienated" from trade unionism Islamists were, the better the outcome. In Egypt, where Muslim Brotherhood members took part in political life as "independents" the prospect of an Islamist unionist was perfectly conceivable. Young activists from both unions and the Muslim Brotherhood had taken strides to work together in the strike wave that preceded the revolution. Leaders were hopeful that some accommodation of one another could be made. This stands in stark contrast to Tunisia, where an "Islamist unionist" for many members of the UGTT was almost a contradiction in terms. Any Islamist members likely hid this identity within the trade union movement until after the revolution, and both rank-and-file and leadership cadres felt confident in the political affiliation of the bulk of the membership. Despite this alienation, a direct confrontation, often through street power, during the reconsolidation phase led to a far more politically expedient negotiation process than happened in Egypt. Egyptian unionists in the independent movements felt betrayed by their erstwhile allies, each side accusing the other of "selling out" to the military interregnum. Familiarity bred contempt. ETUF-affiliated unionists felt encircled, with new Islamist leaders appointed, or announcing themselves in the rank-and-file. Mutual mistrust and fear ruled the day. As a result, Egyptian Islamist–union relations fared far worse than their Tunisian counterparts did even in the absence of outright confrontation. This apprehension also drove unionists of all stripes to embrace a military solution to the political impasse the country faced in 2013. Understanding the history of these relationships is helpful.

The Muslim Brotherhood, the ETUF, and Independent Unions

Egypt has a bifurcated system of workplace organizations. Professional syndicates cover traditionally white-collar jobs such as doctors, lawyers, journalists, and engineers. Trade unions, part of the ETUF, cover conventionally blue-collar workers in transportation, construction, and other industries. Some professions, such as bureaucrats, fall under the banner of trade unions for historic and economic reasons. This leads to crosscutting interests within the same union. For instance, the Teacher's Syndicate is officially a professional syndicate, despite representing a largely working-class, and increasingly militant, membership. The Lawyer's Syndicate covers both wealthy private lawyers and (relatively) poorer public defendants. In the 1980s the professional syndicates became a venue in which political parties could compete.[1]

The Muslim Brotherhood, prevented from forming a political party and increasingly harassed in the 1980s and 1990s, sought to increase its influence in the professional syndicates during this time. Members first rose to prominence in the Doctor's Syndicate, later taking on leadership roles in the Engineer's Syndicate. The Brotherhood's growing interest in the professional syndicates mirrored an increase focus on the middle and upper classes in the organization. The neoliberal turn in the organization mirrored other such pivots at the same time in Turkey and other countries. Brotherhood leadership in this era consisted of many individuals involved in business who had been formally excluded from the kleptocracy of the Mubarak regime, forming a counter-elite of business-oriented Islamists.[2] The experience within the professional syndicates influenced, and was influenced by, the "Centrist" trend in Islamist thinking, which eventually led to the emergence of the breakaway Wasat Party of ex-Muslim Brotherhood members.[3]

Many trade union activists interviewed aggressively rejected the notion that the Muslim Brotherhood ever established a foothold in trade union politics, either within the ETUF or the new independent unions of the 2000s. At the rank-and-file level, this may be true. Gaining access to

---

[1] Ninette S. Fahmy, "The Performance of the Muslim Brotherhood in the Egyptian Syndicates: An Alternative Formula for Reform?" *Middle East Journal* 52, no. 4 (October 1, 1998): 551–62.

[2] Rejwan has named this type of individual the "pious bourgeoisie," a clever term that captures much of the dynamic. It is worth noting that this brand of capitalism is not the Anglo-American variety, despite it occasionally sharing methods with it. This is explicitly Islamic capitalism with concepts of Islamic finance and certain religiously sanctioned redistribution built in. Nissim Rejwan, *The Many Faces of Islam: Perspectives on a Resurgent Civilization* (Gainesville, FL: University Press of Florida, 2000).

[3] Joshua A. Stacher, "Post-Islamist Rumblings in Egypt: The Emergence of the Wasat Party," *Middle East Journal* 56, no. 3 (July 1, 2002): 415–32.

trade unions, as they had professional syndicates, certainly did not seem to be a strong concern of the Brotherhood prior to the revolution. It would be inaccurate, however, to suggest the Brotherhood showed no interest in worker issues. As has been well documented by blogger and activist Hossam El-Hamalawy, a combination of generational changes and shared commitment to street politics generated a rapprochement between worker-oriented leftists and Muslim Brothers in the late 2000s.[4] Unsurprisingly, given its activities with professional syndicates, one of the first groups the Muslim Brotherhood worked with was an independent-oriented teacher's organization. Starting in 2001, labor activists Saber Barakat and Khaled Ali worked with teacher activists on a pressure group called "Teachers without a Syndicate." According to Barakat, the organization was eventually coopted by Brotherhood members, and non-Brotherhood activists went on to form an independent union. Of these early days of joint action, Barakat states,

The Muslim Brotherhood was there in all movements, you can say they supported them ... After the revolution they filled the gaps of the Mubarak regime.[5]

These early efforts at forming or coopting "worker's organizations" or "pressure groups" such as "Teacher's Without a Syndicate" shows that the Muslim Brotherhood had an interest in independent union organizing as far back as the early 2000s. Despite this, the organization was fundamentally conservative. A leader of the independent teachers' union stated that Muslim Brotherhood-affiliated teachers supported their early organizing but "turned against them" as they did not support using strike action.[6]

Despite the re-emergence of tensions, the Brotherhood gave both tactical support, in the form of hosting meetings of independent unionists, and rhetorical cover, by trumpeting labor issues in its English language media, as well as criticizing the ETUF's political role and incompetence in its Arabic-language media.[7] The organization's

---

[4] Hossam El-Hamalawy, "Comrades and Brothers," *Middle East Report*, no. 242 (April 1, 2007): 40–43.

[5] Saber Barakat, Activist, interview with author, April 1, 2012.

[6] Abdul Hafeez Tayal, Independent Teacher's Union Founder, interview with author, April 21, 2012.

[7] "The Rising Class Struggle – Ikhwanweb," accessed May 21, 2014, www .ikhwanweb.com/article.php?id=25221&ref=search.php; "إخوان اون لاين انتقاد-" برلماني لشروط اتحاد العمال لمنح صفة المرشحين," accessed May 21, 2014, www .ikhwanonline.com/Article.aspx?ArtID=69671&SecID=250.

position on the ETUF changed once Brotherhood members were added to the organization's leadership board. As one long-serving unionist said, "[S]ince they joined the ETUF, they changed their point of view. They want to control the ETUF and all unions."[8] The story is the same from many of the independent unionists from across sectors who became active after the revolution. In the words of one, "[T]here was no outreach from the FJP, they are ETUF."[9]

Even leaders of the independent union movement spoke of the pivot of the Muslim Brotherhood to supporting and bolstering the ETUF with a tone of disappointment. Asked about their involvement before the revolution, Kamal Abbas said,

The Muslim Brotherhood was involved long before the revolution. They adopted the rhetoric of worker's rights ... but they don't want to empower workers. Their tools are charity. We have two problems with them: they don't have non-discrimination, and they don't have equality. Many of them are businessmen with a conflict of interest.[10]

The description holds from the Muslim Brotherhood side as well. Former member of parliament Saleh Noman Mubarak, a long-time trade unionist and Muslim Brother, stated,

At one time, we coordinated. Once we had a good relationship. Now they mix politics with trade unions ... As an activist in trade unions I was worried the trade union would collapse. Abu Eita wants to destroy it. The MB stood in (joined) the ETUF to destroy their plans ...

Having worked together previously, the Muslim Brotherhood and union activists were particularly frustrated by the other group taking political action following the revolution. Under authoritarianism, it was easier to paper over differences and focus on issues of agreement: resisting torture and jail sentences for their colleagues, calling for more openness in government, and reforming the legal system to be fairer. Following the revolution, the hard work of governing, including building the institutions of governance in industrial relations, left each side resentful.

---

[8] Habib Ayeb, "Social and Political Geography of the Tunisian Revolution: The Alfa Grass Revolution," *Review of African Political Economy* 38, no. 129 (2011): 467–79.

[9] Walid Sayyid, PetroTrade Union Activist, interview with author, April 23, 2012.

[10] Kamal Abbas, CTUWS Founder, interview with author, November 14, 2012.

The main axis of dispute during late 2012 was between Morsi's administration and the judiciary. Largely unreformed from Mubarak's era, the judiciary declared the parliamentary elections of late 2011 and 2012 unconstitutional due to its use of both first-past-the-post and proportional list election formulas. This decision rendered one-third of the parliament illegal. The FJP held a majority of the seats, and Morsi attempted to reinstate the parliament soon after his election, bringing him into conflict with both the military and judicial elites. Eventually conceding to a second court ruling, Morsi gave up hopes of re-seating the Islamist-dominated parliament.

Throughout the fall, the judiciary also debated the constitutionality of the constituent assembly that was charged with drafting Egypt's new constitution. The constituent assembly also had an Islamist majority, which only grew following boycotts by liberals, leftists, and Christian members. Morsi and the judiciary further clashed over his attempt to replace the prosecutor general, sending the former to the comically distant post of ambassador to the Vatican.

At the end of 2012, Egypt suffered from widespread discontent with the pace and nature of the postrevolutionary consolidation. The Muslim Brotherhood's popularity had plummeted from its postrevolutionary high. Ambitious left and liberal parties who saw an opening even if it meant exploiting labor discontent. Trade unionists, both within the ETUF and in the independent unions, were particularly alienated by the decisions taken by President Morsi on November 22, 2012. Morsi issued a new constitutional declaration, replacing the general prosecutor, reopening investigations into officials of the ousted regime, and stating that the decree was not open to any review by any authority. A less noticed decision taken at the same time allowed the minister of manpower to replace members of union boards who had reached retirement age. The decision could have had serious impacts on union leadership, especially with an FJP member serving as minister of manpower.

Decree 97 of 2012 was passed on November 24, 2012, two days after the constitutional declaration. The law amended an ETUF rule that said trade union officers could serve until any age. Age restrictions were a long-running topic of concern in the trade union movement, and in a period of less polarization may have gained wider support. Both the timing and the particulars of the amendment, however, furthered fears of "Brotherhoodization" in the ETUF. Morsi took the step in part because of a crisis that was manufactured during Al-Borai's term as minister of manpower. The temporary board originally appointed in the months after the revolution was about to exhaust its term in office. Morsi extended this term, now being filled by an unlikely constellation of old regime officials and members of the Brotherhood for another six months. The decree liquidated all board members over the age of 60, a substantial number. They were to be replaced by the second-highest vote getter from the 2006 trade union elections, an election that had already been declared fraudulent. In many cases, due in part to the ban on independent-minded trade unionists from running, trade union officials ran unopposed. In any instance in which there is no runner-up in the 2006 election, the minister of manpower, Khaled Al-Azeri, a member of the FJP, would be able to appoint the replacement. Those who feared a massive expansion of Brotherhood influence over the trade union movement and its associated structures suddenly looked more rational and less hysterical.

By late 2012, the ETUF board had only a handful of independent or independent-leaning members, with almost all control resting with ex-Mubarak loyalists or Brotherhood members. Either an explicit or tacit bargain had been struck, giving the Brotherhood influence over the ETUF in return for keeping out the independent unionists. This arrangement suited the Brotherhood, whose main interest was in preserving its power, and the ETUF, which feared the emergence of trade union pluralism. The ETUF appealed to the deep conservative streak in the military, which sought labor quiescence.

Late-2012 protests brought the conflict between Islamist and secular forces to the streets, specifically to the gates of the Presidential Palace. While many reports at the time showed that anti-Morsi protesters (possibly including members of the security services) were the first to fire live rounds, the decision of young Muslim Brotherhood members to "arrest" protestors and extract "confessions" under abuse in a make-shift camp near the site reinforced many in the anti-Morsi block's opinion that the Brotherhood remained lawless terrorists. The combination of Morsi's amendment to trade union laws in the November constitutional decree with the increasingly harsh actions of Brotherhood members in defense of his legitimacy alienated the leadership of the independent trade union movement. Worried about losing the advances made during the first military interregnum and

Borai's term as Minister of Manpower, they were increasingly open to cooptation by the weak but growing secular opposition. The ground was set for the final conflict in which labor would be mobilized to support a resurgent military element.

Ennahda, the UGTT, and Independent Unions

The Islamist movement had in Tunisia had taken steps toward involvement with the UGTT in the 1980s that were rebuffed by both rank-and-file unionists and the regime. While Egypt's Muslim Brotherhood saw the ETUF as another part of the Mubarak regime to coopt, Ennahda had only limited ambitions to do so with the UGTT. The movement itself, while strong nationally, had little opportunity to copy the top-down approach the Muslim Brotherhood used in Egypt, as UGTT elections were independent. Ennahda's position as one of three ruling parties gave it a more limited grasp on institutional power. Even if it did have more complete control over the bureaucracy of the country, no mechanism for the external replacement of the UGTT board existed in Tunisia as it did in Egypt. Unlike the ETUF's system of elite cooptation, the UGTT's ties to the RCD were lateral, with ties from local offices to the local government. This meant that capturing the leadership would do little, especially after the politicization of the base in the revolution. Moreover, Ennahda was no doubt chastened by its previous attempts at working with the trade union movement. In the 1980s the movement, drawing inspiration from the broader social message promulgated by the Muslim Brotherhood in Egypt, attempted to gain a toehold in the UGTT.[11] The effort was short lived, however. The movement failed to appeal to large numbers of workers, and the leadership mostly focused on an elite strategy. The government interfered with union elections, pushing out both the MTI and communists and ensuring a quiescent center.[12]

---

[11] Alexander argues, convincingly, that inspiration was also drawn from Khomeini's appropriation of leftist themes using Islamist framing in the Iranian revolution.

[12] Christopher Alexander, "Opportunities, Organizations, and Ideas: Islamists and Workers in Tunisia and Algeria," *International Journal of Middle East Studies* 32, no. 4 (November 1, 2000): 465–90.

The lack of Islamist involvement with the UGTT persisted until the time of the revolution. Ali Laarayedh, a long-serving Ennahda leader, described it forthrightly, "[W]e didn't find ourselves in the syndicate." Other Islamists disagreed with the assessment. Ennahda MP Jamila Ksiksi also spoke to the role of Ennahda-affiliated unionists working quietly before the revolutionary period stating:

Before the revolution, Islamists were banned from practicing civil society work, so the only available or acceptable place was in the UGTT ... The UGTT regime protected me personally. The UGTT gathered all ideological and political groups within it. When Ennahda won political power, the position of Islamists inside the UGTT was weaker.[13]

At the same time as Ennahda was growing in political power, the UGTT was growing in social power. The flexibilization law passed in 1996 focused on short-term contracts in a variety of private-sector jobs, many of which grew throughout the 2000s, leaving more workers alienated and disconnected from the union structure. ILO reports from 2011 show 15 percent of the labor force serving on a short-term contract, with numbers reaching 58 percent in the hotel and tourist sector, and 68 percent in the textile sector.[14] While the UGTT may have been slow to realize workers' agitation over the issue, it soon came to take center stage in the ongoing social dialogue.[15] Workers took the opportunity brought by the revolution to push back on the issue of precarious short-term contracts.[16] Under the pressure of industrial actions, many worksites converted short-term contract workers to permanent-contract positions. These newly secure workers generally became members of the UGTT, and had every reason to support its strength.

While new members may have included Islamists, the 2011 Tabarka conference mostly empowered more leftist and militant segments of the

---

[13] Jamila Ksiksi, Ennahda MP, interview with author, January 18, 2016.
[14] International Labour Office and International Institute for Labour Studies, *Tunisia: A New Social Contract for Fair and Equitable Growth* (Geneva: ILO, 2011).
[15] "Textile Workers Strike for Jobs and Wages in Tunisia," Solidarity Online, accessed September 22, 2014, www.solidarity.net.au/mag/back/2011/41/textile-workers-strike-for-jobs-and-wages-in-tunisia/.
[16] "Social Revolt Boosts Struggle against Casual Employment at Coca-Cola Tunisia – Union Negotiates Abolition of Agency Work," accessed September 22, 2014, http://cms.iuf.org/?q=print/724.

federation, many of who had been dissatisfied with the support offered to the Ben Ali regime. While promising to negotiate with all elements of society following his palace coup in 1987, Ben Ali accelerated conflict with Islamist elements in Tunisian society. Unsatisfied with the Egyptian model of Islamist participation in the parliament under the ruse of "independent" candidates, Ben Ali banned Ennahda and drove its leadership to prison or exile. While Ennahda's brief flourishing under the early Ben Ali regime had included overtures to the trade union movement, its long period underground during the later Ben Ali years left it estranged from the trade union movement.

Ennahda's earnest attempts to reassure international finance of its commitment to liberal markets after the revolution only further distanced it from the UGTT's increasingly militant leadership. Islamist energy may also be divided across the trade union movement. When conflicts erupted between the UGTT and Ennahda in 2012, some Islamist members left. Ennahda MP Jamila Ksiksi stated, "There were a lot of Islamists and non-Islamists cancelling their membership ... some cancelled, some joined other organizations ... There are a number who signed with CGTT, UTT, etc."[17]

At the moment of the revolution, it would appear to outsiders that Egypt would be a more fruitful ground for unionists and Islamists to come to some form of agreement than Tunisia. Tunisian Islamists were underground, having no real relationship to the trade union movement's leadership. The Islamists within the UGTT "separated" their work with Ennahda from their work as trade unionists, fearful of regime reprisals. Even during 2012, when Islamists and unionists clashed in the streets during the memorial of Farhat Heched, it seemed unlikely that these forces could find a peaceful solution. On the other hand, Egyptian Islamists had worked with trade unionists before, supporting pressure groups and independent organizing committees. Some of the young activists in each movement had stood in solidarity against the repression of the Mubarak era. Despite this, Islamists and unionists were almost immediately at odds with one another, increasingly insecure and untrusting of the others motives. With no mechanism to discuss issues effectively, their alienation was disastrous.

While struggling with the rise of Islamists in governance, and potentially misplaced fears of increasing numbers of Islamists in their own

---

[17] Jamila Ksiksi, Ennahda MP, interview with author, January 18, 2016.

ranks, the UGTT had an easier time forging connections to secular and left-wing parties. Unlike Egypt's National Salvation Front which offered labor as a sacrificial lamb, Tunisia's National Salvation Front did not dare. Following the assassinations of 2013, the NSF began to call not only for the fall of the Ennahda government but of the NCA itself.

Constituent Assemblies

In Egypt, the constitutional process laid out by the SCAF was opaque from the beginning, and beset by problems. SCAF began by issuing a constitutional decree. It appointed an eight-man committee to propose revisions to the constitution. Included in this review committee were legal scholars who represented liberal and Islamist strands of jurisprudence.[18] The committee proposed several changes to the suspended constitution and recommended a new constitution be drafted following the election of parliament. A popular referendum was held in support of this document in March.[19] This document stated that the to-be-elected parliament would draft a new constitution within 60 days of being seated. Debate over the referendum centered on whether to hold elections for the parliament or write the constitution first. Despite this debate, the referendum passed easily.

As predicted by the new constitution's detractors, Islamist parties dominated the new parliament in 2012. The interim constitution had punted on the makeup of a new, full constitutional assembly, leaving the decision to the Islamist-dominated new parliament. It was decided that sitting parliamentarians would hold fifty seats of the proposed one hundred-member constitutional assembly, ensuring an Islamist foothold. The Muslim Brotherhood's Freedom and Justice Party secured the largest number of votes, with the more conservative Salafi parties securing an unexpected number of seats. These Islamist victories led to the selection of a largely Islamist constitutional assembly.

---

[18] Kristen Stilt, "The End of 'One Hand': The Egyptian Constitutional Declaration and the Rift between the 'People' and the Supreme Council of the Armed Forces," *Faculty Working Papers*, January 1, 2012, http:// scholarlycommons.law.northwestern.edu/facultyworkingpapers/208.

[19] Casey Britton, "Press Release: Egyptian Military Constitutional Proclamation," http://worldanalysis.net, February 13, 2011, http://worldanalysis.net/modules/ news/article.php?storyid=1742.

Several seats were given to "syndicates," broadly defined. Sameh Ashour, from the Lawyers' Syndicate, was joined by Mamdouh El-Wali of the Journalists' Syndicate and Ashraf Abdel Ghafour of the Actors' Syndicate. These leaders all represented elite professional associations not affiliated with working-class trade union movements in the country. Two more representatives from elite professional associations, Dr. Mohamed Abdel Gowad of the Pharmacists' Syndicate and Mohamed Khalosy of the Engineers' Syndicate, were also members of the Muslim Brotherhood. Two seats were given to active trade union activists, Khaled Al-Azhari and Abdel Fatah Khatab. Khaled Al-Azhari was a leader within the Brotherhood and would later be appointed minister of labor. Abdel Fatah Khatab represented the Tourism Union that itself was undergoing major divisions between his ETUF-affiliated union and competitors associated with the new independent unions.

Most of the political parties with platforms more amenable to labor, including the Socialist Alliance Party, withdrew from the assembly entirely. The Nasserist Karama Party, of which independent labor leader Kamal Abu-Eita was a founder, received one seat on the assembly. Islamists dominated with sixty-six of one hundred seats. Liberal and leftist parties soon withdrew from what was seen as an Islamist takeover of the constitutional process.

Thus, the first constitutional assembly in postrevolutionary Egypt failed to represent the interests of the independent trade unions who took part in the revolution. Instead, to the extent it functioned at all, it represented the interests of liberal political parties and Islamist parties, both of whom shared a generally neoliberal economic orientation.[20] The automatic inclusion of workers' representatives in the constitutional assembly seems, at first blush, to be a victory for unionists. If anything, it was a detriment. Besides not speaking for a unified trade union movement, workers' representatives became bogged down in constitutional infighting. With no electoral process behind them, the constitutional assembly had problems of legitimacy, with frequent withdrawals and protests by members. Unions, which had influenced and directed street politics throughout the country since the strike wave started in 2006, were left without an organizing

[20] Mohamed Gouda, Freedom and Justice Party Economic Adviser, interview with author, March 18, 2012; Tarek Al-Tohami, Wafd Leadership, interview with author, March 26, 2012.

structure to mobilize protests, or effective connections to political parties to press their advantage.

Egypt's supposedly more "balanced" second assembly collapsed before its work was complete. Islamist members, who still enjoyed a majority, pushed for more explicitly Islamic elements in the constitution. In reaction, liberal, leftist, and religious minority representatives variously froze, suspended, quit, or failed to show up to the meetings of the assembly. Independent trade unionists announced an unwillingness to work with the Brotherhood until the constitutional assembly was dissolved.[21] Eventually, an organized boycott emerged that encompassed almost all politically active non-Islamist members. While this anti-Islamist movement had different visions for the country, the possibility of an overtly religious constitution united them. In the week following Morsi's constitutional decree, the constitutional assembly, shorn of the Islamists' most bitter critics, finished a draft constitution in a marathon session. The constitutional referendum was held in two rounds in December 2012, and passed despite losing in Cairo governorate. The Muslim Brotherhood's Freedom and Justice Party supported the constitution, while all other major political parties opposed it as being too favorable to Islamists.[22] The constitution, rammed through without support, created a crisis of its own.

In Tunisia, the constitutional assembly had temporary governing powers, though expectations were for a constitutional draft to be completed within one year. The first actions included the drafting of a so-called mini-constitution, which would guide governmental action in the final months of 2011 and into 2012. This mini-constitution allowed for the seating of the Troika government, despite opposition concerns over its piecemeal nature. The UGTT, fresh from its first postrevolution convention, and in the process of successfully facing down competing union federations, saw the NCA as a means to obtain further influence. While Egypt's trade unionists demanded a new trade union law to enshrine trade union freedom, Tunisia's trade union already had a legal status it was comfortable with.

While the Egyptian constituent assembly reserved seats for the trade union movement, the UGTT managed to more directly affect the constitutional process than their counterparts in Egypt without any

---

[21] Emad al-Arabi, Media Coordinator for EFITU, interview with author, November 7, 2012.

[22] Abdel Ghaffar Shokr, Founder of Socialist Popular Alliance, interview with author, November 22, 2012.

designated seats. It was able to cast itself as a nationalist body not bogged down in political infighting. It could focus on building power in the streets, negotiating with employers, and securing its own potentially wayward members by fending off competing unions instead of pushing for seats in the NCA.

A draft constitution was circulated in August 2012, causing outrage among secular and leftist segments of society. The draft, composed by six committees of the NCA, drew condemnation both domestically and internationally.[23] While groups like Human Rights Watch identified several problematic sections of the new constitution, what attracted the most consternation domestically was the language around gender relations. Tunisia had a long history of French-influenced "liberal" laws regarding the status of women, their personal and family status, and participation in government. While the left and liberal segments of society were far from ideals of equality, the UGTT's all male leadership being a notable example, comments by Islamists left many women feeling threatened. The new constitution reflected Ennahda's thinking in its choice of a specific Arabic word to describe gender roles. The word, "yetekaamul" can be translated as "complementarity" or "fulfillment" but is distinct from "musawa" or "equality."[24] Regardless of Arabic semantics or even the intent of the drafters, this part of the constitution became a lightning rod. Ennahda denied any ulterior motive in this phraseology. It pointed to other sections of the draft that ensured equal protection under the law for all citizens, but the damage was done. The clause became a rallying point for the non-Islamist bloc, including the UGTT. The union stood with the Association of Women's Rights and other segments of civil society to reject the draft.[25] The setback added to a profound sense of frustration and the climate of fear around the activities of the NCA. It bolstered the UGTT's role not just as a voice of labor but also as a counterweight to Ennahda.

---

[23] "Tunisia: Fix Serious Flaws in Draft Constitution | Human Rights Watch," accessed October 7, 2014, www.hrw.org/news/2012/09/13/tunisia-fix-serious-flaws-draft-constitution.

[24] Monica Marks, "'Complementary' Status for Tunisian Women," *Foreign Policy Blogs* (blog), August 20, 2012, http://mideastafrica.foreignpolicy.com/posts/2012/08/20/complementary_status_for_tunisian_women.

[25] Borzou Daragahi, "Term Used for Women in Tunisia's Draft Constitution Ignites Debate, Protests," *The Washington Post*, August 16, 2012, www.washingtonpost.com/world/middle_east/term-used-for-women-in-tunisias-draft-constitution-ignites-debate-protests/2012/08/16/c6045e24-e7bf-11e1-a3d2-2a05679928ef_story.html.

Following the violence at the end of 2012 during clashes between the UGTT and Islamists at the Farhat Heched memorial, and even more so following the assassinations in spring and summer of 2013, the anti-Ennahda coalition began to call more forcefully for a change in government. In addition to asking for Ennahda to step down, they began to call for the NCA to resign as well.

Dissolving the government, gripped by infighting and strikes almost since its inception, carried widespread support. Dissolving the NCA was more divisive. Sentiment at the time varied. Some pointed to the ineffectualness of the NCA, the many slowdowns and stalls over contentious issues. Others were still angry over earlier drafts of the constitution. However, the NCA had reflected a broad constellation of political interests when it was formed, and smaller parties no doubt feared the loss of all influence if new elections were called. The stalemate dragged on for weeks. During this time the UGTT took on the role of mediator.

The UGTT at first glance seems like an unlikely interlocutor between Ennahda and its competitors. The union shared both historical and recent ties with the groups represented within the so-called National Salvation Front of secular parties. It had only its recent, and fractious, relationship with Ennahda. It had organized the national strike that coincided with the launch of the NSF, and broadly shared its aims. However, in the previous year leaders had come to enjoy their independence from party politics, and saw an opportunity to extract maximum concessions by remaining above the fray. The organization's "national dialogue," launched after Belaid's death, became even more vital after Brahmi's. While Ennahda had at first rejected the national dialogue, it now saw it as a safer exit from the crisis than the full resignation of its prime minister and cabinet, or even the dissolution of the NCA itself along the Egyptian model.

The UGTT made its national dialogue more appealing than its earlier incarnations by broadening its base of support. This broadening took place not with traditional political parties, but with other civil society groups. The UGTT's successful negotiation with UTICA helped make this possible. Both the UGTT and UTICA feared continuing political violence and deterioration in the conflict between Ennahda and the secular parties. It was, simply, bad for business. The union also incorporated two other prominent civil society organizations into the dialogue. The first was the Tunisian Human Rights League (LTDH).

The organizations shared a long history, with LTDH activists working from UGTT offices around the country since the 2010 uprising. The LTDH had a long national history, having been founded in the late 1970s, and had experienced repression under both Bourguiba and Ben Ali. Finally, the national dialogue incorporated the national lawyers' association. In addition to professional prestige offered by the lawyers' association, the organization enjoyed revolutionary legitimacy having gone on strike early in the 2010 uprising.

The four organizations, termed the Quartet, jointly hosted the national dialogue beginning in September 2013. The national dialogue emerged as a back-channel for decision-making, outside the gridlock that had gripped the NCA. Deals could be hammered out among other sectors of Tunisian society, leaving the main national cleavage unresolved. The fact that the union itself hosted (both metaphorically and physically) the national dialogue gave it both a steady stream of information on decisions being made in the NCA, and the ability to influence the emerging legislation toward its desires. With no political party possessing a large enough base of supporters to intimidate the government, the parties had no trump card to play against Ennahda and would instead need to rely on the UGTT's organization capacity and street power.

Removing Governments

The Tamarod Movement set the anniversary of Morsi's election as a day for mass protests in Egypt. In the months running up to it, representatives of all major trade union factions had participated in the signature-collecting efforts. The desire to remove Morsi from office, following his Islamist-dominated constitutional process and violence outside the Presidential Palace late in 2012, cut across political differences. June 30 saw a major protest across the country. Independent unions participated vigorously, as did the ETUF. On July 1, the military gave the president and the opposition 48 hours to respond to the people's demands. Independent unionists called for a national strike that did not materialize, as political events moved forward without them.[26]

---

[26] Heba El-Shazli, "Where Were the Egyptian Workers in the June 2013 People's Coup Revolution?" accessed April 26, 2014, www.jadaliyya.com/pages/index/13125/where-were-the-egyptian-workers-in-the-june-2013-p.

On July 3, 2013, Morsi was removed in a coup d'état that also saw the suspension of the constitution. Once again, Egypt was under military rule. Much like SCAF's interregnum after the January 25th revolution, a vague constitutional process was outlined. A new constitutional assembly largely composed of the leftist, secular, and liberal activists who had been so frustrated by the leadership of the Muslim Brotherhood and had flocked to the military coup, was convened. The media reported that two seats were going to unionists, one to the head of the legacy ETUF, Gebali El-Marghary, and one to Ahmed Khairy, listed as head of the "Egypt Worker's National Union." Confusingly, Ahmed Khairy had previously not been associated with trade union politics, and his inclusion in a supposedly labor seat seemed odd. The CTUWS, one of the main independent trade union organizations, put out a press release decrying the selections and Khairy's unlikely inclusion as a trade unionist. Khairy's page on the constitutional assembly website was later changed to state his role as leader of the Council of Nile Basin Countries.[27] As in the previous assembly, several seats went to professional syndicates outside the structure of the ETUF. Despite this relative stasis at the level of constitutional design, much political agitation took place in the political realm outside of the assembly.

The aftermath of the coup held some promise for labor. For the first time since the mid-2000s all major labor federations were on the same page backing Sisi's coup and Mansour's appointment as interim president. Mohammed ElBaradei, leader of the Dostour Party, was appointed as vice president. While ElBaradei's party was liberal in orientation, it enjoyed good relations with the independent labor movement and had Ahmed Hassan El-Borai, as a leader. El-Borai took the position of minister of social solidarity, and his appointment was followed by the appointment of Kamal Abu Eita as the new minister of manpower. Abu Eita was the most prominent leader of the independent trade union movement, president of EFITU, and a trade union activist. While the remainder of Prime Minister Hazem Al Beblawi's

---

27 "الدكتور/ احمد خيري إمام عمر عفيفى | الموقع الرسمي للجنة الخمسين لإعداد المشروع النهائي للتعديلات الدستورية",
("The 50 Member Committee" and the person's name is Dr. Ahmed Khairy Imam Omar Afifi"), accessed September 17, 2015, http://c50.dostour.eg/?p= 421; CTUWS, "Labors Representatives in the Constitution Committee Hostility to Independent Unions," September 3, 2013, www.solidar.org/ IMG/pdf/labors_representatives_in_the_constitution_committee_hostility_to_ independent_unions.pdf.

cabinet was liberal and technocratic, the appointment of two independent labor leaders, representing left-liberal and Nasserist political currents, opened up the possibility of progress. Egypt was not the only country, however, to get a new government in 2013.

With the sit-in outside the NCA dragging on, Ennahda had few options. The government began to grind to a halt, with even the national bureaucracy failing under the weight of the political crisis. While the crowds in the Bardo area never reached the size they did on the days after Brahmi's death, their tenaciousness wore Ennahda down. The party's support in the country waned, as it appeared recalcitrant in comparison to the patriotic Quartet. The claims of electoral legitimacy wore thin, as no date for new elections was announced while the damaged NCA lacked the capacity to do so. In September, Ennahda capitulated to the demand that its government resign, following a guarantee that it would be replaced by a technocratic government as opposed to the "national salvation government" proposed by the opposition.

Ghannouchi himself was on hand for the signing of the roadmap document that ended the Troika government on October 5, 2013. The document called for negotiations to form a technocratic government that would last no more than three weeks, and a finalization of the election law. Abbassi, the UGTT secretary general, enjoyed pride of place as convener of the signatories, which included more than two-dozen political parties. Included in the list were Ennahda, Nidaa Tounes, Brahmi's former People's Movement, and an assortment of leftist and liberal organizations. Reports from the event suggest that the wrangling lasted into the final minutes, with Ghannouchi claiming it was not a binding document, but instead a basis for negotiation. This statement was largely symbolic, however. There would be no backtracking on the document. Ennahda could stall, but not backtrack on its commitments.

Despite seeming to yield to pressure, Ennahda removed some of the worst options in their negotiation. No military coup and resulting violence took place as it had in Egypt. The NCA was not liquidated, and was able to resume its work toward a constitution. A late emerging demand that Marzouki be replaced, floated by Essebsi (presumably to be replaced with himself), also failed. Ennahda, long in the opposition, was playing multiple games at once. On one hand, its decision to step down demonstrated a willingness to return to the electoral process, even if that might mean its diminished influence over a future parliament. The UGTT had stared down Ennahda, both in the halls of power and in the streets, and had come to a modus vivendi with the most successful Islamist party to emerge from any of the Arab Uprisings.

In January, the technocratic minister of industry, Mehdi Jomaa, became prime minister. Jomaa, an independent, led the nominally nonpartisan government. Jomaa's greatest strength as a candidate for the post was that he equally annoyed the main constituencies. Nidaa Tounes, still pushing a maximalist line, wanted no one who served in the Laarayedh government to take the post. Ennahda delayed his appointment for nearly a month. Jomaa was acceptable partly for his political inexperience. Unlike other prominent figures, including Essebsi, he spent the Ben Ali years in the private sector. Jomaa promised to focus on putting together an electoral commission to carry out parliamentary and presidential elections by the end of the year.

Despite the torturous and divergent paths that took them there, Egypt and Tunisia formally established their new regimes only a few months apart. Interim President Adly Mansour appointed his first interim cabinet in the summer of 2013, the new constitution was voted on in January 2014, and coup leader Abdel Fattah el-Sisi won the presidency with 96.91 percent of the vote in May 2014. Tunisia's Ennahda Party joined the national dialogue in October 2013, with an understanding that Prime Minister Laarayedh would step down, which he did along with the passing of the new constitution in January 2014. New elections held in the fall produced four leading parties: Nidaa Tounes, led by Beji Caid Essebsi, Ennahda in second, the Free Patriotic Union, a center-right and populist party, and the leftist Popular Front in fourth. Beji Caid Essebsi would go on to win the presidential election in December 2014, with 55.68 percent.

The UGTT's greatest victory in the constitution was the fact that a constitution existed at all. The *content* of the constitution took a back seat to the *context*. After threatening to use the strike weapon to exclude articles perceived as Islamist, and actually using the strike weapon after the assassination of an NCA member, the UGTT was deeply invested in the constitution's passage. Despite this, the constitution did not give the UGTT much in the way of new protections.

The most notable clause of the constitution was an explicit enumeration of the right to strike. The document preserved the language of the 1959 constitution on the right to form unions. The right to strike, originally limited in an earlier draft to "non-vital" areas, was guaranteed in all sectors barring the military and security apparatus. This change seemingly abrogated the 1994 labor code, which similarly restricted strikes to the "non-vital" sectors. This change spoke more to the changing nature of the UGTT than to the preferences of the NCA, as expanding strike rights was not an agenda item for the UGTT in the 1990s negotiation. As noted previously, the only party interested in expanding strike protection was rank-and-file members, and the inclusion of this clause in the constitution demonstrated their increased influence in the UGTT.

The constitution also included a provision on the right to work, adequate working conditions, and a fair wage. The state is also enjoined to ensure the availability of work on the basis of competence and fairness. Whether the "right to a job" provision proves to be more aspirational than actual remains to be seen, but with the UGTT and UTICA's increased roles in managing the transition, this clause only furthered their influence over policy-making, which is now charged specifically with tackling the unemployment problem in the country.

Egypt's final constitution, signed in 2014, did not substantively change the labor system in the country. Peaceful strikes were "regulated by law," presumably a still forthcoming revision to Law 35 of 1976. Unions were to be formed on a "democratic basis," leaving open the possibility of fights over what constitutes a fair union election. The constitution also eliminateed the "workers and farmers" clause for parliament that both reduced the power of the ETUF, the authority that declared a candidate a worker, and restricted what was designed to be a boon to the working classes.

Consolidating the New Regimes

Egypt

Kamal Abu Eita's appointment to head the ministry of manpower was the most definitive break with ETUF influence yet, but one that caused consternation among his own comrades in the EFITU. Their fears were not misplaced. Abu Eita issued a statement saying that the "workers who were champions of the strike" should become "champions of production," echoing calls for an end to strikes. Abu Eita was not the only labor activist given a new title following the coup. Kamal

Abbas, director of the Center for Trade Union and Worker Services (CTUWS), was appointed to the National Council for Human Rights (NCHR). Abbas's CTUWS served as a central organizing platform for labor in the country and spawned EFITU's main competitor, EDLC. The new regime had now swept up the most notable labor activists in the country into governmental and quasi-governmental roles.

Appointing notable labor leaders to positions of authority was not a new tactic. The target merely shifted from the ETUF to EFITU and EDLC. Despite the logic, it fundamentally misunderstood the nature of independent industrial action in the country. Abbas and Abu Eita were unable to reconcile their differences and form a united independent labor front in the country, even when heavily incentivized to do so by both domestic and international actors. Furthermore, the leaders had little top-down leverage even within their own confederations. Many disgruntled workers in the country, notably the Mahalla workers, had never joined up with EFITU or EDLC, yet remained stalwart and militant, striking even when it meant the possibility of repression by the security services. Coopting Abbas and Abu Eita was no guarantee of labor peace.

Abu Eita's term as minister of manpower was marked not only by shifting rhetoric on the right to strike but also continued divisions in the trade union movement. The rifts inside his own federation were mirrored by similar infighting in EDLC. After the ousting of EDLC's President Yousri Marouf, Abu Eita intervened to freeze the account of his old competitors in the independent trade union movement. Ironically, this drew sharp criticism from the ETUF, who feared the possibility of an empowered ministry mucking about in the financials of a trade union federation. Abu Eita's meddling in trade union affairs was yet another sign that his inclusion in the cabinet would do little to advance the cause of independent unionists within the country.

Abbas similarly failed to bring a loyal contingent of unionists along with his inclusion in the government. His decision to accept may have also driven further wedges in the federation associated with his CTUWS non-profit, the EDLC, including the aforementioned ousting of their president in early 2014.

The regime also hedged its bets on the recruitment of independent labor leaders by continuing to work with the leadership of the ETUF. Adly Mansour joined in the now-traditional extension of the term of the ETUF board of directors. Despite the intervention of Al-Borai during his term as minister of labor, and the efforts of Mohammed Morsi and the Muslim Brotherhood to gain a toehold in the organization, the ETUF board remained dominated by old regime loyalists. By preserving them, Mansour's administration guaranteed some stability in one segment of the trade union movement.

Following the sacking of the Beblawi cabinet, Abu Eita left his post as minister of labor. Nahed Al-Ashry succeeded him. Al-Ashry was a long-serving staffer at the Ministry of Labor and rose through the ranks to lead the Dispute Resolution Bureau. The bureau's purported responsibility was to help workers negotiate and solve problems. In practice it served as one of the main units of the ministry devoted to breaking strikes. The "deals" struck by Al-Ashry's bureau often included firing or forced retirement of workers that caused "trouble" on the worksite. EFITU and EDLC were vociferous in their condemnation of her appointment, while the ETUF unsurprisingly remained silent.

With neither Abbas nor Abu Eita able to bring disgruntled workers to heel reliably, the regime introduced new restrictions on public gatherings that applied also to workers. Mansour's interim government pushed through a protest law in November 2013 (Act 107/2013) mandating a written notification to the police station 15 days prior. The act precluded public gatherings at mosques or their surrounding areas, or marching to or from them. It banned protests at "vital facilities," including a wide swath of public spaces. This was not the first protest ban issued in the country. During the Supreme Council of the Armed Forces' brief rule in 2011 a similar restriction was put in place and used to violently repress trade union sit-ins and strikes around the country.

The legal restrictions on strikes were married to a powerful national narrative against "terrorism." Workers at the Cleopatra Ceramic works in Sinai were threatened with terrorism charges if they did not end their strikes, which had been ongoing since 2011.[28] The anti-terror rhetoric was also adopted by the ETUF, with its new president, Gebali El-Marghary, stating that the goals of the federation were to guarantee

---

[28] Erin Cunningham, "From Cairo to Suez, Egypt Workers Defy Government with Labor Strikes," *The Washington Post*, April 11, 2014, www.washingtonpost.com/world/middle_east/from-cairo-to-suez-egypt-workers-defy-government-with-labor-strikes/2014/04/11/674171d0-a713-494d-a76b-b33f5d4bc505_story.html.

production and fight against terrorism.[29] In a statement reiterated by an ETUF press release, former director of state security Amr Abdel Razek stated that labor strikes were a "kind of terrorism" and denied "investor rights."[30] At the same time, the government was pushing through a terrorism bill that expanded the death penalty for leaders of organizations that "harmed the national interest."

The expansion of anti-terrorism rhetoric from the Muslim Brotherhood to other groups had a chilling effect on trade union organizing. Several of the independent union movement's erstwhile allies, including the April 6th Movement and socialist organizations, saw their leadership harassed or imprisoned. The outcome was limited push back. With no sitting parliament to raise objections in, efforts to restrict the restrictions were largely in vain.

The CTUWS catalogued dozens of strikes, protests, and sit-ins and circulated them to international audiences to rally support.[31] The El-Mahrousa Center, an independent research center in Cairo, claims workers carried out 2,274 protests during 2014, a staggering number.

Tunisia

Tunisia's UGTT struggled during the immediate transition in 2014 but generally in a more institutionalized way. Union leadership was particularly bothered by the new government's unwillingness to codify and implement the social pact signed in 2012 and use a new national corporatist bargaining scheme. Speaking in 2015, UGTT Deputy Secretary Sami Tahri stated, "[E]ven now they haven't made this the law. We want to improve the purchasing power (cost of living) ... Development can be made in accordance with the demands of the people."[32]

---

[29] Etuf Media Center, "محلب لـ"عمال مصر": اتخذنا احتياطاتنا تجاه مظاهرات 28 نوفمبر.. وعلى العمال مواصلة العمل والإنتاج," "Mehleb: We have taken precautions against demonstrations November 28th, and for workers to continue to work and produce," accessed October 29, 2015, http://etufegypt.com/archives/21440.

[30] Etuf Media Center, "رئيس أمن الدولة السابق: الإضرابات العمالية الحالية نوع من الإرهاب لأصحاب العمل," "Former Head of State Security: Current Labor Strikes are a Kind of Terrorism for Employers," accessed October 29, 2015, http://etufegypt.com/archives/17372.

[31] "EGYPT: Center for Trade Union and Workers Services '2014 – Assassination of Union Freedom' – IFWEA," accessed November 3, 2015, www.ifwea.org/?x637150=824858.

[32] Sami Tahri, UGTT Deputy Secretary General, interview with author, July 23, 2015.

The overarching goal of union leadership was to return the union to its conventional role as opposed to the outsized role it enjoyed spearheading the National Dialogue. Tahri describes this as, "the UGTT doesn't need to become a political party ... the experience of changing to a political party, [in] Poland, Brazil, always a problem. UGTT would never ask for power. Demanding power is the role of the political parties."[33] Leaders in Nidaa Tounes, the new secular bulwark against Ennahda, felt the same way. Mahdi Abd Al Jawad of Nidaa Tounes stated, "UGTT needs to work in parallel [with the parties] hand in hand, in its next congress it will get away from direct political work, and focus on social work."

National politics made it increasingly hard for the UGTT to focus on its role as a trade union, however. Fourteen soldiers were killed in a terrorist attack in July 2014. The unravelling of the Libyan state led to increased concerns about the porous border between the two. Political parties, eager to build support, capitalized on these concerns to blame both the Troika government and the new caretaker regime of Mehdi Jomaa. The fall elections loomed large, and the UGTT struggled to gain traction in its core demand for full scale social dialogue, including wage setting, and possibly the drafting of a new trade union law, throughout the year.[34]

Linkages to the political parties were stronger in 2014 than they had been previously. The struggles over the NCA resolved, the UGTT strengthened its relationship with the growing Nidaa Tounes and consolidated Popular Front. Even Ennahda, from its position outside the government following the appointment of the technocratic caretaker regime, was more willing to work with the UGTT. Ali Laarayedh, the former prime minister who was forced to resign as a condition of the National Dialogues roadmap, reflected on this time saying, "[S]yndicates are partners in politics. We must continue to find a solution to the crisis of trust."

Promise and Peril in Pacts

Egypt's Mehleb government, appointed earlier in 2014, included no representatives of the independent trade union movement. Nahed Al-Ashry, appointed minister of manpower in March, began promoting

---

[33] Mahdi Abd al-Jawad, Politician of Nidaa Tounes and Machrouu Tounes, interview with the author, June 27, 2015.

[34] Belgacem Ayari, UGTT Deputy General, interview with author, July 30, 2015.

the idea of a 12-month moratorium on strikes. The idea was not new, and had been floated by the Muslim Brotherhood-affiliated labor minister Khaled al-Azhari several years prior. It came this time, however, with renewed interest from the regime and support from the ETUF. The ETUF was accustomed to moderating demands, as this was its main purpose under the Mubarak regime. Furthermore, strikes produced new labor leaders and strike committees outside its control, many of whom affiliated with competitor federations. A social pact to end strikes was completely logical to the ETUF, and the idea described as a voluntary reduction of "partisan demands" began to appear as early as March.[35] These statements were followed by the announcement in the media of just such a moratorium being signed with the leadership of the "National Federation of Egypt's Workers," a federation that had the dubious distinction of being described by both the independent unions and the ETUF as imaginary. Whether a minor federation saw the opportunity to seize the national limelight or Al-Ashry propped up a faux union to corral the actual organizations remains vague. Despite this, Al-Ashry promised an even hand between the independent unions and the ETUF, but the regime increasingly relied on the older federation during 2014 and 2015.[36]

Calls for a social pact or social peace dominated Tunisian politics following the successful elections of late 2014. Following Essebsi's election to the presidency, Ennahda agreed to join a coalition government with Nidaa Tounes, yoking the fates of the two largest parties, at least in the short term. The agreement brought Ennahda back to some semblance of power following its removal from power during the National Dialogue. Nidaa Tounes benefited by having a party with whom to share the blame if its plans faltered, as seemed increasingly likely due to the fractious nature of the party itself.

---

[35] Etuf Media Center, "خبراء اقتصاديون: مطالب العمال عادلة ومهلة الـ6 شهور مقبولة بشروط," "Economic Experts: The Demands for Just Employment and the 6-Month Delay on Acceptable Terms," accessed November 3, 2015, http://etufegypt.com/archives/17267.

[36] Etuf Media Center, "ناهد عشري وزيرة القوى العاملة في حوار لـ"صدى البلد".. مرصد عمالي للإضرابات.. ولجنة حكماء لفض المنازعات," "Nahed Al-Ashry, Minister of Manpower in an Interview for El-Balad … An Observatory for Labor Strikes and a Committee of Elders for Dispute Resolution," accessed November 3, 2015, http://etufegypt.com/archives/17207.

Tunisia, and especially its unions, was challenged in 2015 by a string of violent attacks. Twenty-one people, including many tourists, died in an assault on the Bardo National Museum in Tunis in February. The Islamic State took credit for the attack. Four months later a gunman killed thirty-eight people, thirty of whom were British tourists, at a resort in Sousse. In addition to the security threat, the actions decimated the Tunisian tourism industry, responsible for 7.4 percent of the Tunisian economy directly, and likely more than double that in total activity. Pressure mounted on the UGTT to quickly sign a social pact that would eliminate the strikes that continued to plague the country. November alone saw strikes at the country's largest airport, among its students, and in private sector businesses across the country. Following yet another terrorist attack, this time on the Presidential Guard, President Essebsi addressed the nation on three topics: security, strikes, and divisions within Nidaa Tounes. In the same period of time, the UGTT, along with its partners in the National Dialogue, was awarded the Nobel Peace Prize, bringing unprecedented scrutiny to the Tunisian transition.

The UGTT successfully negotiated an increase in wages in the private sector in the final days of 2015. Rhetoric, especially from the president, called for replacing the existing government with a national unity government that would include the UGTT and UTICA. How a union and business association would "join" a government remains vague. The idea of a national technocratic government with the backing of the business sector and trade union follows a similar logic to Nidaa Tounes' embrace of Ennahda as coalition partner: spread the blame. Legislative action in 2015 and 2016 focused on a package of austerity measures that would likely harm the interests of the UGTT, and "rehabilitation" of former crony capitalist ties to the previous regime, rejected by a wide swath of political actors in the country. Cooptation of both the UGTT and UTICA would likely allow Essebsi and Nidaa Tounes to push through both plans with a reduced threat of major strikes or a withdrawal of support by business leaders.

Cooptation also ruled the day in Egypt. The renewed relationship between the regime and the ETUF followed a series of apparent tit-for-tat exchanges. The regime extended the term of the incumbent board for another year without elections. The board endorsed Sisi for president and agreed in principle to a strike stoppage (ironically, as the strikes were not called by the ETUF). In perhaps the most mixed-bag decision of the group, in April the government called for specialty labor courts to adjudicate disputes between employers and workers. Despite the mixed history of labor courts, the ETUF welcomed the change.[37] The ETUF celebrated Labor Day in the country with a "code of conduct," which was, effectively, a one-sided promise to stop strikes and focus instead on social dialogue. The fact that the union had not called for any of the strikes happening at the time did not hamper its willingness to promise an end to industrial action.[38]

The pivot away from the independent unions and to the ETUF served as a component of Sisi's larger political and economic vision for the country. Sisi's governance thus far has hinged on the success of key, massive, national projects: the announcement of a new administrative capitol, a major economic conference to secure external funding, and the widening of a portion of the Suez Canal. While each projects' wisdom (or feasibility) was suspect at best, the general approach reveals itself: nationalistic, conservative, grandiose, and devoid of ideological trappings. A natural partner in such endeavors was the ETUF, which offers stability and quiescence as opposed to authentic reform.

The Sisi regime acted to reign in the civil service, which accounted for nearly half the public sector and nearly 7 million workers, with a new presidential decree. The new law, designated Law 18 of 2015, had several components, notable among them was a new review policy that would allow for halving of salary or termination following second and third year reviews. It also restructured the compensation scheme for civil service employees that had previously been 50–75 percent, comprising "bonus" or "variable pay." Labor flexibilization in the civil service is not simply a cost-saving measure. Many authoritarian regimes, as well as democratic regimes seeking greater control of workers' movements, used flexibilization to break militant unions.[39]

---

[37] Etuf Media Center, "النقابيون: قرار إنشاء المحاكم العمالية ينهي الإضرابات والاعتصامات", "Trade Unionists: The Decision to Establish Labor Courts Will End the Strikes and Sit-Ins," accessed November 3, 2015, http://etufegypt.com/archives/18141.

[38] "Egypt Trade Union Federation Calls for Stability – Politics – Egypt – Ahram Online," accessed November 6, 2015, http://english.ahram.org.eg/NewsContent/1/64/128756/Egypt/Politics-/Egypt-Trade-Union-Federation-calls-for-stability.aspx.

[39] Dae-Oup Chang, "Korean Labour Relations in Transition: Authoritarian Flexibility?" *Labour, Capital and Society* 35, no. 1 (April 2002): 10–40.

The ETUF gave the law a measured response, highlighting the increased regularity in pay. Independent unions protested vociferously. For the first time under the Sisi regime, a labor decision had the prospect of causing real strife on a national level. Unsurprisingly, workers from the independent unions in the civil service reached for a standard repertoire of protest techniques, focused on sit-ins and assemblies in central areas of the capital. The practice had a long history, starting much earlier than the protests in Tahrir Square that captured national attention in 2011.

Protests in August and September of 2015 were stymied by the restrictive new protest law. They were moved from the cabinet building to the journalism syndicate. The second round of protests were to take place in Fustat Park, a designated protest zone, but were still harassed by security services.

As for the independent unions, even the new umbrella grouping called Tadamon (Solidarity) has demonstrated its weakness with the failure of the August and September protests. Even with the powerful real estate tax collector's union, which gave Abu Eita his platform prior to the revolution, the independent movement cannot muster the support it needs to impact the creation and implementation of laws.

The recent strike in Mahalla began over the issue of a proposed bonus promised by Sisi in September 2015. The bonus of 10 percent was to be paid in the mid-October paycheck, but failed to materialize. Strikes soon followed, and Minister of Manpower Sorour gave the workers a 48-hour ultimatum, threatening them with legal measures if they "obstructed work," language that matches proscribed activity in the anti-demonstration laws the government has used over the past year to break strikes. Sorour, however, was forced to appear in person at the worksite to meet with striking employees, which, while not a new practice (his predecessors in the mid-2000s visited on several occasions), does demonstrate the seriousness with which the government took the strike.[40] Workers were later threatened with termination

---

[40] "وزير القوى العاملة يتوجه إلى المحلة لاحتواء أزمة عمال الغزل"*/الوفد* "Minister of Manpower to Go to the Camp of Spinning Workers in Crisis," accessed November 6, 2015, http://alwafd.org/-وزير-929043/تقارير-وأخبار-الغزل-عمال-أزمة-لاحتواء-المحلة-إلى-يتوجه-العاملة-القوى.

if they did not return to work.[41] While the 48-hour window passed without violent repression, the strike ended on November 3 following a commitment to disburse the bonuses by the government and the holding company responsible for the factories.

The ETUF, for its part, strove to both denounce the strike and take credit for its resolution. The union was demonstrably unable to control dissent within Mahalla, and issued the dubious statement that the resolution only came after the strike ended.[42] In fact, they had been attempting to negotiate with the local strike committees (made up of their own nominal members) throughout the strike to limited success.[43] The exact origin of the debate remains opaque. President Sisi issued the bonus months before the strike began, and somewhere in the tangled path of implementation, Mahalla workers were excluded, but it is unclear if this was intentional, an oversight, punishment, or testing the waters. In the face of repression, it was impressive that workers managed to obtain a governmental concession.

In Tunisia, President Essebsi tapped Habib Essid to form a government in early 2015. The government was challenged by both economic stagnation and terrorism threats. Despite this, it successfully negotiated a new round of wage-setting negotiations with the UGTT and UTICA. In early 2016, President Essebsi effectively announced his loss of confidence in the Essid government by calling for a new government of "national unity" that would include the UGTT and UTICA in early June.

The new national unity government, and its mandate, needed an alternative basis of legitimacy. It came about through elite bargaining, not through electoral legitimacy. To provide this, the president convened the "Carthage Agreement." While the Carthage Agreement seemed to extend to a variety of political actors, including not only

---

[41] ‏عمال المحلة: «وزير القوى العاملة بيهددنا بالفصل عشان علاوة 50 جنيه»،" "Mahalla Workers: Minister of Manpower Threatens Dismissal of Workers Over 50 Pounds" accessed November 6, 2015, http://www.elwatannews.com/news/details/827336.

[42] Jano Charbel, "Textile Workers End Strike, Warn of Escalation If Bonuses Don't Materialize," Mada Masr, accessed November 6, 2015, www.madamasr.com/news/textile-workers-end-strike-warn-escalation-if-bonuses-dont-materialize.

[43] Julius Dihstelhoff and Katrin Sold, "The Carthage Agreement under Scrutiny" (Carnegie Endowment for International Peace, November 29, 2016), http://carnegieendowment.org/sada/66283.

the four ruling parties, but all major parties of the opposition, the UGTT, UTICA, and the Union tunisienne de l'agriculture de la peche (Tunisian Union of Agriculture and Fisheries), its real origins appear to lie in informal negotiations between Nidaa and Ennahda. The document itself mostly consists of platitudes with few actual priorities. The main categories included:

Winning the war on terrorism, increasing growth in development and employment, fighting corruption and promoting good governance, managing the budget and implementing social policy, setting up policies for local communities, and strengthening institutions.[44]

Every element in the document is already covered by the Tunisian Constitution in some form or another, with many established explicitly. Others are covered by existing Tunisian law and had been major components in the National Dialogue that took place during the transition. What, then, were the practical impacts of the document?

The Carthage Agreement did not make good on the president's call to bring UTICA and the UGTT into the government. Youssef Chahed, a member of the cabinet and Nidaa Tounes member, headed the "national unity government" that was formed following the document's signing. None of the cabinet ministers were active leaders of either the UGTT or UTICA, both of which demurred from taking on this more formal role. Despite this, two ministers were seen as being particularly close to the UGTT, namely the minister of social affairs, Mohamed Trabelsi, and minister of public service, Abid Briki. Despite this supposed "inclusion" of the UGTT in the cabinet, Trabelsi had not held a major position in the UGTT since before the revolution, having spent time abroad as a representative of the International Labor Organization. Similarly, Briki had been out of the UGTT leadership since its National Congress in 2011. While these ministers could be seen as a backchannel to the UGTT, this fell far short of the idea of UTICA and the UGTT "joining" the government. Over a dozen interviews conducted in 2016 and 2017 saw UGTT leadership adamant that the UGTT must preserve its independence.

---

[44] "Carthage Agreement," July 13, 2016, www.businessnews.com.tn/bnpdf/accort-carthage-2016.pdf.

Whither Tripartism?

Elite cooptation as a tool of quiescence failed entirely in Egypt, and thus far in Tunisia as well. The UGTT had managed to resist calls to "join" the government, and managed to negotiate wage increases for its members, even if the protracted negotiations angered both parties. Egypt's inclusion of Kamal Abu Eita in the first post-coup government and the appointment of Kamal Abbas to the National Council for Human Rights had no meaningful impact on the strike propensity of independent trade unions. The regime misjudged the capacity of these leaders to influence striking and protesting workers. Tunisia's leaders, notably President Essebsi, rightly recognized that UGTT leaders could call large sectoral strikes, but seemingly fails to understand that rank-and-file unionists could turn on these leaders with ease.

Trade unionists in both countries have had to deal with draconian terrorism laws. Tunisia has been under intermittent states of emergency since 2015, and the Sisi regime has passed anti-protest and anti-strike laws. Neither has stopped strikes, both organized and wildcat, from taking place throughout the country. Egypt's compliant national media reinforces the idea that protests are contrary to public order. Several threats of general strike followed by cancellations, including most recently in fall 2015, may be weakening the strike weapon in Tunisia. The two attempts to organize major protests against the Egyptian Civil Service law both ended with no real success and serious disruption by the security services.

The UGTT has decisively, for now, beaten the alternative confederations for pride of place in Tunisia. It is the go-to partner for the government, the business association, and political parties. Its main challenge will be in resisting efforts at cooptation and continuing to deliver for its members.

Egypt's once-promising independent trade union is stymied and unlikely to contribute to national politics for the foreseeable future. Tunisia's UGTT is threatened by being asked to contribute too much to national politics, at the expense of workers' concerns. Both regimes have struggled to control long-simmering worker agitation and industrial action. Time will determine which movement manages to authentically restore corporatist bargaining in their country and resist the temptation to be coopted by a powerful reconsolidating state.

Conclusion

This chapter was motivated by twin paradoxes in the postrevolutionary transition in Egypt and Tunisia. Egypt's independent trade unionists had forged some ties and familiarity with Islamist groups in the country prior to the revolution, yet fell prey to fighting and cooptation with them. Tunisia's trade unionists were largely alienated from Islamist groups but managed to forge a working relationship with them.

A second paradox took place in each country's constitutional assembly. In Egypt, seats were reserved for trade unionists, yet they had almost no influence on the creation or passage of the new constitution. In Tunisia, seats went only to political parties, yet the trade union was instrumental in both the creating and passage of the document.

These twin paradoxes show the complicated nature of institutional arrangements at times of transition, and shed light on what may help or hurt trade unionists amid revolutionary change.

7 | Conclusion

For those with normative concerns tied to the fate of the working class, the conclusion of this analysis comes with some frustration. While Tunisian trade unions have succeeded in advancing their agenda, it is within the difficult framework of the UGTT, which faces constant pressures at cooptation. Even more dishearteningly, Egyptian trade unions have failed to capitalize on their early promise, and after the 2013 coup face the heavy hand of repression felt by the entirety of civil society in that country. Despite this, the theoretical bounty yielded by the experiences in Egypt and Tunisia is only beginning to be explored by scholars both within the region and beyond it. In this chapter, in addition to recapitulating the two causal stories, I will seek to situate these processes in historical and present day battles being waged between trade unions and regimes around the world.

Prospects for the Future

Puzzle 1: Corporatist Collapse

This book identifies the collapse of corporatism as a key factor in understanding revolutionary politics in both Egypt and Tunisia. This corporatist collapse was born of the decision to simultaneously implement corporatist structures with new neoliberal policies of structural adjustment. Structural adjustment, coupled with the flexibilization of labor laws and the removal of trade unions from political power, combined to rend the corporatist bargains, leaving workers open to new revolutionary mobilization.

In Egypt, a structural adjustment program launched in 1991 was only partially implemented. This slow-down was seen as a victory for the state bureaucracy and its trade union allies, but predictions of the death of neoliberal reforms came too soon. In the mid-2000s privatization was pursued with renewed vigor. State-owned enterprises were sold off to an emerging oligarchic elite, and a cabinet of business-men oversaw a withdrawal of state support for workers. The Egyptian Trade Union Federation was coopted and its elections corrupted, destroying its capacity to "aggregate and advocate" and producing a cadre of disaffected workers. A new labor law failed to provide real power to workers and instead trapped an increasing number in short-term flexibilized contracts, further alienating them from their union and their government.

In Tunisia, structural adjustment was launched along with a recon-solidated authoritarian regime following the ouster of former president Habib Bourguiba. The new president, Ben Ali, secured his legitimacy through the so-called Tunisian miracle of economic development. This miracle required labor quiescence, achieved through removing or coopting the leadership of the country's formerly powerful union, the UGTT. His extended family benefited from privatization while the unemployment rate led to an alienated generation of youth. Labor flexibilization failed to fix the unemployment problem and served to weaken the union's hold on rank-and-file workers even more. Militant local labor activists took it upon themselves to organize not only for employed workers but also for unemployed former workers and stu-dents with no job prospects. Corporatist bargaining broke down, as the union was unable or unwilling to address the country's fundamen-tal problems.

It is useful at this juncture to consider how these important variables could play out in the future as both the economies and political systems of these two countries evolve. Looking closely at these prospects also can inform the extent to which the theories presented can travel to other cases.

The particular constellation of domestic and international forces that led to the original corporatist bargain and those that produced its destruction are unlikely to recur, either in the cases under review or internationally. Corporatism, as a labor management strategy, was originally coupled with developmentalist interventions and imported substitution industrialization, variants of state intervention tied to the global politics of the era including superpower competition. Even those forces that caused corporatist collapse would be difficult to replicate exactly, following changes to the world economy globally and the revolutionary wave locally.

Ironically, structural adjustment policies were launched in both Egypt and Tunisia just a few years before a major revision in the nature of these programs was launched. The ongoing failure of these programs to successfully "restore" productivity to the economies targeted combined with growing evidence for the side-effect of worsening conditions for poor communities under structural adjustment led to revisions in the 1990s and 2000s.[1] While some of these changes made their way to Egypt and Tunisia (including in the form of continued World Bank support for the Social Development Fund in Egypt), the benefits that accrued to the economic elite and the push to greater political participation among wealthy industrialists helped perpetuate a partially discredited model of development. The IMF was explicit in this regard when a new round of development lending was proposed following the revolution in Egypt.

Labor flexibilization, unlike the structural adjustment policies, is less context-dependent. While Tunisian trade unions have taken some small steps to push back the labor law passed in 1996, Egyptian trade unions have been characteristically incompetent. The mechanism by which labor flexibilization produced corporatist rupture, as described in Chapter 2, would also not be reversed simply through "tightening" the labor market. Workers would need their new job security to directly intersect with trade union politics, either through national bargaining or a resurgent labor movement. Some of this process has taken place in Tunisia, which is why I describe it as "reestablishing corporatism." While the UGTT is highly incentivized to lie about its membership numbers, it has undoubtedly grown, even with the threat of independent unions.

Labor flexibilization has evolved globally in addition to its effects on the two cases under consideration. The International Labor Organization has responded to increased pressure on workers through flexibilization with its "decent work" agenda, formulated in a series of reports and actions through the early 2000s and enshrined in 2008's

---

[1] John Pender, "From 'Structural Adjustment' to 'Comprehensive Development Framework': Conditionality Transformed?" *Third World Quarterly* 22, no. 3 (June 1, 2001): 397–411; William Easterly, "What Did Structural Adjustment Adjust?: The Association of Policies and Growth with Repeated IMF and World Bank Adjustment Loans," *Journal of Development Economics* 76, no. 1 (February 2005): 1–22.

Declaration on Social Justice for a Fair Globalization.[2] The ITUC continues its pushback on IMF efforts to promote labor market flexibilization, with varying results. The policy prescription emerged again following the Great Recession, as several states took on austerity and flexibility measures. International institutions have also promoted the "flexicurity" model pioneered in Europe. Egypt and Tunisia are among the only countries on the Africa continent to offer unemployment benefit insurance, a component of flexicurity, though its implementation, like that of subsidies, has been viewed as corrupt and spotty. If an emphasis on flexibilization or flexicurity remains a feature of policy proposals in Egypt and Tunisia, it does not bode well for trade unions in either country. Trade union politics depends on the socialization of membership and the distribution of club goods, both of which are difficult to maintain with short-term or generally "flexibilized" labor markets.

Labor flexibilization remains a challenge to other countries using corporatist bargains to ensure worker quiescence or regime stability. Countries using corporatism to distribute resources or buy loyalty of the public may need to shift to weak or nonexistent party structures in the presence of flexibilization. If corporatism is designed to ensure quiescence, regimes will face the challenge of wildcat strikes or alternative labor organizing. Region-based trade union structures may feel pressure to continue to advocate for workers who are not formally on their membership rolls, as UGTT officials felt in southern Tunisia. Sectorial-based unions may avoid this pressure by not encountering disgruntled, laid off, or "flexibilized" workers in the same way, but will have little to offer the government in controlling the agitation of these workers.

The third variable behind corporatist collapse, the ability of trade unions to aggregate and advocate demands of their members to the government, depends on the politics of the country. In both Egypt and Tunisia, regimes pivoted to a new base among wealthy elites. At the same time, increasing fears of Islamist penetration and the general threat of a more restive civil society led to crackdowns on trade union representatives. Both strategies neglected trade union officials' role in

---

[2] "ILO Declaration on Social Justice for a Fair Globalization," Document (August 13, 2008), www.ilo.org/global/about-the-ilo/mission-and-objectives/WCMS_099766/lang–en/index.htm.

legitimately securing benefits for their members. Egypt's decision to corrupt the elections in the ETUF led to ineffective (though compliant) officials. Tunisia's "decapitation" of the UGTT leadership left it with a complicit upper echelon, but frustrated rank-and-file members. The former strategy leaves trade unions open to the emergence of competitors, while the latter allows for rank-and-file revolt. Both can be challenging in regime maintenance.

The new corporatist bargain struck in Tunisia seems likely to ensure the UGTT's continued role in economic policy. The union's victories in the drafting of the constitution and the toppling of the Ennahda-led government demonstrate its political power. All of the political forces that have emerged in the country, Ennahda and its Islamist allies, nationalist/liberals clustered around Nidaa Tounes, and the leftist/ socialist bloc, have reconciled themselves to the UGTT's influence. The UGTT is also more capable of aggregating the demands of its own rank-and-file members than it was before the revolution. The organization still faces the possibility of truly discontented members joining the rival independent unions, or even a resurgent push of Islamists to create a union confederation of their own; these efforts have been limited so far. The UGTT conference held in 2012 may have left some of the most radical and socialist members out in the cold, but did a better job integrating a centrist bloc. The resumption of national-level wage bargaining took place in 2015, and at least token gestures have been made toward the integration or representation of unemployed workers in the impoverished interior.[3] The 2017 Congress saw a real competition between a "consensual" list and an insurgent one, with the consensual list winning.

For Tunisian trade unions, the biggest threat is not being excluded from government decision making but being tied too closely to it. Essebsi's goal of "inclusion" seems certain to link the UGTT to a host of less popular macroeconomic choices: international loans, a reduction in spending, government lay-offs. This would make it harder for the UGTT to protest such decisions, as it would be implicated in them. The UGTT would run two risks here: First, it could become enmeshed with Nidaa Tounes and the government, returning it to the bad old

---

[3] Hella Lahbib, "Tunisie: Nouveau Gouvernement – UGTT-UTICA – Nouvelle Étape, Priorités et Défis," *allAfrica.fr*, accessed February 9, 2015, http:// fr.allafrica.com/stories/201502041649.html.

days of quiescence; second, it could be completely replaced. The liberalized atmosphere that has seen an increased use in social media, a roll back of the police state, and a flourishing of civil society might lead to another rank-and-file revolt, this time benefiting a competitor institution.

As long as trade union interests are navigated through competing confederations, as in Egypt, advancement for workers will be ad hoc at best. The return of military-backed authoritarianism in that country coupled with restrictions on the right to protest do not bode well for the ability of trade unionists to aggregate their demands. The general purge of Muslim Brotherhood-affiliated Islamist elements from all facets of the trade union structure, and more broadly throughout civil society, will no doubt have a chilling effect on any aggressive calls for reform from trade unionists. How the new Sisi regime will manage trade union elections, or the prospects of competing federations at the shop-floor level, remains to be seen; however, the appointment of long-time ETUF officials does not bode well for those hoping for revolutionary change. After five years of bureaucrats with at least some distance from the ETUF, it appears that the ministry has been placed directly under their control again, with a renewed emphasis on cooptation in the Mubarak style.

Continued Divergence?

Puzzle 2: Divergent Outcomes

Since 2011, Egypt and Tunisia have taken starkly different paths. This empirical puzzle drove the second half of this project and remains evident in each country today. This project has proposed several key processes that produced the variation in trade union impact on the transition thus far: external links, internal links, incorporation. These factors led to different splits, namely a federation versus federation split in Egypt and a rank-and-file versus central split in Tunisia.

The Egyptian trade union movement consisted of a legacy union, the ETUF, and upstart independent unions. The independent unions won the attention of "global labor," a constellation of international labor organizations, global union federations, nonprofits, and quasi-governmental organizations that deal with workers' issues, including the ITUC and the Solidarity Center. The ETUF was alienated from these sources of rhetorical and financial support. Internally, the ETUF remained close to the old regime, while the independent unions formed multiple links to small parties, with many of its notable leaders getting directly involved in politics. The ETUF's long association with the old regime left it faring badly in the competition for members, while the independent unions' relatively recent emergence left them with weak infrastructure. The trade union movement as a whole faced federation versus federation fighting, leaving them open to successive rounds of attempted cooptation, first by the Muslim Brotherhood and then by a resurgent military. Labor wound up impacting the transition process very little.

The Tunisian trade union movement managed to face down its internal critics and bring some (or at least their concerns) into the leadership of the organization. Its challengers were weak, and failed to gain substantiation rhetorical or financial support from global labor, which continued to flow to the UGTT. The UGTT avoided forming an electoral alliance with any party, casting themselves as "above" the political fray. It drew on a deep reserve of revolutionary and anticolonial legitimacy that helped to restrain potentially wayward members and discourage defection. The movement faced a rank-and-file versus central split, which was largely healed by 2012, allowing the union, despite internal differences, to directly impact the transition process, first through legitimate general strikes and later by hosting the National Dialogue and having its preferences written into the new constitution. Given these recent histories, the question remains: Are we inclined to see continued divergence and varying outcomes between Egypt and Tunisia?

The least changeable process is incorporation. Tunisian and Egyptian trade unions were able to draw on distinctly different rhetorical wells during and after the uprisings in their countries. The ETUF was forced to reckon with its coopted nature under the Mubarak regime, but its origins as a weak advocate for workers went back to the 1950s. It had no enduring symbols, revolutionary legitimacy, or nationalist folk hero to invoke when faced with challenges to its role in the country. Changing a founding myth would be incredibly hard for the ETUF. If anything, its competitors can lay claim to a more resonant, if recent, origin story, opposing the Mubarak regime and resisting the Muslim Brotherhood.

The UGTT is keenly aware of the continuing power of its internal narrative of revolutionary, anti-imperialist legitimacy. This legacy helps regulate internal dissent. It can be seen in the organization's competitors taking on the names of previous trade union organizations, attempting to anchor themselves in groups as old, or older, than the UGTT itself. Even craven and coopted UGTT leadership can draw on this rhetorical well, as they did in the 1980s and 1990s. The rhetoric of revolutionary legitimacy only amplified in the years after 2011. Defenders of the organization describe its role in the 2011 revolution as part of its "historical concept and historical tradition."[4] The fact that UGTT rank-and-file workers, not its core leadership, were involved in early protests has been papered over as current leadership takes credit (some rightfully so, following the 2012 conference) for starting or leading the revolution. The ability to draw on this revolutionary legitimacy will hold the UGTT in good stead. This legitimacy was enhanced greatly when the National Dialogue Quartet was awarded the Nobel Peace Prize. Someone entering the office of the UGTT following this award would not be foolish enough to mistake the prize itself as the official symbol of the union as it adorns posters, cards, and photos. The imprimatur of international legitimacy has improved the organization's standing nationally. On the other hand, the ETUF's reliance on regime-derived legitimacy leaves the organization in a more precarious position.

While this project has highlighted the importance of external linkages to global labor for both material and rhetorical support, it has left largely unexplored the origins of global labor's preferences in each country. This is an important question and a path for future research. Interviews with leaders of the ITUC, the Solidarity Center, and Friedrich Ebert Stiftung highlighted a few components, notably the presence or lack of a viable alternative to the legacy trade union on the ground and the idiosyncratic beliefs or preferences of the activists assigned to the country. Some of these preferences are influenced by (and recursive with) the perception of revolutionary legitimacy in Tunisia and regime-backed legitimacy in Tunisia. The role of the independent unions in the country seem to be a matter of timing, with Tunisian independent unions emerging a bit later and lobbying a bit more weakly for international recognition than their Egyptian counterparts.

---

[4] Sofienne Ben Hamida, Journalist interview with author, April, 2012.

International support for the independent trade unions in Egypt was vociferous before and during the uprisings. It was encouraged throughout the transition. Efforts at reconciliation focused exclusively on the warring independent factions, never with the legacy union. Repeatedly, these efforts at reconciliation, specifically with Kamal Abbas and Kamal Abu Eita, failed. The ILO has one active case looking at violations of trade union freedoms in the country, active since 2013, but ILO Committee of Experts reports are slow moving. Despite being staffed in ACTRAV by many labor-affiliated bureaucrats, the ILO maintains relationships with labor, business, and government. Its activities seem to favor progress of tangible goals, explaining in part its continued support for the UGTT and critique of the ETUF.

Other segments of global labor took a more forceful stand during the transition than the ILO. The Solidarity Center wound down its relationship with the ETUF and shifted both financial and rhetorical support to independent unions. Despite this, and the concerns of ILO officials that local independent activists were growing complacent being feted by global labor, support seemed to be drying up in 2012 and 2013. The increased pressure on foreign actors inside the country, as evidenced by the raids on the International Republican Institute and National Endowment for Democracy and later trials of their staffs, limited the ability of global labor to impact the domestic scene in Egypt.

Global labor's relative lack of attention to alternatives to the UGTT in Tunisia is likely to persist. International media has supported the UGTT's positive role in the transition, and the efforts of independent unionists in the country have never attracted much support from foreign unions. The Global Union Federations maintained their ties with UGTT-affiliated unions. Solidarity Center never experienced a break with the UGTT, and has kept most of its criticism focused on lack of representation for unaffiliated workers and the limited prospects of women in the trade union leadership. The UGTT's role in the National Dialogue makes it corecipient of the Nobel Peace Prize, a fact that the union has used to great effect in its self-promotion internally and externally.

The continued support for the UGTT in Tunisia and the diminishment of international influence in Egypt could produce any number of outcomes. This project has identified global labor's pluralist framing and monetary support as important to the generation of a federation versus federation split in Egypt. Despite this, the split may now be self-reinforcing. The pluralism genie was out of the bottle in Egypt following the revolution, and instead of replacing the former union, Egyptian federations turned on one another, fighting and proliferating. Some, at least, were able to both financially and rhetorically sustain themselves after global labor began to push for reunification, and international financing dried up.[5]

While institutional legacies and rhetorical framing are important to the process, trade union positions, federation versus federation or rank-and-file versus central cleavages, were driven by material incentives. Up until now the most realistic threat to the UGTT's sole leadership of the union movement was its disgruntled, militant rank-and-file members. This challenge has largely been muted since the 2011 and 2017 conferences, which included competition and different visions for the union.

The federation versus federation cleavage is likely to persist in Egypt. Despite a staggering number of interventions from both local and international trade union activists, no reconciliation took place between Kamal Abbas and Kamal Abu Eita. Disgruntled unionists varied widely on their loyalty to Abbas and Abu Eita during the transition period with neither consolidating a strong majority of independent workers. Both sides also saw a slow secession of members to the ETUF and competition from region-based union federations. The return of Mubarak-era leadership to the top positions in the Ministry of Manpower and the ETUF suggests that the new Sisi regime is doubling down on the federation as a means of control. The depersonalization of the independent union movement may be beneficial for it, but the current repressive environment is not.

What does this mean for the capacity of trade unions to influence the consolidation of these new regimes in each country? In Tunisia, any conflict between trade union confederations is likely to mirror the broader cleavage between Islamist and secular politics in the country. The UGTT has entrenched its position and enshrined its priorities in law. It has passed through the crucible of the transition with an even stronger relationship with its "social partner" UTICA and is a

---

[5] Ironically, the AFL-CIO, parent organization of the Solidarity Center, faced internal revolt over efforts at trade union pluralism in the United States at the same time it was advocating pluralism in Egypt.

necessary component of the coalition that won the presidency and
parliamentary majority in 2014. In Egypt, trade unions are unlikely
to influence the consolidation of the Sisi regime, though it is difficult to
tell who or what (if anything) will. Wildcat strikes have continued
unabated despite the authoritarian measures taken up in Sisi's new
"war on terror." The new government seems poised to tackle the 30-
year old subsidy issue in a comprehensive way, but has done little in
the way of presenting broader economic visions. During his campaign,
Sisi argued for greater use of the military's economic and distributive
capacity, a frightening move for workers in the military sector who are
subject to the military legal system, which can be harsh on striking.

Despite these challenges, Sisi is not faced with the same constellation
of problems previous Egyptian leaders have been. There is no reasonable competitor he must keep the labor movement away from, with an
almost nonexistent leftist community and a completely run to ground
Islamist movement. Despite its elite interventions, the Muslim Brotherhood never had a deep hold on the labor movement inside the independent unions or the ETUF. Islamist trade unionists were often
Salafis, a group whose political parties generally backed Sisi and are
well integrated into the regime.

Despite this, Sisi's "war on terror" has severely damaged the capacity of the trade union movement to coalesce any demands. Sisi's
rubber stamp election, in which almost every major political party in
the country endorsed him, only exacerbates the situation. The UGTT
was able to influence the trajectory of the Tunisian constitution and
political process in part because it was able to wield a credible strike
weapon. Even its competitors were often dragged into national solidarity strikes called by the organization, and only the most recalcitrant
(and Islamist-influenced) unions could stand outside of them. No one
will be holding a national strike in Egypt any time soon. The draconian
counter-terror laws effectively insure that any protests will be seen as a
threat to the regime, leaving them effectively outlawed.

As for tangible benefits, the differences continue. The new Egyptian
minimum wage, set at 1,200 EGP ($150 dollars), matches, not the
current demands, but those established at the start of the strike wave in
2007 and are roundly ridiculed as insufficient given both inflation and
the possibility of reforms to the subsidy system. The increase, which
was announced under Morsi and reannounced under Sisi, is only
designed to go to a fraction of the country's workers, mostly in the

public sector and on full-time contracts. The number actually seeing an increased wage may be as few as 7 million out of over 25 million workers. Tunisia's most recent minimum wage increase went to the private sector, and seems well enforceable and universal. Despite this, Tunisia remains threatened with inflation that erodes even this increase. Ongoing economic protests in 2017 show that some issues, including interior development and unemployment, linger.

Theoretical Contributions

This project has yielded several theoretical contributions as well as pointing at a series of new questions to be examined in the future. Among the most notable contributions are understanding corporatist collapse in revolutionary politics, explaining differing trade union impacts on regime transitions, and furthering our understanding of trade union competition.

This project puts forth a theory of corporatist collapse under neo-liberal reforms and structural adjustment.[6] While many theorists have written about the failure, transformation, and endurance of corporatist pacts, this project explicates how corporatism failed in two novel and recent cases. As the global political economy evolves and policy prescriptions change, the types of corporatist collapse may evolve as well, necessitating a continuous effort to understand this important phenomenon. Egypt's and Tunisia's corporatist collapses do not match those of Scandinavian countries in the 1980s, not only because of the evolution of structural adjustment, flexibilization, and loss of power among unions but also because North African corporatism is not the same as Scandinavian (nor fascist Europe or authoritarian Latin America, other common sites of corporatist analysis.) Despite this, it shares many of the hallmarks of these other projects and as such deserves to be analyzed alongside them. One of the subtler aims of this project is to join the decades' long push to topple Middle East exceptionalism by showing that recognizable processes undergird the political economy of Egypt and Tunisia despite the quirks inherent in any world region.

---

[6] While I have established a slightly different meaning here, credit for first using the phrase goes to Lange et al. "The End of Corporatism: Wage Setting in the Nordic and Germanic Countries," by Peter Lange, Michael Wallerstein, and Miriam Golden in Sanford M. Jacoby, *The Workers of Nations: Industrial Relations in a Global Economy* (Oxford: Oxford University Press, 1995).

By positing a mechanism for corporatist collapse that transcends simply identifying its symptoms, we can better assess the political ramifications of this event. In Egypt and Tunisia corporatism extended far beyond wage setting or collective bargaining. Corporatism was a means of ensuring worker quiescence, corralling a restive segment of society, and precluding the emergence of an alternative power base in labor. Corporatism was part and parcel with state building, independence, developmental, and regime consolidation programs. Collapsing corporatism is not simply the end of an economic system, but the erosion of a key support structure of these regimes. As such, this project links corporatism to larger analysis of the antecedents to contentious politics.

It is too neat and tidy to suggest that workers were the cause of the revolutions in Egypt or Tunisia. A broad-based revolution cannot be reduced only to workers. It is also reductionist to claim this as it strips the revolutionary mantle from other groups long oppressed who joined the revolutionary coalition: Islamists, liberals, the middle classes, the youth, communists, socialists, civil rights campaigners, artists, and internet activists. But worker mobilization was vital to the revolution. The number of workers in each country dwarfs the interests labeled in the previous sentence. Without being freed up by corporatist collapse, workers' mobilization in the revolution may have never happened. The debilitating strike wave and conflicts between workers and the security services, as well as Abu Eita's successful sit-in in downtown Cairo, all helped form the new repertoire of contentions in Egypt. The open-ended strikes, solidarity marches, and circulation of youth activists on the coast and working-class activists in the interior formed a similar repertoire in Tunisia.

The project has also contributed to our understanding of trade unions in transitional contests. So far, Egypt and Tunisia have served as a stark reminder that transitions from authoritarianism are open ended, and can result in democratic opening, reconsolidation of authoritarianism, or anywhere else on the spectrum between these ideal types. All institutions of political control and regime maintenance deserve a close analytical look following an uprising. This project borrows the term "legacy union" from Caraway's work on trade unions in transition. While Caraway sought to determine how legacy unions hold on to or lose power to independent challengers, this project looks instead at the impact of trade union movements on transitions themselves. Poland, Russia, South Africa, Brazil, South Korea, and Taiwan have all seen a major role for trade union organizations in their transitions. The long-term consolidation of democratic norms depends in part on the participation of the working classes, and trade union politics is one path to participation. Empirically, within the cases selected we see the major impact of the UGTT in Tunisia. While political science generally, and transitions literature specifically, has recognized the important role trade unions can take on, this project contributes to the how and when of trade union influence.

Little attention has been paid so far in either trade union or transitions literature to what I term "global labor." Global labor is, in one sense, a transnational advocacy network, as described by Keck and Sikkink.[7] TANs have been important to transitions around the world and are acknowledged as a key component of the international system. Despite this, both literature on trade unions and members of these advocacy networks themselves rarely recognize their power over not only domestic labor unions but also political trajectories within countries. Global labor solidarity, both through rhetoric and funding, is key to trade union movements seeking autonomy from the government. Poland's Solidarity received funding, support, and training from a variety of international unions, including the AFL-CIO.[8] The AFL-CIO's predecessor the American Federation of Labor was a long-time ally of the CIA in intervening in Latin American politics during the Cold War.[9] Despite this history, the perception among both labor scholars and labor leaders was that the heyday of international solidarity was long in the past. The perception exists that international trade union politics were exclusively a side-project of Cold War competition and had no independent impact on domestic politics. The cases analyzed showed that this was wrong-headed. The rhetorical framing of unity versus pluralism and the financial support to break away and form independent confederations was all vital to the trajectory of trade union politics in Egypt and Tunisia.

[7] Margaret E. Keck, *Activists beyond Borders: Advocacy Networks in International Politics* (Ithaca, NY: Cornell University Press, 1998).
[8] Gregory F. Domber, "The AFL-CIO, The Reagan Administration and SOLIDARNOŚĆ," *The Polish Review* 52, no. 3 (January 1, 2007): 277–304.
[9] Anthony Carew, "The American Labor Movement in Fizzland: The Free Trade Union Committee and the CIA," *Labor History* 39, no. 1 (February 1, 1998): 25–42.

In some ways, trade union activism in the Arab states fell in a blind spot between Marxian approaches that predicted labor at the vanguard of an explicitly anti-bourgeois revolutionary front and Polanyian approaches that predicted broad "societal" reactions to neoliberalism. The labor uprisings in Egypt and Tunisia were neither. While labor disseminated new tactics, it did not lead the vanguard of the revolution, and workers joined protests on Habib Bourguiba Avenue and Tahrir Square as individuals first and workers second. No workers' party emerged in either country. Polanyi's expectation of societal pushback and double movement also fails to capture the story.[10] Polanyi and his followers describe a broad societal demand for state intervention against savage market logic. The corporatized trade union organizations were themselves a state intervention and in other context might be hailed as part of the counter-movement against neoliberal reforms. The context of North African variants of neoliberalism and corporatism meant this was not the case. With neither Marxian nor Polanyian models explaining the actions of workers their movement was largely ignored in the region.[11]

Even those who have championed and analyzed so-called new solidarity, most notably among them scholars like Peter Evans, have missed the form that trade union activism in the Arab states would take.[12] These are not examples of social movement unionism in any European or Anglo-American sense. They combined crosscutting nationalist concerns, but not in the way that advocates of social movement unionism or "fusion" politics advocated.[13] The intervention of global labor did not follow on the basis of equal-footing ties of solidarity between workers pressured by common forces in the global north and global south. Instead we find paternalistic global union forces changing the incentive structure of local actors along with their rhetorical framing. The process more closely resembles a bidding war

[10] Gareth Dale, "Double Movements and Pendular Forces: Polanyian Perspectives on the Neoliberal Age," *Current Sociology* 60, no. 1 (January 1, 2012): 3–27.

[11] This assessment of traditions in global labor is strongly influenced by Michael Burawoy, "From Polanyi to Pollyanna: The False Optimism of Global Labor Studies," *Global Labour Journal* 1, no. 2 (May 31, 2010).

[12] Mark Anner and Peter Evans, "Building Bridges across a Double Divide: Alliances between US and Latin American Labour and NGOs," *Development in Practice* 14, no. 1–2 (February 2004): 34–47.

[13] Dan Clawson, *The Next Upsurge: Labor and the New Social Movements* (Ithaca, NY: Cornell University Press, 2003).

for international attention than a utopian emergence of transnational union solidarity.[14] Trade union activists had to absorb market logic to present their movements in a way that would gain international sympathy.[15]

The Tunisian and Egyptian cases should also inform future thinking on the relationship between party, regime, and trade union politics. The idea that trade union politics do not matter in the region is long standing. For many, the European narrative of trade unions and democracy moving in lock step has given the impression that trade union politics will not matter in authoritarian regimes. Too often political scientists do not recognize the importance of labor and industrial relations in shaping the policies and capacity of a state, and vice versa. Egypt and Tunisia, as late industrializing states, share more in common with Latin American, Eastern European, and East Asian cases than they do with the Western European and Anglo-American examples. Many of the theories of democratization popular in Middle East studies are closely related to European readings of state–society relations far removed from the North African context. Researchers on trade union politics do a better job of recognizing the role of trade union politics under authoritarianism and in transitioning regimes, but unfortunately little of this research has taken place in the Middle East region.

The trade unions in Egypt and Tunisia faced a series of decisions regarding political parties and movements that are related to previous struggles that trade unions have faced. The North African context mostly varies in the legacy of colonialism, a variant of neoliberalism that fails to protect property rights, and the legacy of large powerful security sectors. The regimes that the ETUF, the UGTT, and their competitors all faced were characterized by late, dependent development. Successive waves of nationalization and crony capitalist privatizations left weak institutional commitments to property rights (despite a wave of judicialization that sought to protect them). Security of property was a key component in the development of labor-party linkages in European history, often determining the nature of the

---

[14] Bruce Robinson, "Solidarity across Cyberspace: Internet Campaigning, Labour Activism and the Remaking of Trade Union Internationalism," *Work Organisation, Labour and Globalisation* 2, no. 1 (2008): 152–64.

[15] Bob Clifford, *The Marketing of Rebellion: Insurgents, Media, and International Activism* (Cambridge; New York: Cambridge University Press, 2005).

coalition between socialists, anarchists, and liberals.[16] This was not the salient cleavage in Tunisia or Egypt, where the relationship between secularists and Islamists was dominant. The relationship to parties was therefore based on other facets of ideology as well as the relative strength of the unions, the choices they made, and the decisions of the parties themselves. Party politics were never going to be the vehicle of trade union political empowerment as they were in some European and Latin American contexts. Even in Tunisia, where the UGTT eventually managed to directly influence the transition it was at the expense of political parties, not through their strength. The capacity and ideology of new political parties is worthy of further study, though parties were not the only actor at play in Egypt and Tunisia.

Both Egypt and Tunisia had to reckon with Islamist movements joining the political process formally for the first time. In both cases the parties formed by Islamists were bourgeois and conservative in their policy proposals, despite drawing much of their support from the working classes. Their leadership was economically liberal and drawn from a contra-elite of "pious middle class" business owners and university graduates. These movements were different in each country, however. The Muslim Brotherhood was part of the old regime, broadly defined. Members held seats in the parliament and respected the red lines established by the Mubarak regime. Tunisia's Islamists were more repressed, with much of their leadership in long-term exile. This project looks specifically at the economic priorities and power-politics interests of the Islamist parties in Egypt and Tunisia and largely eschews analysis of Islamist parties as "Islamic" in any substantive way. An emerging group of scholars have explicitly critiqued the way political Islam has been studied and broadened what is a reasonable field of inquiry in Islamist politics.[17] In the case of both Tunisia and Egypt, Islamist parties promised good governance and an end to corruption that was extremely popular in either case. Appeals to social

---

[16] Adam Przeworski and Fernando Limongi, "Political Regimes and Economic Growth," *The Journal of Economic Perspectives* 7, no. 3 (July 1, 1993): 51–69.

[17] Jillian Schwedler, "Studying Political Islam," *International Journal of Middle East Studies* 43, no. 1 (February 2011): 135–37; Even those who are deeply skeptical of Islamist politics have expanded the discourse on their parties and how they operate, including Tarek Masoud, whose general thinking is available at *Tarek Masoud on Political Islam*, 2013, www.youtube.com/watch?v=bQU-Fs3JB1k&feature=youtube_gdata_player.

justice and economic development, couched explicitly in Islamic precepts, also helped drive their popularity. The analysis of the rise of these Islamist parties (and their fall) is just beginning. Tarek Masoud has provocatively argued that the Muslim Brotherhood in Egypt turned out working-class voters by appealing to a strong redistributionist preference despite their neoliberal policies. The future of the relationship between Islamist parties and trade unions in both countries is difficult to predict and will depend on whether non-Salafi Islamist politics has been permanent banished from the Egyptian regime, and whether Ennahda can regroup into a potent electoral force again.

A major point of variation between the two cases is the role of the military. Tunisia's military was small and professional, dwarfed by other components of the state's coercive apparatus. Egypt's military is massive, swollen by a lucrative relationship with the United States and multiple wars with Israel. It also served as a commercial interest in the regime, with current and former military officials owning several businesses. Military production extended far beyond guns and bullets and into refrigerators and bottled water. Strikes were a sore point for the military, leading them to a different disposition toward trade unions. The relationship between unions and the military in Egypt evolved during the transition and included conflict, cooperation, and cooptation at different points. Historically, trade unions can be bitter enemies of military-backed authoritarian regimes or a constituent part of them, and neither was precluded in a mechanistic way in Egypt. Future research into the Sisi regime's relationship to labor will help illuminate the linkages between the two.

Predictions and Possibilities for Future Research

The prospect of corporatist collapse under neoliberal reforms, especially those brought on by structural adjustment and austerity politics, is not confined to the two cases considered here. I have argued that the combination of corporatist control and neoliberal reforms can bring on corporatist collapse and that workers freed from old corporatist bargains can be put to new revolutionary purposes as they were in Tunisia and Egypt. While the larger universe to which this theory extends includes only authoritarian regimes, risks exist even for democratic states that seek to combine neoliberal reforms and corporatism.

Austerity politics have severely challenged corporatist bargains in Europe since 2009. While governments may rise and fall, bringing even "radical" parties like Greece's SYRIZA to power, the system can generally accommodate this. While social dislocation, protests, and even violence may emerge, prospects for revolution are slim. Not so in authoritarian contexts.

The Dogs That Didn't Bark: Jordan and Bahrain

Closer geographically and culturally to the Egyptian and Tunisian cases, Jordan and Bahrain also face the possibility of worker discontent. Each of these countries has several of the preconditions found in Egypt and Tunisia. Despite that, Jordan's economic protests never coalesced into a revolutionary movement, and while Bahrain's did, the movement was crushed. These two cases, which require further elaboration, provide support for many of the ideas in this project, but also some of its potential limits, pointing us toward areas of further research.

In Jordan labor flexibilization was expanded in the labor law of 1997. Structural adjustment led to a diminishment of subsidies in the 2000s. Global labor has actively taken up the issue of workers' rights in the country.[18] A Free Trade Agreement signed with the United States mandated the country uphold the ILO's Core Labor Standards, but the country restricts freedom of association. The official, government-sponsored trade union movement, the General Federation of Jordanian Trade Unions (GFJTU), represents only around 10–15 percent of workers, and its capacity to strike is sharply limited.[19] Given these facts, it is not surprising that Jordan has seen the emergence of a General Federation of Independent Unions, which, like Egypt's independent union movement, emerged from the institutionalization of wildcat strike committees.[20]

[18] "The Struggle for Worker Rights in Jordan: Solidarity Center," accessed March 5, 2015, www.solidaritycenter.org/publication/the-struggle-for-worker-rights-in-jordan/.

[19] Melani Cammett and Marsha Pripstein Posusney, "Labor Standards and Labor Market Flexibility in the Middle East: Free Trade and Freer Unions?" *Studies in Comparative International Development* 45, no. 2 (May 13, 2010): 250–79.

[20] "The Emergence of a New Labor Movement in Jordan | Middle East Research and Information Project," accessed March 5, 2015, www.merip.org/mer/mer264/emergence-new-labor-movement-jordan?ip_login_no_cache=ccc51060f12405205d883443b72cc89b.

Bahrain granted trade union rights only in 2002. The General Federation of Workers Trade Unions in Bahrain was organized that year and quickly enmeshed itself in global labor activities, including joining the ICFTU (now part of the ITUC). The revision had the makings of an attempt at corporatism, with the trade union leadership negotiating at a national level despite the difficulties of organizing in a country where more than half the population are not citizens of the state. The GFWTU was restricted to private sector employees, explicitly banning government employees from the organization. Labor in Bahrain is extremely flexible and prone to abuse as a large number of workers come from developing countries and are wholly dependent on their employer "sponsors."

Even with these restrictions, the GFWTU joined Bahrain's 2011 uprising, calling for two national strikes following the extreme violence meted out to protesters in the capital of Manama. After a resumption of fighting, a second strike was called in March 2011. When the revolution was crushed by a combination of Bahraini and Saudi security services that year, over 3,000 employees were fired, with many trade union leaders among them.[21] In 2012, a new trade union was formed whose position was explicitly pro-regime.

Why, given all of these similarities to the dynamics in Egypt and Tunisia, did these cases turn out so differently, and to what extent do they still face the possibility of revolutionary change? Neither Bahrain nor Jordan made labor a bulwark of stability in their regime. Labor movements were not part of the emergence of an independent state or an important sector in the consolidation of a ruling coalition. The official labor union was a small part of Jordan's system of regime maintenance. Bahrain's inclusion of an official trade union came about during a round of liberalization during the reconsolidation of the regime in the early 2000s. Both countries draw on alternative claims to legitimacy. As monarchies, both the histories of incorporation and then rhetoric that undergirds them are different from single-party republics. As such, unrest in labor is less likely to present serious

---

[21] "'Interfere, Restrict, Control' Human Rights Watch," accessed March 5, 2015, www.hrw.org/node/116416/section/8.

threats to the regime itself, even when caught up in revolutionary politics as it was in Bahrain.[22]

The prospect for future revolutionary action emerging from the labor sector is dependent on the regimes making workers a key constituency or the emergence of economics as a key justification for regime maintenance. This is certainly possible, as both regimes face serious challenges to the fundamental legitimacy of hereditary rule, especially after the recent revolutions in the region. That being said, old corporatist pacts were created in a different era of the global economy, and the (re)distribution systems that made them appealing are increasingly challenging to maintain for small, export-oriented economies. More research is required to both understand the reasons why corporatist collapse failed to emerge in these regimes and why nascent revolutionary politics failed to topple their authoritarian governments.

Historical Cases in the Developing and Post-Communist World

Two historical cases also lend credence to the theories advanced in this analysis. The rise of Solidarity in Poland saw many of the same dynamics as Egypt's and Tunisia's independent trade union movements. Born of a wildcat strike, the movement forced the government to recognize its existence and eventually became synonymous with the revolutionary independence and reform movement itself. Its leader, Lech Wałęsa, was elected president and became an international symbol for workers. Wałęsa visited Tunisia in 2011, and trade unionists discussed the successes and failures of Solidarity during the transition. Among other similarities, Solidarity benefited from massive funding from the United States, and was active in international solidarity efforts. Solidarity's decision after the fall of the Soviet Union and election of a democratic government were also influential in Tunisia. The trade union elite discussed the possibility of forming a political party, as Solidarity did, but chose not to, a decision that was ultimately to their benefit.

Another model discussed and debated in Egypt and Tunisia was that of the Congress of South African Trade Unions (COSATU). Formed

---

[22] For more on the unique fate of monarchies in the uprisings, see Jason Brownlee et al., *The Arab Spring: Pathways of Repression and Reform* (Oxford: Oxford University Press, 2014).

during apartheid, COSATU entered into an alliance with the African National Congress (ANC) and the South African Communist Party to struggle against white rule. The decision was fraught, as the ANC, upon coming into power, pursued a more conservative and neoliberal economic policy than the one espoused by its coalition partners. While the decision to work together was vital to the revolutionary movement that ended apartheid, it limited the flexibility of the trade union to impact the regime's decision during the transition.

The frequency and repetition of the dynamics under review in this book is striking. Despite the distinct differences in state functioning, level of development, and system of governance, trade unions in transitions are forced to make challenging decisions regarding their relationship to political parties. The two historical cases presented in brief here lend further credence to the argument that the UGTT's decision to form flexible ties, as opposed to the rigid ties of COSATU or the cooptation of the ETUF are more advantageous to trade unions in transition. Solidarity's decision to directly form a political party also led to challenges, including elite fracture and an eventual drift back toward more conventional trade union activities.

East Asia

As outlined in the first chapter, the project was motivated in part by empirical questions and in part by two shadow cases that helped develop the theories presented: Taiwan and South Korea. Given these East Asian historical cases as background it is perhaps not surprising that the greatest, and most troubling, prospect for extension of the corporatist collapse theory is the People's Republic of China.[23] The PRC is in the middle of a massive strike wave, with over 3,000 strike actions being reported in the last four years by the opposition China Labour Bulletin. China has moved in the last 20 years away from managing industrial relations within the structure of the Communist party-state to a system of legalistic and contractual management. An increasingly militant cadre of disaffected workers threatens the All-China Federation of Trade Unions (ACFTU), the official trade union organization. The party-state in the past few years has sought

---

[23] "China Labour Bulletin Strike Map," *China Labour Bulletin*, accessed March 5, 2015, www.numble.com/clbmape.html.

to institutionalize the conflicts within the ACFTU with mixed results. The PRC, historically, has been a more competent authoritarian institution than its counterparts in Egypt and Tunisia, and the rapid economic growth in China give the party-state more flexibility in controlling militancy.

None of these facts are good news for the other possible extension, the PRC. The PRC, as a nominally Marxist-Leninist state, did make workers a key component in both the founding mythology and actual regime maintenance. The strike wave taking place now looks eerily similar to the industrial actions that gripped the interiors of Tunisia and Egypt before the revolutions. While China has a faster-growing economy, more resources, and one of the world's most robust coercive apparatuses, the emergence of corporatist collapse in Egypt and Tunisia should give scholars and policymakers who are concerned about China pause.

Transitions

This project's focus on the reconsolidation of new labor regimes and the impact on transitions also extends beyond the region. It has identified three factors as critical to the success of a trade union movement having a significant impact on a new regime. Two of these, the linkages to political parties and the mode of incorporation, are well known to scholars. Party–labor linkages are well explored in the European context and were key factors in the emergence of welfare states, corporatist bargains, and social democracy.

External linkages, as discussed previously in this chapter, remain underexplored by researchers, many of whom considered international solidarity efforts a prelude to social movement unionism, or a relic of Cold War competition. They are neither. The Solidarity Center, with copious funding from the National Endowment for Democracy, is active in a number of authoritarian and hybrid regimes, including Burma (Mynamar), Zimbabwe, and Nicaragua. Their preference for and focus on unity or pluralism varies from country to country, and they are far from the only organization in the global labor movement to be involved in such efforts. Friedrich Ebert Stiftung from Germany is involved in union consolidation efforts in Botswana, while the UK's Trades Union Congress (TUC) is raising funds for trade unions in Burma (Myanmar). The ILO is mandated by its charter to produce reports and interact with labor in all signatory countries, and as revealed from the North African cases can have an enormous impact with training and framing for trade unionists or those who aspire to form a trade union.

Research on the decision-making processes of the groups that make up "global labor" is rare. The interviews cited in this project suggest an arbitrary, politically motivated, and opaque process by which global labor chooses to support or ignore local labor actors. This process has a major impact, especially in transitioning regimes. Instead of seeing themselves as beneficent external actors, activists in the global labor movement need to instead recognize that they shape and constrain the incentives and opportunities open to local advocates in substantive ways. More than this, these interventions determine whether countries have united or fractured trade union movements, a major predictor (for better or worse) of their efficacy. Brownlee has rightly identified foreign aid and political support for "democracy promotion" as being highly suspect and likely to entrench authoritarianism in the interest of the home country. The same critical eye must be turned to global labor politics, as "pluralism promotion" can become "pluralism prevention" with the fate of millions of workers hanging in the balance.

Egypt and Tunisia, along with the other countries that saw mass movements in 2010–13 (Syria, Libya, Yemen, Bahrain, Morocco, Sudan, and Iraq), demonstrate the tenuous and uncertain paths states attempting to transition out of authoritarianism must take. While examples of powerful authoritarian legacies in Latin America, Eastern Europe, and East Asia already served to deflate some of the sky-high expectations of democracy promoters, the dynamics of the legacies remain opaque. Fortunately, new research into the role of authoritarian persistence and reconsolidation is increasing our understanding. Applying these insights to labor relations will be key to understanding both the political and economic outcomes of transitions to and from democracy. Many of the variables addressed in this project are being explored in diverse contexts to better understand authoritarian legacies.[24]

---

[24] Teri L. Caraway, Maria Lorena Cook, and Stephen Crowley, eds., *Working through the Past: Labor and Authoritarian Legacies in Comparative Perspective* (Ithaca, NY: Cornell University Press, 2015).

This project brings attention to an alternative history of the Arab Uprisings, a history still being written. It seeks to return some agency to those who helped make the uprisings possible, and have seen only some of their promises fulfilled. Understanding the future of Egypt and Tunisia requires a keen understanding of the forces of labor within the country, as they have demonstrated their ability to make or break regimes.

Index

Abbas, Kamal, 67, 183, *See also*
  CTUWS *and* EDLC
  appointment to NCHR, 182, 192
  denounces ETUF corruption, 87
  establishes CTUWS, 37
  French Human Rights Prize recipient,
    37
  global labor support, 83, 158
  and ILO conventions, 45
  imprisoned, 49
  independent union movement, 64
  legitimacy claims, 89
  on Mahalla strikes, 54
  meeting with Habib Guiza, 111
  on the Muslim Brotherhood, 166
  relationship with Abu Eita, 89, 162,
    182, 202–3
  use of new media, 46
Abbassi, Amara, 113
Abbassi, Hacine, 132, 142, 179
Abdaljawad, Mahdi, 127
Abdel Gowad, Mohamed, 173
Abdel Hadi, Aisha, 41, 48, 60
Abid, Lassâad, 137
Abu Eita, Kamal, 151, 183, 192, *See
    also* EFITU
  background, 46
  establishment of RETA, 49, 52–53,
    75
  global labor support, 158
  independent union movement, 64,
    189
  Karama Party, 50, 173
  Kefaya movement leader, 47
  legitimacy claims, 89
  as Minister of Manpower, 178,
    181–82
  pay inequality protests, 47
  relationship with Abbas, 89, 162,
    182, 202–3

  use of new media, 46
  worker mobilization, 206
Achour, Habib, 95, 98, 109
Actors' Syndicate, 173
ACTRAV. *See under* ILO
Adouani, Sami, 150
advocation, defined, 4
AFL-CIO, 150, *See also* American
    Federation of Labor
  funding for ETUF projects, 51
  funding for Solidarity Movement, 85
  international operations, 81
  Solidarity Center. *See* Solidarity
    Center
  support for international unions, 207
African Development Bank, 28
African National Congress (ANC), 215
African-American Labor Center, 51, 81
aggregation, defined, 4
Al Jazeera, 46
Al Masry Al Youm, 46
Al-Aridah, 133–34
Aleimi, Hichem, 114
Alexander, Anne, 57, 59
Alexander, Christopher, 99, 103
Algeria
  civil war, 101
  support for Tunisian movement, 115
Al-Ghad. *See* Ghad Party
Ali, Khaled, 165
All-China Federation of Trade Unions
    (ACFTU), 215
Al-Massar, 141
Amamou, Slim (aka Slim 404), 120,
    128
American Federation of Labor, 95, 207,
    See also AFL-CIO
Amin, Idi, 127
Angry Friday, 54, 62
Ansar Al-Sharia, 141

privatization
  effect on UGTT, 11
  in Egypt, 10, 29, 32, 36, 42, 195
  in Tunisia, 102
professional syndicates (Egypt), 163–65
Progressive Democratic Party, 127
property rights, in North African
  context, 209
proto-unions, 135
Public Service International (PSI), 151

Qualified Industrial Zones (QIZs), 34

Rais Lebled (song), 120
rank and file vs. leadership split
  (Tunisia), 12, 18, 108, 110, 158
rank-and-file unionists, 14
rank-and-file vs. central split
  in Tunisia, 199
Rasheed, Rasheed Mohammed, 40
Rassemblement Constitutionnel
  Démocratique. *See* RCD
Razek, Amr Abdel, 184
RCD, 133
  and UGTT, 113–16, 129–30, 154,
    162, 169
  documents hacked, 120
  established, 99
  in revolutionary government, 54
  protests against, 128
Real Estate Tax Authority Union. *See*
  RETA
reconsolidation of new labor regimes,
  216
regimes, in transition, 84
repression
  under Mubarak regime, 50, 171
Republican Party, 141, 149
RETA, 49, 66, 151, 189
revolutionary politics
  union involvement in, 2
Revolutionary Socialists, 75
revolutionary-since-birth narrative
  in Tunisia, 126
rhetoric
  as a form of support, 84, 120,
    158–59
  Egyptian vs. Tunisian unionists, 156
  Ennahda, 137, 140
  ETUF, 61–62, 64

framing of unity vs. pluralism, 207
Nasserist, 61
of independent unions, 62
of the Tunisian miracle, 101, 114
of union leadership, 45, 58
UGTT, 18, 131, 144, 187
Rider, Guy, 144
Romdhane, Ali, 110

Sabbahi, Hamdeen, 50
Saber, Karam, 30
Sadat, Anwar, 26, 28, 39
Sahbani, Ismail, 114, 126, 135, 155
  as UGTT secretary general, 101, 109
  ties to AFL-CIO, 136, 153
Salafi Dawa, 77
Salafi Front, 77–78
Salafism, 20, 204, 211
Sawiris, Naguib, 92
SCAF, 68, 71, 88, 172, 178, 183
  and transit worker strike, 70
  declares strikes illegal, 69
  removes Mubarak, 68
  vetos new trade union law, 69
security services, increased use of in
  Egypt, 39
Selmani, Chokri, 114
Shafik, Ahmed, 68
Shaping the Political Arena (Collier and
  Collier), 58, 60–61, 124
Sharaf, Essam, 66, 70
Sharif, Nawaz, 127
Shokr, Abdul Ghaffar, 75
Sisi, Abdel Fatta el-
  and union elections, 199
  as military chief, 92
  as president, 180
  endorsed by ETUF, 187
  militarization of economy, 70
  military intervention, 178
  relationship with labor, 211
  wages policy, 204
  war on terror, 204
Social Democratic Party, 75
Social Development Fund (SDF), 196
Social Fund for Development (SFD), 30
social media
  use of in organizing strikes, 49
Social Pact, 144, 153, 159
social pact, tripartite (Tunisia), 143